## DATE DUE

| | |
|---|---|
| | |
| | |
| | |
| | |
| | |
| | |
| | |
| | |
| | |
| | |
| | |
| | |
| | |
| | |
| | |
| | |

BRODART, CO.                          Cat. No. 23-221

D1058195

# TRUSTING WHAT YOU'RE TOLD

# TRUSTING WHAT YOU'RE TOLD

How Children Learn from Others

✦

PAUL L. HARRIS

The Belknap Press of Harvard University Press
Cambridge, Massachusetts
London, England
2012

*Library of Congress Cataloging-in-Publication Data*
Harris, Paul L.
Trusting what you're told : how children learn from others / Paul L. Harris.
p.   cm.
Includes bibliographical references and index.
ISBN 978-0-674-06572-7 (alk. paper)
1. Learning, Psychology of.   2. Children.   I. Title.
BF318.H363   2012
155.4'1315—dc23       2011046701

# Contents

# TRUSTING WHAT YOU'RE TOLD

# Introduction

✦

$W$e adults could scarcely find our way in the world, either literally or metaphorically, if no one told us anything. Imagine planning a journey to a distant city you've never visited before. Even to conceive of that plan—to know of the city's existence and to want to see it—calls for a wealth of geographic information that only other people can supply. Deprived of the testimony of others about the land in which we live, our spatial horizon shrinks to the places we have already seen and those we see just ahead of us. Much the same can be said of our temporal horizon. If no one ever told us about the past, it seems unlikely that we would ever think about the Great War, the Roman Empire, or the Stone Age, let alone the eons that preceded life on earth. Our intuitions about the span of history would be cramped by our own short biography.

In spite of this manifest dependence on information supplied by other people, progressive educators have conceived of young children as hands-on learners who learn best in the here and now from their own active observation and experimentation. The possibility that children's early learning might be intimately linked to what they can conjure up in their imagination on the basis of what other people tell them has been downplayed. Maria Montessori offers a well-known example of this emphasis on the priority of first-hand experience. In the Montessori classroom, the teacher aims to take a back seat, on the assumption that young children's engagement with concrete materials is the optimal vehicle for learning. Indeed, for Montessori, the teacher's quiet withdrawal was the hallmark of good teaching.

Montessori's focus on children's autonomous learning is part of an influential tradition. In many ways, she echoes the stance taken by Jean-Jacques Rousseau in his writing about education. For example, Rousseau offers the following stern warning against answering children's questions: "To nourish his curiosity, never hasten to satisfy it. . . . Ask questions that he can handle and leave them to him to resolve. Let him know things not because you have told him, but rather because he has understood it for himself. Let him not learn science; let him invent it. If you ever substitute authority for reason in his mind, he will no longer reason; he will only be the plaything of other people's opinions" (from *Emile*, 1762/1999; my translation).

Following in the footsteps of his compatriot, Jean Piaget also insisted that children should learn primarily from their explorations and from active interpretation of data that they themselves gather. Like Rousseau, he was dubious about whether children can truly learn from what other people tell them. They may be able to parrot what they have been told, but any understanding based on verbal input is likely to remain superficial. One of Piaget's telling examples is children's counting. Young children can often produce a number sequence correctly— "One, two three, four, five . . ."—but further probing shows that they have a limited grasp of quantity. For example, they may not realize that the number of items in a row remains the same whether the items are spread out or bunched up.

Yet a moment's reflection shows that there is a profound limit to the role that first-hand experience can play in cognitive development. In many domains, children cannot gather the relevant data for themselves. The objects or processes in question are remote or invisible, so that children have to depend on what other people tell them. Admittedly, in the course of development, children would do well to exercise their autonomous judgment by sifting and reinterpreting what they are told—just as they sift and reinterpret their own firsthand experience. Still, the testimony of other people is likely to be just as important as firsthand experience for setting such reflection in motion.

Consider a couple of examples. By the time they are 6 or 7 years of age, many children realize that our mental processes depend on the functioning of the brain. Their knowledge of brain function is not superficial. They can give considered and appropriate answers to questions that they have not met before. Asked, for example, how a pig might prefer to sleep after receiving a brain transplant from a child, many 6- and 7-year-olds plausibly claim that he would "like to get tucked in, all cozy in bed at night," rather than sleep "in the sloppy mud" (Johnson, 1990). Similarly, preschoolers are beginning to realize that the earth is not flat. Most 4- and 5-year-olds in England and Australia deny that they would fall off the edge of the world if they "walked for many days in a straight line," and by the age of 8 or 9 most of them understand that people can live all over the earth and that the sky is "all around" and not just "on top" (Siegal, Newcombe, Butterworth, 2004). Clearly, children do not arrive at these conclusions about the brain or the shape of the earth by direct observation. They learn about them from what other people tell them—even if some intellectual work is needed in order for children to appreciate the full ramifications of what they are told.

Children's dependence on what other people tell them is not limited to scientific phenomena. In discussing adults' reliance on testimony, the Scottish philosopher David Hume focused on reports of miracles: the parting of the seas, resurrection from the dead. He argued forcefully that we ought to be dubious about such reports. After all, he wrote, it is more likely that the person affirming the miracle has been misled—or is trying to mislead us—than that the laws of nature have been violated (Hume, 1748/1902). Children are no better than adults in following Hume's skeptical advice. They accept the extraordinary claims that are widespread in their community. They come to believe in the miraculous powers of God, in the efficacy of prayer, and in an afterlife. Such beliefs can even infuse what children say they have seen and heard. When 5- and 6-year-old believers in the Tooth Fairy were asked to describe her last visit as truthfully as they could, not only did they often weave in implausible details—"She flied in the window" or "My cat got her stinking fairy dust all over her fur"—they claimed to have personally witnessed her visit: "I heard her close my window," "She told me to go back to sleep," "I sawed her tippie-toed into my room," "She looked like a tiny little princess" (Principe & Smith, 2008ab).

In this book, I take for granted children's capacity to engage in autonomous reflection. The long research tradition from Rousseau to

Piaget, and from Piaget to recent analyses of the young child as scientist, has amply demonstrated that capacity. But I ask how children learn from, and reflect upon, what other people tell them. Once we grant that children trust the testimony of other people, it becomes clear that the direction of cognitive development is necessarily open-ended. We need to abandon the idea that children steadily move toward objectivity and enlightenment. Even if they construct a set of more or less universal and objective truths about the physical world, about biology, the life cycle, and the human mind, children also come to accept all manner of exotic and unverifiable claims.

I start by looking at the first signs of children's ability to learn from what other people tell them. Well before children go to school, they are capable of engaging in a sustained conversation. They can follow a story or an explanation, can reflect on what they are told, and can ask questions. Young children also have a powerful imagination. They engage in pretend play, often in collaboration with others, in which they contemplate possibilities that they have never actually encountered. The confluence of these twin capacities—for engaging in conversation and for thinking about events that have not actually been experienced—means that young children are well placed to learn from the testimony of other people (Harris, 2000). More specifically, they can listen to claims about unobserved events, form a mental representation of those events using their imagination, and work out the implications.

When children listen to a story, most of the events described will be fictional. We naturally suppose that children use their imagination to represent such events. However, I argue that children also use their imagination to represent real, unobserved events, as well as fictional events. To take a simple example, when they are told that a toy they left in one place has been moved to another, children need to update their mental picture of the world. They must imagine the object in its new location. The evidence shows that toddlers are increasingly able to act on such unseen but reported transformations. Rather than go back to the old place—which is now empty—they search for their toy in the new place. Such findings illustrate how toddlers grasp that what they observed for themselves may not be valid: other people can provide an update or a correction. This self-knowledge—or, more precisely, this insight into their own relative ignorance—helps children to realize that other people can be an important source of valid information. Therefore, it is worth asking other people questions—many questions. Children's willingness to alter their ideas about the world on the basis of someone else's say-so, and to ask questions in order that they may do just that, is discussed in Chapters 1 and 2.

Granted children's sensitivity to two streams of information—the information they gather for themselves via direct observation and the information they gather from others by listening, by posing questions, or by simply watching other people—we can ask what children do when those two streams conflict. Do they insist on the conclusions that they have reached for themselves, or do they defer to other people's suggestions? Children face this dilemma in all sorts of contexts. They may think they know how to use a tool or open a box, but how do they respond if someone shows them a different way? They may think they know how to classify some half-familiar object, but what if someone offers an alternative suggestion? It turns out that children are surprisingly receptive, and even deferential, in these contexts, as described in Chapters 3 and 4.

Does this mean that young children are too trusting? Alongside the claim made by Rousseau and Piaget that children can and should resist relying on what other people tell them, there is also a long intellectual tradition implying that young children are all-too-willing to accept what they are told. Yet even if children are sometimes credulous, they exercise considerable discrimination in choosing whom to believe. Chapter 5 describes how they choose among informants who are likely to be familiar to them. Chapter 6 describes how they choose among relative strangers. Taken together, the evidence shows that children have sensitive antennae: they may not always be in a position to check on or evaluate the plausibility of the message, but they do monitor the messenger.

Chapter 7 shifts the discussion to a fresh domain: moral judgment. Do children make their own moral judgments—independent of the prescriptions laid out by authority figures? Some children are surprisingly autonomous in the conclusions that they reach. Well before adolescence, they are willing to take a moral stand against the habits and prescriptions of their own family. Yet even in taking that stand, these independent-minded children are swayed by what other people tell them about actions that cause pain and suffering.

Earlier, I emphasized that children use their imagination to construct a mental picture not just of the fictional entities that they hear about in a story, but also of real, albeit unobserved entities that they learn about from the claims and attestations of other people. This latter type of testimony ranges over a huge variety of phenomena. Children learn about invisible scientific phenomena, such as germs and oxygen; they learn about spiritual phenomena, such as angels and the afterlife; and they learn about historical figures and events, such as Julius Caesar and the Civil War. Despite the heterogeneity of these phenomena, children's knowledge of them ultimately derives from the same source: the testimony of other people. This raises an intriguing but neglected question. Do children regard all of these phenomena as having roughly the same status? Do they think of germs, angels, and ancient Romans as equally real or as real in the same way? This question is visited and revisited in the course of Chapters 8, 9, and 10.

What does children's trust in testimony imply about the nature of cognitive development? One possible answer is that testimony serves to amplify children's cognitive capacities but does not fundamentally change the ultimate direction of cognitive development, which is toward greater objectivity and enlightenment (Harris, 2002). On this view, children come into the world already equipped with observational skills and a reflective capacity. The main function of testimony from other people is to supplement the observational data at their disposal by providing them with information about entities that are too microscopic, too distant, or too embedded for the children themselves to observe. Thus, despite the important role of testimony, children can still be seen as pursuing an agenda of objectivity. The testimony provided by other people serves only to further children's mastery of that agenda.

I believe that this conception of cognitive development and the impact of testimony upon its direction is far too narrow (Harris & Koenig, 2006). There is no inevitable march toward objectivity or enlightenment. It is true that most children arrive at a set of rational ideas about some of the fundamental categories of existence—including space, identity, number, and time. Nevertheless, in the course of development, guided by the testimony of others and supplemented by their own imagination, children also come to entertain various culturally specific ideas about where human beings have come from and where they are going. They take these ideas on trust, not on the basis of rational scrutiny. Indeed, rather than seeking coherence, they sometimes accept ideas that are fundamentally incompatible with one another. The endpoint of cognitive development is not objectivity and equilibrium. It is a mix of the natural and supernatural, of truth and fantasy, of faith and uncertainty.

# CHAPTER 1

# Early Learning from Testimony

**W**hen children first start to talk, they talk about what is right in front of them, and so do the adults who talk to them. So there is virtually no discussion of the future, the past, or faraway places. That early restriction makes sense. It is precisely because children can use their grasp of the immediate situation as a kind of mental dictionary with which to decipher other people's intended meaning that they can acquire language in the first place (MacNamara, 1972). There is a sense, therefore, in which children encounter a recurrent correlation between what they are told and what they observe. Without that correlation, it is hard to conceive how children could acquire language in the first place. Nevertheless, little by little, children start to produce "displaced" speech—to move beyond the here and now (Hockett, 1960). They engage in conversations about people who are not present, events that took place some time ago, and places that they may never have seen. This expansion of their mental universe is especially obvious when children begin to enjoy stories, picture books, and television.

Most of the research on children's displaced communication has concentrated, not surprisingly, on the remarks that children themselves make. They are easy to record and analyze, and I start with an overview of what has been found. But a key question for the theme of learning from testimony is when and how children begin to update and enrich their conception of the world on the basis of what other people say to them. So long as other people's remarks are mainly tied to the immediate context of the utterance, children can derive no major benefit. What people tell them is more or less equivalent to what children can observe for themselves. However, when the remarks are about events and entities that are displaced from the time and place of the conversation, that equivalence between testimony and observation is reduced and even eliminated. Children can begin to learn something about the world that they have not observed for themselves.

By the end of their first year of life, infants are able to point to objects of interest or to objects that they want. They can even use pointing to request an object that is missing from its usual location (Liszkowski, Schäfer, Carpenter, & Tomasello, 2009). For example, if they want a toy they, will point to a container that normally holds toys—suggesting an embryonic, prelinguistic capacity for communication about an absent object. Nevertheless, at the onset of language acquisition, early in the second year, children's remarks are overwhelmingly directed at the here and now. Only very occasionally do they make any reference to some nonpresent object, action, or object feature. For example, on being handed a toy mirror wrapped in foil, a 16-month-old child commented: "This is for looking with." At that moment, she could not see her reflection—because of the foil covering the mirror—but she was able to invoke its customary use.

The frequency of displaced references increases dramatically (Morford & Goldin-Meadow, 1997). At 16 months, only 1 percent of children's utterances include a displaced reference; but in the course of the next two years, such references come to occupy a much bigger proportion of children's output—more than one third by 36 months. Displaced references also increase in complexity. At around 21 months, children begin to talk not just about object features but about entire events, typically those that have just taken place or those that are about to take place. For example, immediately after doing a somersault on the couch, one 21-month-old said: "See, I flipped over." By 30 months, children begin to talk about events that are more remote in time and space. As one 2-year-old explained: "And after three, I'm going to be four." Two-year-olds also start to talk about hypothetical or fantasy events. For example, having watched an adult either shake pretend talcum powder or pour pretend tea over a toy pig, they described what had happened in this miniature fantasy world. They said that the pig was "powdery" after the shaking of pretend talcum powder, but "wet" after the pouring of pretend tea (Harris & Kavanaugh, 1993). Of course, because this was a game of make-believe, the pig was actually neither "powdery" nor "wet," but children could imagine these pretend outcomes and talk about them.

What drives this expansion of the child's conversational horizon? Perhaps older and more experienced interlocutors include children in conversations that increasingly draw them into thinking about non-current or fantasy events. However, when Morford and Goldin-Meadow (1997) looked at who had initiated the conversation about a displaced topic, it was generally the child rather than the caregiver. Only in the case of conversations about the nonimmediate past was it the parent who mostly took the lead. Apparently, children themselves have a strong, natural predisposition to strike up conversations about remote objects and events.

Support for this conclusion emerged in a creative study by Morford and Goldin-Meadow (1997). They observed four deaf children being raised in homes where no family member was able to use sign language. In the absence of meaningful access to any conventional system of communication, be it spoken language or sign language, all four children invented their own form of sign language. The signs that they used were not just those gestures that are widespread among hearing children, such as pointing or nodding. These deaf children also created gestures—for example, holding the hand vertically near the chest, palm out, and then moving it in an arc away from the body, to signal objects distant in space or time. Eventually, the children were able to produce quite complex ideas with these invented signs. For example, David pointed to a picture of a sand shovel (a picture that he used to indicate any kind of shovel), then pointed down toward the basement (where the family's snow shovel was kept), produced a "dig" gesture, a "pull on" (boots) gesture, and then a "snowing" gesture. He thereby managed to convey the idea that when it snows, he (or another family member) puts on boots and digs with a snow shovel (Butcher, Mylander, & Goldin-Meadow, 1991). Using such self-created signs, the four deaf children displayed an increase in both the frequency and the scope of their displaced references, just like hearing children. Indeed, they displayed an even stronger tendency than the hearing children to be the initiator of such conversations about displaced topics—not surprisingly perhaps, given the paucity of any comparable signing skill by other members of their family. So even among children who are obliged to take the lead in their own self-generated medium of communication, there is an autonomous expansion beyond the here and now.

Still, important differences between deaf children and hearing children also emerged. For the deaf children, the entire sequence of development started later—at around 30 months, rather than 18 months—and the increase in scope was less dramatic. Moreover, references to noncurrent events remained less frequent, and only one of the four deaf children made any references at all to future events, even though such utterances expand markedly among hearing children (Adamson & Bakeman, 2006).

In summary, children appear to enjoy a natural disposition to communicate about absent objects and events. Even when they invent their own sign language, children use it to produce displaced utterances. Still, the opportunity to engage in sustained conversation by means of a shared symbolic system, be it a spoken language or an established sign language, plays an important role in helping children to make an early and full use of that disposition. Children like to talk about the not-here and the not-now, but they do that best when someone talks with them. Left to their own devices, children do eventually produce displaced utterances but later and in a narrower fashion.

## Understanding Displaced References

So far, we have looked at the natural history of children's own displaced utterances. But when do children start to understand those of a conversation partner? That understanding is obviously critical if children are to gather new information about the world from the testimony of others. The available research is quite fragmentary, but we can tentatively trace a developmental path. In one of the first studies, Janellen Huttenlocher (1974) found that children around the age of 13 to 14 months show clear signs of understanding references to an absent object or person. Provided that the absent object is located in its customary place, children go in search of it. For example, when Wendy was 13 months, she was asked: "Where are the fish?" In response, she went around a large barrier to another room where the fish tank was located. Similarly, when asked, "Where is the mirror?" Kristen at 13 months was able to crawl from any position in her parents' bedroom and enter the closet where the mirror was housed.

Soon after, infants start to respond appropriately even when the absent object is in an unusual or temporary location. For example, at 14 months Wendy had been feeling cranky and her mother gave her a blanket. This was eventually discarded and left on the couch. Some ten minutes later, when she was asked, "Where is your blanket?" Wendy crossed the room to the couch in order to retrieve it. Similarly, at 16 months Craig was in the kitchen when he was asked if he wanted a cookie. He went to the living room and returned with some of the cookies left on the floor where he had spilled them earlier.

Saylor and Baldwin (2004) also found that 15-month-olds respond appropriately when an absent person or toy animal is mentioned. For example, when 15-month-olds were asked, "What's Daddy doing?"— either when Daddy was present in the room or when he was absent— they responded differently to these two situations. If Daddy was absent, they were more likely to look toward the door or produce a relevant remark: "He's busy at work." Toddlers also extend such reactions to newly learned names for a missing character. Ganea (2005) taught 14-month-olds the name of a stuffed toy: "Max." Max was then put aside, and children listened to a story. On hearing Max mentioned in the course of the story, children often turned to look or point in his direction, and some even got up and went toward him.

These various behaviors show that children in the second year of life grasp a key feature of human communication—namely, that a speaker can refer to an invisible or absent referent. This understanding is initially manifested in children's nonverbal reactions, such as the direction of their gaze or their active search for the missing referent. Of course, when a speaker refers to a person or object that is not present, it is not always appropriate to go looking for the thing mentioned. Children's attempts to physically find a story character—as in Ganea's study—suggest that they may not fully appreciate the way that conversation can be more or less completely severed from the surrounding context. By the middle of their third year, however, children are increasingly likely to confine themselves to a verbal comment (Saylor & Baldwin, 2004)—consistent with the realization that displaced references should not be automatically interpreted as a request to physically recover the absent referent, but rather should be seen as an invitation to share information about it.

Acquiring new information from the testimony of other people is complicated. Recognizing that someone is talking about an absent referent is an important first step. Children have to somehow represent in their mind the object or person referred to. But in addition, if they are to respond appropriately, children may have to retrieve, on the basis of that verbal reference, other stored information—such as where the object is or what the person is doing. There is, however, a further step that children must take if they are to acquire new information and not simply retrieve what they already know. People offer us new information via testimony, information that we have not had the opportunity to gather for ourselves. When do children start to grasp this fundamental property of other people's testimony? In particular, when do children start to update or alter their beliefs about the world merely on the basis of someone else's say-so?

Some initial clues are buried in a report by Jacqueline Sachs (1983) on the emergence of displaced speech in her daughter, Naomi. At 22 months, Naomi asked: "Where's Daddy?" Her mother replied: "Daddy is working. Daddy will be home tonight. You'll see him tomorrow morning." One month later, at 23 months, a similar exchange occurred. Naomi again asked: "Where's Daddy? Daddy's in work?" Her mother replied: "Daddy's at work, honey." Notice the subtle but telling difference between the two conversations. In the second exchange, at 23 months, Naomi asks where her father is—as she had done one month earlier—but this time she also suggests a tentative answer: "Daddy's in work?" The most plausible explanation for Naomi's suggestion is that she has learned where Daddy usually is from what her mother has told her on past occasions. She has, in short, learned from testimony.

More exotic examples of the same phenomenon appear around the same period. At 22 months, Naomi asked, "Where's the moon?" and received the following reply: "Where's the moon? The moon is sleeping. The moon is not out now." It seems as if Naomi accepted this whimsical response, because during the same month, the following exchange took place. Adult: "Where's the moon?" Naomi: "Moon." Adult: "Uh huh. Where is it?" Naomi: "Moon sleeping."

These two serendipitous examples suggest that even before their second birthday, children can acquire new information via testimony. They can encode and retrieve information that they could not easily discover for themselves. Presumably, Naomi did not discover from firsthand observation that when Daddy was away from home, he was working. Nor, presumably, did she establish via direct observation that when the moon cannot be seen, it is "sleeping." Rather, she had acquired both of these "facts" from talking to other people.

Still, in these examples, and indeed in any examples where the evidence is based on what children say, it can be objected that children are doing little more than "echoing" what they have been told. Indeed, as noted earlier, traditional criticisms of children's learning from verbal input have frequently implied that such knowledge remains superficial: it is just something that children repeat back verbally, and not something that genuinely alters the way they think about the world. Certainly, in the case of the two examples involving Naomi, close scrutiny of her remarks shows that this objection may have some force. In what sense does she really understand that the moon is "sleeping," or, for that matter, that Daddy is "working"? Such remarks might index nothing more than "verbalism," as Piaget called it—a tendency to parrot back an adult's statement with no genuine understanding of what it means.

To demonstrate that children's learning from testimony goes beyond parroting, we need to show—ideally in the context of a well-controlled experiment—that it has a noticeable impact on the way children subsequently think about the world and behave toward it. In a pioneering study, Patricia Ganea and her colleagues designed a persuasive experimental demonstration with 22-month-old toddlers (Ganea, Shutts, Spelke, & DeLoache, 2007). Each child first learned that a particular toy frog was called Lucy. Lucy was then left to "sleep" in a basket while the child went to an adjacent room to listen to a story. In the middle of the story, an adult passed by with a bucket, explaining that she was going to clean the table in the room next door where Lucy had been left. However, she soon came back saying: "I'm so sorry! I was washing the table, and I spilled water all over Lucy. Lucy is wet now! She's covered with water." The experimenter reiterated this information: "Oh no! Did you hear that? Lucy got wet! She's all covered in water" and invited the child to go see Lucy. Once back in the toy room, the child was asked to pick out Lucy from three choices: a wet frog, a dry frog, and a wet pig. Most 22-month-olds successfully picked out the wet frog.

This setup, simple though it is, provides compelling support for the claim that very young children are not just able to understand and repeat other people's testimony, but can also update their knowledge or beliefs about the world on the strength of that testimony. When children left Lucy in the basket on the table, she was dry. When they went back to look for her, they realized that she was now wet and chose the wet frog rather than the dry one. Their only clue to the change in Lucy's state was the testimony provided by the two adults. Apparently, by the end of the second year, children can learn from, and act upon, others' testimony about the way things stand in the world.

How exactly did the children manage to choose the right stuffed animal, appropriately basing their choice on the most recent, testimony-derived information about Lucy? One way to get a sense of the complexity involved is to consider the choices that we make when we want to store some new information on a computer. Initially, we have two options. We can open up a fresh file, one we will dedicate to the new information, or we can retrieve a file that we have already created and add the new information to that existing file. Similarly, when children hear the claim that Lucy is wet, they might open up a new mental file and enter the information into it. Alternatively, they might retrieve an existing file and add the new information to that file.

One tacit implication of the first possibility—the opening of a new file—is that children create new files whenever they are presented with a new verbal claim. This seems psychologically implausible. It would lead to the proliferation of thousands of mental files. In particular, it would mean having distinct files for firsthand as compared to testimony-based information. We would do well to think carefully about the more psychologically plausible alternative: the reuse and editing of existing files.

Before the children left the room to listen to the story, they had played with Lucy and then put her in the basket "to sleep." Presumably, such firsthand experiences are entered into a mental file. When children subsequently learn something new about Lucy—they are told that she is now wet—it would seem economical and efficient to retrieve this preexisting file and to edit it in light of the subsequent, testimony-based information. For example, any default representation of Lucy in this preexisting file might now be enriched by the new, testimony-derived information that Lucy is "wet." However, such editing is not unproblematic. It means that earlier information would be lost. Children would keep files nicely up to date but have no record of the past. The fact that Lucy was once dry would be gone. More generally, children would live in a transient, testimony-derived present.

It's worth thinking about a plausible variant of this overwriting system. Suppose that when children receive new information regarding a given entity, they retrieve a previously created file concerning that entity and then edit that file, as described earlier. But when they save this new, enriched file, they also keep a copy of the old file. Then, when they return to the room where they have left Lucy and are asked to pick her out from the array of three animals, they review potentially relevant files but choose the one containing information about "wet" Lucy, on the grounds that it has the most recent date.

An analogy with our everyday editing of computer files will highlight the advantages of such multiple storage. We often press "Save As" rather "Save," so that in saving a newly edited file we retain access to the file in its initial state. The new file may be flawed or valid for only a short time. Yet if we allow overwriting and deletion to occur, we lose the possibility of referring back to the old file. Any storage system faces this dilemma: how to reflect the way things currently stand, while at the same time preserving potentially useful information about the way things were. Multiple-stage storage, in which old information is not systematically deleted but supplemented by new information, can offer the best of both worlds.

Is there any disadvantage to such a storage system? One potential bug is easy to imagine. Suppose that children retrieve a newly edited file as well as an older file. They may be unsure about which file to act on. In fact, children do have such problems in file management, as we discovered when we told them where to find a hidden toy (Ganea & Harris, 2010). Toddlers aged 23 and 30 months were shown a living room with four different hiding places, such as a cabinet, a basket, and so forth. On any given trial, children put a stuffed animal into one of these hiding places and then went to a room next door, where they received one of two types of information. In the observation condition, children were lifted up so that they could watch through a window as an adult moved the toy to a different hiding place. In the verbal condition, children did not look through the window themselves. Instead, an adult who was looking through it told them about the change of location. In both conditions, children then returned to the living room, where they were asked to retrieve the stuffed animal.

At 30 months, children rarely made errors in either condition. Most of them correctly retrieved the stuffed animal from its new hiding place, whether they had seen the move or had only been told about it. By implication, 30-month-olds listen carefully and navigate their mental filing system just as effectively, whether information about the new location is taken in via firsthand observation or via what they are told. In either case, they appropriately choose the mental file they should act on: the one that indicates the most recent location for the stuffed animal.

The pattern of responding was quite different among the 23-month-olds. Although most children searched correctly at the new location when they had seen the change of location for themselves, they made a mistake when they were merely told about it: they went back to look for the toy where they had left it. By implication, 23-month-olds opted for the file they had initially constructed on the strength of their own observation, not the more recent file, updated via testimony.

Support for the proposal that 23-month-olds had file management problems—rather than problems with simply understanding what they had been told—emerged in a follow-up study. Instead of being hidden in a container, the animal was left visible in the middle of the room as children left. It was then moved from that visible location and hidden elsewhere. Under these conditions, most 23-month-olds searched for the toy at its new hiding place, irrespective of whether they had seen the object moved or were told about it. Indeed, even when younger toddlers (19-month-olds) were told about the change of location, they, too, were almost always correct. Hence, the mistakes observed in the first study were not due to difficulties in understanding testimony about an object being moved to a new location. Rather, the 23-month-olds in Study 1 had difficulty in selecting the appropriate file.

Why was that selection process more successful in Study 2 than in Study 1? Two differences between the studies stand out. In Study 1, just before children left the room, they put the toy in a container. In Study 2, by contrast, they simply left the toy on the floor in the middle of the room. So children presumably had a detailed and specific mental file about the toy's initial location in Study 1, but a fuzzier file in Study 2. Maybe the specificity of the initial file in Study 1 was especially compelling when the time came to search for the object. But there is a second possibility. When children returned in Study 1, they could see the original container but not the fact that it was now empty. By contrast, when children returned in Study 2, they could see that the toy was no longer where they had left it on the floor. Maybe this visible evidence of the toy's displacement helped them to search correctly in Study 2.

Study 3 was designed to help distinguish between these two possibilities. Children aged 23 months again put the toy in a container and left the room. However, on one trial the container was fully opaque, whereas on the other trial it had a window cut in its front panel. This meant that the children could immediately see that it was empty on their return. If children's file management problems in Study 1 had occurred because the initial file was quite specific, they should mistakenly go back to the first container, whether it was fully opaque or had a window. On the other hand, if their problems in Study 1 had occurred because they could not see that the toy had been moved on their return, the container with a window should help them by revealing that the toy had been moved.

In line with the first hypothesis, most children searched in the initial container on both trials. Even when they could see through the container window that it was empty—consistent with what the adult had just told them about the toy having been moved—children often approached the container and looked inside. Apparently, these 23-month-olds, remembering that the toy had been in the container, found it difficult to set aside such a specific piece of information and to act instead on what they had just been told. By contrast, when they had simply left the object in the middle of the room—where there was no container to mark its exact location—they had a fuzzier mental representation of its location, one that was more easily set aside in light of subsequent verbal testimony.[1]

In miniature, these studies illustrate a ubiquitous process in human cognition. We form an idea, but we often update that idea, sometimes on the basis of what we see and sometimes on the basis of what we are told. At first glance, this updating process seems obvious and ought to be seamless. Children are told about a change of location or a change of state. They take in that testimony-based information, update their mental filing system, and act upon it. However, as revealed by the studies just described, the updating of mental files is a complex process and may work imperfectly, especially when the updating is based on information gathered via testimony. A preexisting file may compete inappropriately with the newly gathered information.[2]

## Updating, Enrichment, and Revision

Once a mental file has been opened, newly gathered information entered into that file can stand in various types of relationship to preexisting information. It can provide more recent information, so that an *updated* version of a preexisting file is needed. This corresponds, of course, to the situation in the experiments just described. An alternative possibility is that the newly gathered information is compatible with all existing information and simply adds to it. In that case, an *enriched* version of a preexisting file is what is needed. For example, children might play with Lucy the frog and then, in her absence, be told about some of her properties that they have not yet discovered—they might be told that Lucy will croak if you give her a squeeze. Children's ability to enrich their existing file about Lucy with this new information—and to appropriately act on the enrichment—would be signaled by their giving her an expectant squeeze on a later encounter.

A third possibility is that newly gathered information may provide information which conflicts with the initial file. In that case, a *revised* version of a preexisting file may be called for. For example, a mother talking to her child about an outing the previous day might claim—contrary to what the child assumed—that they had seen a toad rather than a frog. In this case, the child faces a dilemma. Should the preexisting file be saved along with the newly edited file, or should the new information be allowed to overwrite information in the preexisting file? We will look further at children's responses to this dilemma in Chapter 4.[3]

Let's step back and review. The psychological study of cognitive development has routinely focused on the way that children learn from their own firsthand, empirical experience. Yet children are not just hands-on learners. They have a striking capacity to learn—via testimony—from other people's knowledge and experience. A ubiquitous feature of such learning via testimony is the need to think and talk about objects and events that are "displaced"—that are not being experienced at the time and place of the communication. Children display this ability soon after the onset of language acquisition. Starting in the second year of life, they begin to talk about absent objects, properties, and actions. In the course of the next two years, they increasingly talk about past, future, and possible events. Moreover, when deaf children invent their own sign-based communication system, as they do when no conventional sign language is available to them, they show a similar disposition to talk about absent objects and events, even if, in their case, the onset and augmentation of that capacity is delayed.

Children's capacity for displaced talk shows that they can contemplate and discuss events that they are not currently experiencing. They can even discuss future and fantasy events that they have never experienced. In thinking about how individuals learn from testimony, therefore, we may ask if children can be told about an event that they have not experienced, and come to treat it *as if* they had experienced it. More specifically, at what age are they able to treat what other people tell them as a source of information about the world—equivalent in key respects to firsthand observation? This simple but fundamental question has received little attention, but scattered findings hint that children might be able to do this toward the end of the second year. When they are told about some invisible property of a person or an object—that Daddy is at work or that the moon is sleeping—they assimilate the information and repeat it.

Recent experimental work highlights the fact that belief alteration via testimony affects not just what children say, but also what they do. Told about some change to the world, they update their mental filing system, and act appropriately in light of this new information. Yet such file management is a delicate, error-prone process. When it goes smoothly, children respond to what they have been told as accurately and effortlessly as they respond to their own firsthand observations. However, it does not always go smoothly. Particularly when the new, verbally based input has to compete with detailed and specific prior information, the updating process may go awry. Children try to retrieve an object from an earlier hiding place even when they have just been told that it is somewhere else.

In the next chapter, I discuss children's questions. On the face of it, the fact that children ask questions suggests that they are prepared to learn from others' testimony. But as noted in the introduction, a long tradition in developmental psychology has adopted a withholding, negative stance, implying that when children gather information by asking questions, their ensuing knowledge is superficial—mere "verbalism." I think we should be more generous.

# CHAPTER 2

# Children's Questions

.✷.

In recent decades there have been several attempts to teach chimpanzees to communicate via language. One of the most successful programs has involved Kanzi, a male bonobo. With the help of a "talking" keyboard, Kanzi is able to express his needs and feelings and to make requests. His comprehension of human language is roughly equivalent to that of young preschooler, and sometimes superior. When Kanzi and Alia, a 2½-year-old child, were given a comprehensive test of language understanding, they did quite well. For example, asked to give a particular object to a particular recipient (e.g., "Give the doggie some carrots"), they both performed accurately. Indeed, when asked to retrieve a particular object in a particular location (e.g., "Go get the carrot that's in the microwave"), Kanzi was more accurate than Alia (Savage-Rumbaugh, Murphy, Sevcik, Brakke, Williams, & Rumbaugh, 1993).

Despite this impressive ability to understand language, Kanzi does not put his communication skills to use in the way that a human child does. In particular, he does not ask questions to gather information. Instead, Kanzi devotes more than 90 percent of his utterances to making requests that express his desires and preferences (Greenfield & Savage-Rumbaugh, 1990). Nor does this restriction appear to be due to the linguistic complexities of formulating a question. In principle, a question can be posed by mere repetition. For example, at 35 months David said to his twin, Toby: "My hands are cold." Toby queried this statement via simple repetition: "Cold?" he asked. Yet Kanzi does not even make use of repetition to ask questions (Greenfield & Savage-Rumbaugh, 1993).

It is not clear exactly why Kanzi fails to ask questions. Even if he recognizes gaps in his knowledge and seeks out information to fill them—and research shows that primates, including bonobos, do have such self-knowledge (Call, 2010; Call & Carpenter, 2001; Smith, 2009)—he may find it hard to conceive of human beings as creatures who possess information that he lacks or to think of ways he could get them to supply it. He may not appreciate how the language keyboard could be used as a tool to elicit information. Whatever the explanation for Kanzi's disinclination to ask questions, his tendency to use language primarily for making expressing wants and preferences highlights the very different stance taken by human children. As we shall see, from the very start of their ability to communicate, they ask questions—lots of them.

Before we analyze the suite of psychological abilities that are needed to ask a question, it is worth thinking about the intimate link between asking questions and learning from displaced utterances. As we shall see, when children ask questions they are frequently intent on seeking information from their conversation partner—rather than practical help or attention. If the information they wanted were available to direct perceptual inspection—in the here and now—there would be no need to pose the question. To the extent that a piece of information, displaced from the immediate situation, can be conveyed through conversation, questions can serve to elicit that information. In short, it is plausible to think of children's questions as a deliberate strategy to elicit from other people the type of information that triggers the process of learning from testimony, a process discussed in the previous chapter.

When children ask a well-formed question, they would appear to have mastered several prerequisites. First, they know that they don't know: they have some appreciation, however tacit, of their own ignorance or lack of knowledge. In addition, when they pose a question, they are presumably able to entertain possible answers—answers that are not immediately to hand. For example, when they ask about the location of a favorite toy, they can imagine that it might be upstairs in their bedroom or downstairs in the kitchen. When they ask what's for dinner, they can imagine that it might be soup or pasta. Without the ability to conceive of more than one possible way that things might stand in the world, why ask questions in the first place? In this sense, children's questions imply an increasing flexibility in their ability to build mental models of possible realities.[1] Children's use of questions also implies that they have some insight into the way they can learn from other people's testimony. They realize that it is not always necessary, or possible, to examine the world for themselves; instead, other people may know something that they do not and can supply the missing information. Finally, children's questions imply some grasp of the way that language, specifically a well-formed question, is a device for gathering that information. In summary, children's questions imply the orchestration of several different skills: recognition of a gap or missing piece of knowledge; the ability to imagine the way that things might be—to anticipate possible answers to a question; an appreciation of how other people can serve as informants who help to decide among those possible answers; and the realization that a question is a tool that can elicit pertinent information from an informant.

## The Early Study of Children's Questions

The psychological study of children's questions reaches back more than a century. James Sully, one of the earliest writers on child development, analyzed an intriguing collection of questions—including those asked by his own son—on matters ranging from how the dead reach heaven if they are buried in the ground to why seals are killed for their skins (Sully, 1896/2000). He concluded that even if children's questions are sometimes aimed at getting attention, many are not. Children genuinely seek information, and they often have an inkling of the kind of information that they are after. Sully notes that some early questions have a metaphysical or scientific flavor. The child asks, for example, "Who made God?" or "Why don't we see two things with our two eyes?" Nevertheless, Sully also claims that many questions appear to spring from the child's assumption that everything has been created for a purpose, and typically a human purpose. For example, when the child asks: "Why does the wind blow?" Sully argues that he probably means to find out what purpose is served by the blowing of the wind, rather than to find out its antecedent cause. More generally, according to Sully, the child thinks: "The world is a sort of big house where everything has been made by someone, or at least fetched from somewhere" (Sully, 1896/2000, p. 79).

Some 30 years later, on the basis of an extended diary study of one 6-year-old child observed over a 10-month period, Piaget (1926) came to similar conclusions. He insisted that many of the questions children pose betray their assumption that objects exist primarily for human purposes. Instead of looking for an explanation in terms of mechanism, or spatial contact, or causal laws, children invoke motives and intentions or else invoke a pseudo-necessity, implying that things could not be any other way. So, for example, Piaget claims that when the child asks, "Why can you see lightning better at night?" the question is best interpreted as a request not for the conditions that make it easier to see lightning at night, but for the purpose that such greater visibility serves.

Writing during the same period, Nathan Isaacs (1930) dissented from Piaget's interpretation. On the basis of questions asked by young children at the Malting House School, founded by his wife, Susan Isaacs, as well as the questions cited by Sully and Piaget, he argued that children often put questions to adults when they encounter an anomaly—something that runs counter to their everyday experience. For example, turning some of Piaget's examples against him, Isaacs argued that the child who asks, "Why do animals not mind drinking dirty water?" or "Why can you see lightning better at night?" is not looking for some purpose or intention. Instead, the child is trying to make sense of an unusual occurrence. Human beings don't like drinking dirty water—why do animals not mind drinking it? Ordinarily, we see much better during the day than at night—why is lightning an exception to this general rule?

As Isaacs went on to show, many of the questions posed by young children appear to be motivated by this desire to resolve apparent anomalies. Consider, for example, the following questions, all from children close to their fourth birthday: "Why doesn't the ink run out when you hold up a fountain pen?" "Why does it get lighter outside when you put out the light?" and "Why doesn't the butter stay on top (of hot toast)?" In each case, it seems reasonable to conclude that children are posing these questions not because of a belief in intelligent design, but because they are puzzled by a departure from their regular experience. Ordinarily, liquid runs out of an inverted tube, putting out the light makes the atmosphere darker, and objects are stable on a flat surface. Certainly, we know from decades of research that young children are very sensitive to departures from their regular experience. Even in the first year of life, infants stare—in apparent puzzlement—at an outcome that violates their prior expectations (Baillargeon, 1994).

These early analyses offer a fascinating, albeit contested, glimpse of the child's thought processes. Yet as Sully, Piaget, and Isaacs acknowledge to varying degrees, the analyses that they offer suffer from several restrictions. First, the data-gathering technique is highly selective. Parent-investigators are likely to record questions that are striking or imaginative, rather than routine: "Who made God?" is more noteworthy than "Where are my socks?" Second, such assiduous note-takers are scarcely representative of all parents. Third, the reports concentrate on children of 4 and older; but if asking questions is a basic human capacity, observations of younger children are needed to provide information about its inception. Fourth, all three investigators focus primarily on what prompts children to ask questions. They rarely discuss how far the answers that children receive add to the children's stock of ideas. Finally, with the important exception of Isaacs, they do not consider how the pattern of answers that children receive might shape the children's larger conception of how knowledge is gathered and revised.

In a comprehensive monograph, Michele Chouinard (2007) overcame several of these limitations. She used records of children's spontaneous language (available in CHILDES—see MacWhinney & Snow, 1985) to obtain a much more representative sample of their questions. She looked at the very early stages of children's question-asking, as well as later developments. Finally, she conceptualized children's questions in the way that I believe to be most appropriate: she viewed them as a key strategy for children to gather information—information that is likely have an important impact on the nature and direction of cognitive development.

As a first step, Chouinard analyzed the questions asked by four children ranging from 13 months to 5 years, with the majority of the data coming from the period between 2½ and 5 years. Two were middle-class European American children, one was a middle-class African American child, and one was a working-class European American child. Obviously, this tiny sample cannot be taken as representative of all children in the United States, much less in other countries. Nevertheless, these systematic recordings of children's conversations over many months revealed patterns that recur across all four children, making it feasible to generalize cautiously to a broader sample. Recordings were made in the children's homes when they were engaged in routine activities, typically with their parents or playing with toys brought by the investigators. In total, more than 200 hours of recordings were analyzed, to yield a total of nearly 25,000 questions.

The first result to underline is that the four children bombarded adults with questions, asking somewhere between one and three questions per minute, depending on the individual child—a rate that might be surprising even to parents and teachers. However, frequent questions would not be important for cognitive development if they were not intended to gather information. Children might ask questions for other purposes—for example, to get attention ("Hey, Mom?"), to clarify what the adult just said ("What did you say?"), to ask for something to be done ("Can you fix this for me?"), to request permission ("Can I go outside?"), or to express pretend-dialogue in the context of doll play ("Are you hungry?"). In fact, approximately two-thirds of children's questions—ranging from 62 percent to 75 percent, depending on the individual child—were aimed at obtaining information. Moreover, this proportion remained quite stable from the age of 2 to the age of 5.

Chouinard's data also indicate that adults were quite responsive—they provided a reply to more than two-thirds of the children's questions, and again this pattern was stable in children from 2 to 5. Indeed, especially when responding to 1- and 2-year-olds, adults often provided more information than the child had actually asked for, perhaps sensing that, given his or her limited language skills, the child had not been able to formulate a question targeting exactly the information needed. Further evidence that children were definitely seeking information was revealed by their tenacity. When adults failed to supply the information that they sought, children were likely to persist with their questions.

What kind of information did children ask for? Chouinard divided children's questions into two classes. First, there were questions aimed at getting facts, such as the name ("What's that?"), function ("What does it do?"), or location ("Where is my ball?") of an object or the activity of a person or animal ("What is he doing?"); these were typically *what* and *where* questions. Second, there were questions aimed at getting explanations; these were typically *how* and *why* questions. Until the age of approximately 30 months, children mostly asked fact-oriented, *what* and *where* questions. At later ages, however, questions aimed at getting an explanation became more frequent—amounting to about one-quarter of the total. To translate this into a temporal measure: when they were actively conversing with a familiar adult at home, these four preschoolers asked for an explanation about 25 times per hour.

The shift toward seeking explanations might reflect children's developing linguistic skills. Children might master the syntax of *what* and *where* questions before the syntax of *how* and *why* questions—but such an explanation is unlikely. As Chouinard points out, in principle it is possible to ask for an explanation without producing a well-formed *how* or *why* question. When a child looks at a broken toy airplane and asks, "Daddy broke?" the child is probably seeking explanatory information, even if the question is not well formed. The shift toward questions aimed at getting an explanation may therefore reflect a change in children's cognitive focus, rather than in their linguistic skills. Arguably, children increasingly realize that other people are a good source of causal information, particularly in cases where observation alone is not fully informative. Consistent with this speculation, 2-year-olds who simply observed a causal sequence—a moving block that activated a toy airplane—did not try to reproduce the effect themselves, whereas children who heard an adult offer a causal description—"The block can make it go"—did try to do so (Bonawitz et al., 2010; Muentener & Schulz, 2012). By implication, the adult's explanation helped children to go beyond the registration of two successive events and to realize the causal connection between the movement of the block and the movement of the airplane.

As noted, children not only sought information, they were also quite persistent in doing so. In the absence of a satisfactory reply, they frequently repeated their initial question. Indeed, an initial question was often followed up with a series of related questions. From the age of 30 months, more than half of children's questions formed part of a sequence, rather than standing in isolation, and requests for an explanation were especially likely to be embedded in such a sequence. Frequently, children started off by asking for factual information, and then changed tack to seek an explanation.

If we make the relatively conservative assumption that children will be at home in the company of a familiar caregiver for one hour each day, this study implies that they will produce somewhere between 400 and 1,200 questions each week. From the age of approximately 2½ years, about one-quarter of those questions will be requests for an explanation. Hence, before they go to school, children could ask around 10,000 questions each year, all aimed at probing why and how things happen. Moreover, that number might increase dramatically if a child spent the entire day, rather than a single hour, with a caregiver or other familiar conversation partners. Of course, we need to better understand how children assimilate the explanations that they receive. Still, asking questions is likely to be a vital strategy for early cognitive development.

How far can this portrait of four children be generalized to other children? Most of the data came from children aged 30 months and older. What are very young children capable of? Can they circumvent their limited or nonexistent language skills in order to ask questions? In addition, the children studied by Chouinard may have been unusual in various ways. Three children came from well-educated, middle-class families, and all four families had agreed to have regular recording sessions take place in their own homes over several years. Such families may have taken an exceptional interest in their children's development, and they may have been especially conscientious in answering questions, perhaps reinforcing an otherwise infrequent type of utterance. Would the same results be found with a more representative sample of

U.S. children? Would similar results be found among children growing up in other, non-Western communities? Finally, the children were studied in their own homes, typically talking to a parent. That setting might be especially hospitable to the asking of questions: at home, children have more or less exclusive access to an adult caregiver, and that adult likely knows them very well. Conditions outside of the home—for example, in preschool—may be less conducive.

## When Do Children Start Asking Questions?

Asking questions might be a skill that children gradually master as they acquire language. More specifically, as children come to realize that it is possible to ask questions, they might realize this only because they have been asked questions themselves, or only when they have acquired the appropriate linguistic tools for formulating a question. On this interpretation, children have no inherent inclination to ask questions—they simply emulate others who do so. However, it is worth considering a very different possibility: the disposition to seek information from other people may not ultimately be a linguistic skill, acquired in the context of language acquisition. Children may bring their interrogative stance to language, rather than copying it from conversation partners. To weigh these two possibilities, Chouinard (2007) conducted a diary study. Parents of children ranging in age from 1 to 5 years were asked to keep detailed notes on their children's questions. In order to gather information about how children try to elicit information before they can put their questions into words, the parents of the youngest children ranging in age from 12 to 24 months were asked to make a record of their children's nonverbal behavior, as well as their spoken utterances.

This follow-up study showed that questions asked by very young children were likewise mostly aimed at gathering information. For example, even among children of 12 to 17 months, who mainly used gestures and vocalizations to pose their "questions," the overwhelming majority of their queries appeared to be aimed at obtaining information rather than, for example, obtaining permission or seeking attention. An example will clarify how the youngest children managed to convey their questions in an almost wordless fashion. One mother was unpacking her groceries. The child picked up an unfamiliar item—a kiwi fruit. Holding it toward her mother with a puzzled expression on her face, she said: "Uh?"[2]

Not surprisingly, children in the younger age groups—from 12 to 30 months—almost always asked for factual as opposed to explanatory information, and they tended to ask isolated questions. As in the example just given, they asked a single question about the name or function of an object. It is tempting to think of these questions as pedestrian and unlikely to play much of a role in the child's cognitive development—especially when we compare them to the more exotic questions recorded by Sully, Piaget, and Isaacs. However, it is useful to keep in mind the points made in the previous chapter regarding young children's ability to update their knowledge on the basis of others' testimony. Children's early, factually oriented questions call for such an updating ability. For example, when a 2-year-old asks, "Where is my ball?" she is asking about an object that she cannot see at the time of her question. In addition, no matter what guess she herself might make, based on her memory of the place where she last saw her ball, in order to profit from the answer to her question, she will need to edit that pre-existing mental file in light of what she is told. Indeed, even when children ask about a visible object—as in the case of the child who picked up the unfamiliar kiwi fruit, the information that is elicited—about its name or function, in this particular example—is not something they can easily gather except via the testimony of others. The name or function of an unfamiliar object is often impossible to figure out from direct inspection.

From the age of 30 months on, about one-quarter of children's questions were aimed at obtaining an explanation, and about one-third were part of a series of questions rather than being produced in isolation. So the diary study confirmed that the pattern described earlier, in which children increasingly and persistently probe the how and why of things, is established early in the preschool period—by the middle of the third year. Later, we will look in more detail at the way children go about asking for explanations. First, however, it is important to ask whether the pattern established so far is a general one or limited to certain types of children.

## The Impact of Social Class

The findings with very young children, aged 12 to 30 months, suggest that asking questions is a natural and spontaneous capacity, calling for minimal socialization on the part of adult interlocutors. Still, there is plenty of room for children to hone that capacity in ways that fit their family and culture. Indeed, even within the United States or the United Kingdom, children vary considerably in how often they ask questions and in the tenacity with which they pursue a given line of inquiry, depending on the type of family in which they are raised.

In a careful early study of children's language, Dorothea McCarthy (1930) observed 140 children in Minneapolis ranging in age from 18 to 54 months. She recorded the first 50 utterances of each child as the child talked to the same, unfamiliar adult. Among upper-class as compared to lower-class children, a greater proportion of those 50 utterances were questions. This class difference was already evident at 24 to 30 months, and was still apparent at 48 to 54 months. Moreover, even when children of the same mental age were compared, a robust social-class difference emerged. For example, among upper-class children with a mental age of 48 to 54 months, almost 20 percent of their utterances were in the form of a question. By contrast, among lower-class children with a similar mental age, fewer than 10 percent were in the form of a question.

Some of this variation might be due to the greater confidence of upper-class children in posing questions to a stranger—remember that all children had been asked to talk to the same, relatively unfamiliar adult. However, a similar class difference emerged some 50 years later in a study carried out in the United Kingdom by Tizard and Hughes (1984). They recorded conversations between 4-year-old girls and their mothers at home. The proportion of conversation turns devoted to questions was greater for middle-class as compared to working-class children. Middle-class children were especially likely to ask curiosity-based questions—as opposed to questions that focused on procedural matters or that challenged parental authority. Middle-class children were also more likely to engage in bouts of persistent questioning— called "passages of intellectual search" by Tizard and Hughes. In the course of regular conversation, a sustained focus on any given topic was fairly unusual among the 4-year-olds. Fewer than one-fifth of their conversations lasted for 22 turns or more. By contrast, during "passages of intellectual search" a sustained focus over many turns was evident in more than half. This type of tenacious search for an explanation was observed in most of the middle-class families, but in only about one-quarter of the working-class families.

Why did the middle-class children ask more questions, especially sustained curiosity-based questions? A plausible interpretation is that they had become used to receiving informative replies at home. Indeed, the middle-class mothers were more likely to say that they enjoyed answering their children's questions. However, when Tizard and Hughes (1984) assessed the adequacy of mothers' replies, they found no relationship to children's own question-asking, at least as measured in terms of simple frequency.[3] On the other hand, there was a link to the mothers' own conversational style. Mothers who asked more questions of their children had children who asked more questions of them. Children may be more influenced by their mother's style of seeking information than by the answers she provides.

Hart and Risley (1992) likewise reported evidence suggesting a causal link between question-asking by the parent and question-asking by the child. They carried out a longitudinal study of parent-child interaction in the homes of 40 children, representing the broad range of American families in terms of socioeconomic status. On average, one-third of parental utterances were questions, but across the different families there was tremendous variation around that average—from fewer than 20 percent to almost 50 percent. Moreover, the variation remained stable: individual families continued to display approximately the same proportion of questions across the 27-month period in which observations were conducted.

The tendency to ask many questions appears to be part of a more general style of communication. Those parents who asked more questions were more likely to take up, repeat, or expand on what their child had just said. By contrast, parents who asked fewer questions were more likely to issue prohibitions: "Stop" or "Don't (do that)." Apparently, parents have different attitudes toward talking with their children. Some see it as an opportunity for cognitive exploration and elaboration. Others see it mainly as a tool for controlling what their children do; they communicate in order to stipulate—or rein in—their children's behaviors. Parents who model the exploratory stance—who see dialogue as an opportunity for sharing and exchanging information—are likely to have children who emulate that stance. This would explain why Tizard and Hughes (1984) found that parents who ask a lot of questions have children who do the same.

Despite the plausibility of this emulation hypothesis, it is important to keep another possibility in mind. We know that a considerable proportion of the variation among children in their language ability can be attributed to genetic factors. As they get older, children who have been separated from their biological parents and raised by adoptive parents show more and more resemblance to their biological parents, but not to their adoptive parents, in tests of verbal ability (Plomin, Fulker, Corley, & DeFries, 1997). The same pattern might be found for the disposition to answer questions. Future research could usefully ask whether adopted children display the question-asking style of their biological parents or of their adoptive parents. It will also be important to find out whether children—no matter what their innate language ability—can be prompted to ask more questions when they talk to an adult or peer who asks many questions.

## Cross-Cultural Variation?

All the children discussed so far were growing up in the United States or Western Europe. Do children in other cultures ask questions as often and as persistently? Munroe, Gauvain, and Beebe (2011) studied 3- and 5-year-olds living in small villages or towns of four different countries: Belize, Kenya, Nepal, and Samoa. To varying degrees, the children's parents were engaged in subsistence farming and paid labor.

Children's remarks were recorded as they engaged in their everyday activities, often—but not always—with their parents nearby. Overall, information-seeking questions made up about one-tenth of all the remarks that children made—a proportion quite close to that observed by Chouinard (2007). But whereas about one-quarter of the U.S. children's information-seeking questions were aimed at getting an explanation, these *how* and *why* questions were rarely asked in any of the four non-U.S. communities. In fact, such questions amounted to fewer than 5 percent of children's information-seeking questions.

Drawing on ethnographic data, Munroe and his colleagues note that most mothers in these communities expected their children to be obedient, responsible, and respectful, and they often used punishment, including beating and scolding, to that end. There was little indication that they viewed dialogue with their children as an opportunity for the exchange of information. A possible explanation for their stance is that an appreciation for explanatory dialogue is fostered via education. To varying degrees, schooling provides a powerful model of the way in which information can be transmitted via language—either oral or written (Levine et al., 2012). Those who have been to school are constantly exposed to that model, and they presumably internalize it. When they eventually become parents, they are likely to reactivate that model and use it as a guide in raising their own children. So we can expect more-educated parents to engage in more conversation, especially pedagogic or explanatory conversation, with their children. In the context of such dialogue, it is plausible that questions will be more frequently modeled and emulated.

Indeed, Munroe and his colleagues found that across the four communities, it was the children in Samoa who asked the greatest proportion of information-seeking questions, whereas the children in Kenya asked the least. This fits with the proposal that parental schooling is an important influence. In Samoa, both primary and secondary schooling were available. Many parents had experienced both, and every household possessed books and writing tablets. In Kenya, by contrast, only primary schooling was available in the village, and a third of all households lacked books and writing tablets (Gauvain & Munroe, 2009).

## Home and School

If young children pose many questions, especially *how* and *why* questions, to their parents at home, we might expect them to adopt the same information-gathering stance toward their teachers at school. Tizard and Hughes (1984) examined this issue by making recordings of the same set of children when they were at home with their mothers and when they were at preschool. They found that all children, irrespective of social class, asked many fewer questions at preschool. Indeed, sustained and tenacious questioning of an adult occurred rarely, if ever, in preschool, whereas it was fairly common at home with the mother. As Tizard and Hughes point out, even if children gain various social benefits from being in preschool with other children, they appear to have fewer opportunities for learning via dialogue with an adult.

Why might a child ask more questions of a parent than of a teacher? Two different factors come to mind. In the first place, it is easier—and arguably more appropriate—for a child at home to monopolize the attention of a parent via frequent questioning. After all, a teacher is often trying to look after and communicate with a group of children, as opposed to a single child. Beyond such contextual factors, however, it is also intuitively plausible that deep-seated, interpersonal factors are at work, exacerbating the contrast between school and home. In much the same way that young children come to regard certain adults as available and responsive at times of emotional need, they might also come to regard certain adults as cognitively available at times of puzzlement or cognitive confusion. Moreover, just as emotional availability fosters an affective bond—an attachment—between child and adult, cognitive availability is likely to foster an intellectual bond between child and adult. So when children seek information, they are likely to be selective in whom they question and whose answers they assimilate—just as, when they make a bid for emotional reassurance, they choose whom to approach and whose gestures of comfort to accept. The conditions under which young children display such selective intellectual trust, and the extent to which emotional and intellectual trust are distinct or intertwined, will be discussed in more detail in Chapter 5.

## Learning from Questions

Do children learn from asking questions? It might seem perverse to raise this issue. Surely, provided that their questions are answered in a helpful, informative fashion, children will learn. Moreover, as we saw in the previous chapter, toddlers can update their picture of the world on the basis of what they are told. Nevertheless, a negative or ambivalent attitude toward children's questions recurs in earlier writings on the subject. For example, toward the end of his otherwise sympathetic treatment, James Sully remarks: "It may often be noticed that a child's 'why?' is used in a sleepy mechanical way with no real desire for knowledge, any semblance of an answer being accepted without an attempt to put meaning into it" (Sully, 1896/2000, p. 89).

In *The Language and Thought of the Child,* Piaget also emphasizes that a young child is too easily content with an explanation: "He always thinks he has understood everything. However obscure the explanation, he is always satisfied" (Piaget, 1926, p. 119). Indeed, Piaget seems to have avoided supplying his own children with ready explanations. Lecturing in Geneva in 1971, he described an occasion on which his daughter had twirled round and round, making herself dizzy. Puzzled about her feeling that the world was spinning around her, she looked to her father and asked: "Is it turning around you too, Papa?" "What do you think?" replied Piaget. "You always ask me that!" his daughter remonstrated.

At the Malting House School, children were likewise encouraged to answer their own questions. Susan Isaacs describes the educational aims of the school as follows: "We wanted to stimulate the active inquiry of the children themselves, rather than to 'teach' them; and we wanted to bring within their immediate experience every range of fact to which their interests reached out." In line with those goals, children at the school were given many opportunities to experiment and observe, be it to study the effects of holding a glass rod in the flame of a

Bunsen burner or to examine the innards of a dead mouse (Isaacs, S., 1930, pp. 129, 185). In combination with this philosophy of hands-on learning, the teachers were discouraged from answering children's questions directly: "When the children turned to us, we would, in the first instance, throw the question back to them. 'What do you think? How does it seem to you?'" (Isaacs, S., 1930, p. 40). Indeed, there was a general skepticism about verbal explanation. In a passage that would certainly have earned Rousseau's approval, Susan Isaacs writes: "We avoided offering ready-made explanations to the children not only because we did not want to foster verbalism, but also because we did not want to substitute ourselves as authority for the child's own discovery and verification of the facts" (Isaacs, S., 1930, p. 40).

These various remarks imply that children who are given an answer to their question simply accept it without reflection or analysis. Is this implication correct? Extending the analyses reported by Chouinard (2007), Frazier, Gelman, and Wellman (2009) examined more than 3,000 questions asked by six children in naturalistic settings—typically their own home. The children ranged in age from 2 years through 4 years 11 months. Frazier and her colleagues reasoned that if children ask *why* or *how* questions but do not reflect on the answer, they should respond in much the same way whether they receive an adequate explanation or not. What they found, however, was that children reacted differently in the two cases. When children received an adequate explanation, they were likely to express satisfaction by acknowledging their agreement or by asking a follow-up question on the same topic. On the other hand, when they did not receive an adequate explanation—for example, when their interlocutor admitted ignorance ("I don't know") or queried the premise of the question (Child: "How can snakes hear if they don't have ears?"; Adult: "I don't think they can hear"), children were likely to repeat their initial question or to propose their own explanation.

Like the sample of children studied by Chouinard (2007), these children constituted a small and unrepresentative sample—for instance, four of the six children came from academic families. So it is important to ask if the same pattern is found with a broader range of children. In a follow-up study, Frazier and her colleagues observed children via an experimental procedure rather than in a naturalistic setting. They presented more than 40 preschoolers ranging in age from 3 to 5 years with various anomalies. For example, children were shown a picture that depicted a nest; inside the nest were two baby birds and a turtle. Just as Nathan Isaacs might have expected (Isaacs, 1930), children often remarked on the anomalies, either by asking a question ("Why is the turtle in that nest?") or by expressing surprise ("Hey, that's a turtle!"). When the interviewer supplied an explanation ("You know, I think the turtle crawled in there by mistake"), children tended to agree or move on to a follow-up question; but if the interviewer provided a nonexplanatory answer ("You're right—there is a turtle in that bird's nest"), children behaved as they had done in the naturalistic study: they often reiterated their question, or occasionally volunteered their own explanation. Taken together, these two studies show how wrong Sully and Piaget were. When children ask a *why* or *how* question, not only are they genuinely looking for an explanation, they also notice whether they receive one or not, and respond accordingly.

When children ask a series of questions—either by repeating the same basic question or by engaging in a more wide-ranging "passage of intellectual search"—they might persist until they have obtained the information they seek. This formulation suggests that a given series of questions is guided by the search for a clearly identifiable, missing piece of information, and that questioning will stop once it has been provided. Such a targeted search might apply when children ask factual *what* and *where* questions. However, scrutiny of children's sustained questioning shows that the process is often more complicated. Children's follow-up questions are sometimes intended not to supplement the answer they have received, but rather to qualify or query that answer. So even when they do receive an explanation, children are not always satisfied with it. They do not necessarily accept what they are told—they weigh up the degree to which it satisfactorily resolves the puzzle that they are trying to sort out. Some examples will indicate what I have in mind.

Sully (1896/2000) reports the following exchange between his wife and their 4-year-old son. Having been told that seals are killed for their skins and for oil, the boy turned his attention to stag hunting and asked: "Why do they kill the stags? They don't want their skins, do they?" His mother explained: "No, they kill them because they like to chase them." "Why don't policemen stop them?" "They can't do that, because people are allowed to kill them." The child protested: "Allowed, allowed? People are not allowed to take other people and kill them." His mother countered: "People think there is a difference between killing men and killing animals." "You don't understand me," the child answered with a woebegone look.

Sully was trained in philosophy and eventually became a professor at University College, London. Given his intellectual temperament, perhaps he had encouraged his son to be both articulate and skeptical. However, resistance to the information supplied by a parent is not confined to children with philosophical fathers. Consider the following exchange reported by Tizard and Hughes (1984). Four-year-old Rosy was puzzled about why a window cleaner was given money. In the course of a long exchange, her mother explained: "Well, the window-cleaner needs money doesn't he?" "Why?" asked Rosy. "To buy clothes for his children and food for them to eat." Rosy objected: "Well, sometimes window-cleaners don't have children." Similarly, when Beth (just under 4 years) was offered an explanation by her mother for why roofs slope—"Otherwise, if you have a flat roof, the rain would sit in the middle of the roof and make a big puddle, and then it would start coming through"—Beth responded: "Our school has a flat roof, you know." An exchange reported by Nathan Isaacs (1930, p. 538) reveals a similar alacrity in identifying potential counter-instances. Rose (age 3 years 8 months) asked her mother, "Why don't we milk pigs?" "Because they have little ones of their own to feed," her mother explained. Rose demurred: "So do cows have calves."

These few examples indicate that when children search for an explanation via conversation, two related but distinct processes come into play. Children register and digest the generalizations that adults make—for example, that seals are killed for their skins. Yet they also check how far those generalizations cover other cases already known to them. Having identified a possible exception, children call attention to it: Are stags hunted for their skins? Apparently, when children are offered an explanation, they do not mindlessly swallow what they are told.

Such caution suggests we should not assume that children who receive answers to their questions will be prone to what Susan Isaacs and Piaget refer to as "verbalism"—the tendency to accept adults' claims without fully grasping their implications. Instead, the above examples show that there are important parallels between the way children process phenomena that they learn about via direct observation and phenomena that they learn about via other people's testimony. In the case of direct observation, as Nathan Isaacs argues, children are often puzzled when they encounter an apparent departure from some generalization that they have established. They know that, in general, liquids pour out of an inverted tube. Hence, they are puzzled by, and comment on, the fact that ink fails to pour out when you hold the pen nib down. Similarly, they know that, in general, one solid will stay in place on top of another. Hence, they are puzzled when butter sinks into hot toast, and they comment on it. In a similar fashion, the puzzled queries that children voice in the various conversations just quoted spring from their ability to retrieve a case that is anomalous in light of the generalization that the adult has just proposed. So whether we focus on children's processing of their firsthand experience—the ink that does not pour, the butter that sinks—or alternatively on their processing of the replies that they receive to their questions, we observe the same phenomenon: sensitivity to anomaly, rather than passive acceptance.

Finally, it is worth underlining the fact that the few examples of tenacious questioning described here may underestimate the sheer doggedness of some children's questions. Not only might children ask a series of questions on one particular occasion; they may also bury an issue temporarily, only to unearth it at some later point. Parents report that certain emotionally charged topics—birth, calamity, death—can be revisited several times in the course of a few weeks or months. Neither the diary studies described in this chapter nor the more comprehensive analyses undertaken by Chouinard give us much information about how such questioning evolves as children brood and reengage. In discussing such repeated bouts of question-asking, Tizard and

Hughes (1984) suggest that children may sense that they have not fully understood a topic, and therefore return to it on several occasions. Yet it is also possible that when children receive an adequate and comprehensible explanation, the new information they have received leads to other questions. Recall that Frazier and her colleagues found that children often follow up an adult's explanation with further questions (Frazier et al., 2009). Such additional questions may take time to formulate—they gradually arise as children work through the implications of an explanation that they have been given. This cycle between information-seeking, the active incorporation of newly gathered information, and the formulation of new questions is quite close to what Piaget had in mind when he described children's physical exploration of the world. It is, of course, a cycle that is endlessly repeated in science.

## Taboo, Debatable, and Resolved Questions

Children can ask questions about all manner of topics, but it is likely that some are more fraught than others. More generally, we can think of the landscape of interrogation as falling into at least three domains: the taboo, the debatable, and the resolved. Depending on how their questions are received, children will likely learn that some topics are taboo—questions about them will not be answered and ought not even to be asked. Other topics will elicit conflicting answers. Still others will elicit consensual or incontrovertible answers. What gets assigned to these three different domains, and the overall magnitude of each domain relative to the others, will likely vary dramatically from culture to culture and from home to home. In some homes, there will be ample room for debate, whereas in others, many questions will be treated as settled. So, beyond acquiring particular answers to particular questions, children will also gradually develop a tacit sense of the conversational terrain: what is forbidden territory, what can be explored further, and what can be taken for granted. We know little about this mapping process. Further comparative work in different homes and different cultures would be illuminating.

## Conclusions

Unlike the young of other species, children ask a lot of questions; most of those questions are aimed at gathering information, as opposed to requesting permission, challenging authority, or seeking attention. A question implies that children recognize their ignorance, conceive of possible answers, and realize that other people, if asked, can help them choose among those possible answers. For example, when young children ask, "What's this called?" they can conceive of the object having a name—even if they do not know what it is—and they expect that their interlocutor can tell them what that name is. When they ask, "Where's my ball?" they can conceive of the object being somewhere—even if they do not know exactly where—and they expect their interlocutor to be able to identify that location. We are so used to this information-gathering strategy by young children that it is tempting to take it for granted. But the fact that no other species adopts it highlights its cognitive complexity. Children start to deploy this strategy from the beginning of the second year, before they can even properly formulate their questions in words—a fact suggesting that it is a deep-seated aspect of human mentation. On the other hand, that tendency varies considerably across social groups and social circumstances. For example, the tendency to ask questions, especially a sustained series of related questions aimed at obtaining an explanation or resolving an anomaly, is more evident in middle-class as compared to working-class children in Britain and the United States, and it is uncommon among children in less modern, non-Western settings. It seems likely that children emulate the stance toward conversation that is modeled by their parents; in turn, the parents' stance is markedly influenced by their own level of schooling. As a result, children vary considerably in the extent to which they use questions as a vehicle for exploration and clarification. That said, whatever their family background, young children ask fewer questions, and fewer sustained questions, when they are in school.

Historically, psychologists and educators have not focused on the cognitive benefits that children's questions might bring. Indeed, they have been suspicious, preferring to think of genuine learning in the way that Rousseau did—as flowing primarily from the interaction of a solitary child with the natural world. These writers worry that when children ask questions, they will unthinkingly defer to adult authority. They will not check or test the answers that they receive. To combat that tendency, Susan and Nathan Isaacs thought it was important to provide children with equipment and opportunities for experimentation. Likewise, the Montessori classroom emphasizes the way children can learn from interaction with concrete materials.

Yet various pieces of evidence indicate that children are not always acquiescent when they enter into a dialogue with an adult. When offered an explanation, they call attention to counter-examples and anomalies. They also ponder what they have been told and proceed to ask more questions. Rousseau, Piaget, and the Isaacses sought to make children better scientists by not answering their questions. Ironically, the evidence in this chapter suggests that it is when children have their questions answered that they respond with the cautious reflection and the persistent curiosity of good scientists. By implication, rather than leaving children to their own devices, we should encourage them to join the community of inquiry that is characteristic of science.

Still, Rousseau and his successors were not entirely wrong. As we shall see, even if children are not always acquiescent, neither are they arch-skeptics. The next two chapters describe how children sometimes accept what they are told, even in cases where it goes against their own intuition.

# CHAPTER 3

# Learning from a Demonstration

⋆

$V$ery young children change their ideas about the world on the basis of what other people tell them, and they actively seek information from other people by asking questions about identity, function, location, and cause. But children can also learn a lot from watching other people. Particularly in preindustrialized societies, young children come to participate in a variety of activities, including food-gathering, gardening, fishing, and weaving, through observation and imitation (Konner, 2010).

The study of human imitation is fascinating for several, overlapping reasons. First, it is possible to offer children and nonhuman primates, especially chimpanzees, approximately the same demonstration and compare how the two species imitate what they have seen. This close comparison promises to help identify distinctive or unique features of human imitation. Research on apes has established that they have local traditions of tool use. For example, the way that chimpanzees use sticks to poke into a termite mound varies from one locale to another. To the extent that there are no obvious ecological factors which might explain such variation, we can reasonably speak of local cultures of tool use, cultures that are transmitted fairly faithfully from one member of the group to another and arguably from one generation to the next (Whiten et al., 1999; Whiten, 2005). Indeed, by showing selected chimpanzees a new practice and watching it proliferate more or less unchanged though the group, primatologists have successfully mimicked experimentally the spread and maintenance of such cultural traditions of tool use (Whiten, Horner, & de Waal, 2005). These diffusion experiments highlight the imitative capacity of chimpanzees and its centrality for the tool-based culture of primates (Whiten, McGuigan, Marshall-Pescini, & Hopper, 2009). At the same time, field observation suggests that despite their capacity for imitation, primates display nothing parallel to the progressive increase in tool complexity—the so-called ratchet effect—that is so evident in human technology. In other words, the basic capacity to imitate the manufacture and use of tools is not sufficient to explain how, in human culture, more complex technical forms elaborate on, and displace, earlier forms. If this type of imitation were sufficient, we might expect to see a comparable ratchet effect among primates (Harris & Want, 2005). Since we do not, we should be alert to the possibility that human imitation has some distinctive features that make the ratchet effect possible.

Another body of research, this time in archaeology, shows that before the human ratchet effect got underway, there was a very prolonged period of unchanged tool use in human prehistory. Oldowan stone tools (named after the Olduvai Gorge, an archaeological site in Tanzania) are associated with *Homo habilis,* who lived from approximately 2.2 million to 1.6 million years ago. *Homo habilis* made these tools by using one rock as a hammer to strike another, yielding a large core and a smaller, detached flake. The exact function of the tools remains a matter of debate—they could have been used for animal butchery, scraping hides, woodworking, nut-cracking, or a variety of other such purposes (Schick & Toth, 1993). Acheulean tools (the name comes from a site in northern France)—which display greater standardization, and circular or oval flakes with bilateral symmetry—appeared around 1.6 million years ago and persisted until approximately 200,000 years ago. However, it is only in the recent past—in the last 200,000 years or so—that we gradually begin to see clear signs of a ratchet effect in human tool manufacture, a cumulative increase in complexity over time. For a vast stretch of human history, there was stability, underpinned, so far as we can tell, by imitation, from one generation to the next. This remarkable stability highlights the question of how the ratchet effect was eventually set in motion. One possibility is that a cognitive change led our ancestors to be more creative or planful in their design of tools. Certainly, this would be consistent with other signs—such as the proliferation of cave art and complex burial practices—that an imaginative capacity was emerging in humans during the Upper Paleolithic (Harris, 2000). On the other hand, it is also possible that there was a shift, not so much in the way tools were conceived by individual inventors, but in the process of transmission within and across generations. More specifically, particular types of tool preparation or use may have been increasingly transmitted in a selective fashion, with learners being more receptive to some demonstrations than others. In short, it is worth taking a close look at how human beings, as contrasted with chimpanzees, learn via imitation. Both species imitate, to be sure, but there may be differences in the way they imitate and in the models they choose. In particular, unlike chimpanzees, children may be more inclined to conceive of other people as guides or informants—in line with their frequent and persistent use of questions.

A good comparative starting point is a series of experiments carried out by Victoria Horner and Andrew Whiten (2005). They tested young chimpanzees living on Ngamba Island, a chimpanzee sanctuary in Uganda. The chimpanzees had been born in the wild and continued to have daily access to the forest habitat that is typical for their species. However, following their rescue, generally from the bush-meat trade, they also spent a portion of each day in a holding facility at the sanctuary, where a relatively stimulating environment was made available to them in the form of foraging tasks and novel objects. The rearing history of these young chimpanzees was therefore a mix of their species-typical forest environment and the captive environment of the sanctuary.

To assess the chimpanzees' ability to imitate, the researchers gave them a puzzle box from which they could extract a food reward. The lower section of the box contained an opaque tube with food inside the tube. The mouth of the tube was covered by a door at the front of the box, but the chimps could open the door and extract food by poking inside the tube. The upper section of the box had an empty hole in its top surface, covered by a bolt. A long aluminum rod was also available which the chimps could use to remove the bolt on the upper section and poke into the hole (Figure 3.1a) or to poke into the opaque food tube in the lower section (Figure 3.1b). Food could be accessed only via the lower section, not the upper section.

Some chimpanzees were shown the box with clear sides, so that it

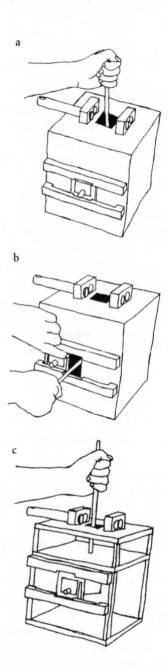

**Figure 3.1.** The puzzle box: actions directed at the upper section of the box, as in (a), were ineffective in extracting food from the lower section, in contrast to actions directed at the lower section, as in (b). Based on Whiten, Horner, & Marshall-Pescini (2005).

was easy for them to see the opaque tube inside the lower section. More important, it was easy for them to see that it would be pointless to try to poke inside the tube via the top section (Figure 3.1c), since there was a ceiling dividing the upper and lower sections. Only an approach via the mouth of the tube in the lower section would be effective. Other chimpanzees were shown the box with opaque sides, so that the best way to obtain the food was not obvious to them. They could reasonably conclude that it would be worth poking the rod either into the hole in the upper section (Figure 3.1a) or into the tube in the lower section (Figure 3.1b).

Before the chimpanzees were given a chance to go to work on the box, the experimenter offered an overly elaborate—and somewhat unhelpful—demonstration. Taking the rod, she hit the bolt and poked the rod into the hole in the upper section. Then, turning to the lower section, she opened the door covering the mouth of the tube, poked the rod inside and extracted the food. From the chimpanzees' point of view, when the sides of the box were opaque, it probably looked as if the actions on the upper section were somehow necessary for a successful attack on the lower section. Not surprisingly, they tended to copy the experimenter in a relatively faithful fashion. On the other hand, when the sides of the box were clear, so that the futility of trying to extract the food via the top hole was evident, the chimpanzees efficiently ignored the experimenter's actions on the upper section of the box, and immediately directed their efforts to the tube in the lower section.

In sum, when their intuitions about the physical layout inside the box were uncertain, the chimpanzees deferred to the experimenter, mimicking her demonstration. However, once they could see inside the box, they ignored her irrelevant actions on the upper section and concentrated on the lower section. Indeed, when chimpanzees were first given a demonstration with the clear-sided box, so that the interior layout was obvious from the start, and then were given a demonstration with the opaque-sided box, they also ignored the experimenter's irrelevant actions. Once they had grasped the physical layout, they were not misled by the experimenter into adopting a roundabout, indirect strategy—even with the opaque box.

This study clearly shows that when a procedure is demonstrated, it may or may not be faithfully reproduced. It is sometimes pruned or reworked. Chimpanzees know something about containers and how to get at what's inside them. They are prepared to apply that knowledge in order to winnow out components of a demonstration that strike them as useless. What about young children? Do they show the same selectivity and efficiency as chimpanzees when they copy a demonstration?

Back at St. Andrews in Scotland, Horner and Whiten tested 3- and 4-year-old children with the same puzzle box. Like the chimpanzees, the children were also given an overly elaborate and misleading demonstration by the experimenter. Moreover, some children were first given a demonstration with the opaque box and then with the clear box, and some were given the reverse order. The results were striking. No matter which box they worked on and no matter which box came first, children reproduced the adult's irrelevant actions on the upper section as well as the relevant actions on the lower section.

How should we interpret children's overimitation—their faithful but inefficient copying of exactly what they had seen the experimenter do? Perhaps, unlike the chimpanzees, they did not grasp the interior layout of the box even when they could see through the clear sides. In particular, maybe they did not understand that the ceiling dividing the lower and upper sections formed an impassable barrier. But this is not very plausible. We have no reason to think that the naïve physics of young children is any less sophisticated than that of young chimpanzees, especially when children live in a much richer world of implements and containers. In any case, in a follow-up experiment with still older children, the children displayed the same pattern of overimitation (McGuigan, Whiten, Flynn, & Horner, 2007).

Two other interpretations are much more plausible. Maybe children thought that it would be impolite or antisocial not to copy what the adult had done, even if they privately wondered why she was wasting her time—and theirs—by poking into the hole at the top. By implication, the less interpersonally attuned chimpanzees treated the demonstration in a businesslike fashion—as a source of useful information about how to get at the food, but not as demonstration to be punctiliously copied. Alternatively, perhaps children are more receptive pupils than chimpanzees. Even when they could see directly into the box, maybe they thought that the experimenter was showing them a useful strategy even though it looked inefficient to them. On this hypothesis, children did not politely "go along" with the experimenter while remaining skeptical. Instead, they assumed that the experimenter's demonstration was teaching them something helpful—albeit mysterious—about the box.

Derek Lyons and his colleagues set out to compare these two interpretations (Lyons, Young, & Keil, 2007). They reasoned that if children were just politely going along with the demonstration, it should be easy to prompt them to abandon its irrelevant components. With this in mind, they gave preschoolers in New England a training session in which the children were encouraged to point out irrelevant actions by the experimenter as he retrieved toys from a series of containers. Children quickly learned to be candid critics. About three-quarters of those older than 4 received the maximum possible score for spotting irrelevancies. Yet, despite their high scores in this training session, children diligently included the experimenter's irrelevant actions when it was their turn to open more complex puzzle boxes in a subsequent test session. These results undermine the theory that children are politely "going along" with the experimenter's elaborate demonstration. Despite being trained to spot its useless aspects, children still conscientiously included them.

Lyons and his colleagues, therefore, focused on the "receptive-pupil" hypothesis. They argued that children are receptive *causal* learners who more or less automatically think of the experimenter's useless actions as having a causal impact, however inexplicable. A moment's reflection on our own everyday activities underlines the plausibility of this hypothesis. When we flick a light switch or turn a car key in the ignition, many of us—if challenged—would be unable to offer an adequate explanation of exactly how and why our actions are effective. We realize that there is some mechanism linking the switch to the light bulb or the car key to the engine, but that's about it. Arguably, young children are just as trusting as adults: they engage in actions whose causal impact is mysterious.

The receptive-pupil hypothesis predicts that children will not imitate actions if they cannot conceive how those actions could have a causal effect. This idea was tested by having 4-year-olds watch the experimenter direct irrelevant actions to a piece of the apparatus that was physically separate from the main puzzle box. The idea was that children would conclude something like the following: "Hey . . . why did the experimenter touch that separate part of the puzzle? There's no way that could ever help to get the toy, so I won't bother to do that!" (Lyons et al., 2007). The results were neatly consistent with this prediction. Children did not copy the irrelevant action directed to a physically separate part of the apparatus. Apparently, overimitation can be switched off. Although it might be tempting to conclude that overimitation is just blind copying, that would be a misinterpretation. Blind copying implies that children faithfully reproduce a demonstration no matter what its components. What children appear to be doing instead is something more selective: they include those components that they can conceive of having a causal effect—however mysterious. But they discard components that they regard as completely ineffective.[1]

## The Role of the Environment?

We adults engage in many actions for which we could not give a comprehensive causal rationale. Clearly, our ignorance of the appropriate causal story is linked to the complexity of the contemporary environment. It is easy to manipulate a light switch, and easy to see its effect, but the intervening causal mechanism is hidden from view and involves operations that we may not understand. By contrast, the causal operations of traditional technologies—for example, a bow and arrow or a fishing line—are more transparent than those of an electric light switch.

This suggests an interesting but narrower interpretation of the findings described so far. Maybe the receptivity to mysterious causal process displayed by the children in the preceding experiments is found only among children growing up in a complicated, industrialized world where the inner workings of the machines and tools that they encounter are hidden from view. On this hypothesis, children growing up in places like Scotland or New England are not displaying a learning stance that is characteristic of human children as a species. Instead, they engage in overimitation because they have found that it is a reasonable way to get started in using the complicated technology that they encounter.

Nielsen and Tomaselli (2010) tested this speculation by comparing two groups of children. In the urban environment of Brisbane, Australia, they tested children ranging in age from 2 to 6 years, using puzzle boxes like those described earlier. In remote regions of the Kalahari Desert, one in South Africa and one in Botswana, they tested children of the same age range growing up in Bushman communities still partially maintaining a traditional hunter-gatherer lifestyle. Nielsen and Tomaselli speculated that there would be less overimitation among the Bushman children because they had grown up in a much less industrialized environment than the Australian children. In fact, however, the two groups of children behaved in the same way. Left to their own devices, they opened the door of a puzzle box in straightforward fashion—by hand. But after watching an adult twirl a stick on top of the box and then use it to pry open the door, children faithfully copied the adult. Apparently, overimitation is not restricted to children growing up in urban settings replete with Western technology. It is a good candidate for a human universal.

The line of interpretation proposed so far implies that children resort to overimitation when they believe that the demonstrated actions are causally effective—however mysteriously. But what happens if they are first given a chance to open the puzzle box efficiently? Do they then suppress overimitation? From a strictly pragmatic point of view, that outcome seems plausible. Why do something needlessly complicated if you already know how to do it simply and efficiently? However, in a further experiment with South African children from the !Xun and Khwe clans, Nielsen and Tomaselli (2010) found that even after the children had efficiently opened the boxes by hand, they still went on to copy the experimenter's subsequent demonstration of a more elaborate method—and this tendency was even stronger among older children. It was as if children said to themselves: "Well, it beats me why he does it *that* way—I know a much simpler way. But, I guess he must be doing it for a reason—so I suppose I'd better do the same." By implication, children's overimitation cannot be based on considerations of efficiency. If their main aim were to get the object out of the box as efficiently as possible, they should copy the complex technique only when they don't know of a simpler one.

Further research by Nielsen and Blank (2011) reinforces this conclusion. Four- and 5-year-olds were each given two demonstrations of how to open a box: one by an instructor using an efficient technique, and one by an instructor using an inefficient technique. One of the instructors then left, and the other handed children the box. Children used the efficient technique to open it only in the presence of the efficient instructor. When the inefficient instructor was present, they reproduced his technique. Clearly, children do not pursue simple efficiency—or complexity, for that matter—across the board. The presence of a person who has demonstrated a given style—be it simple or complex—guides their choice of what to do.

## The Cultural Learner

We've seen that if someone engages in a mysteriously complicated action, children copy it faithfully—much more faithfully than chimpanzees. An initially plausible interpretation of such overimitation is that children are receptive pupils looking for guidance about causally effective ways to solve a practical problem. But we have encountered two problems with this interpretation. First, children copy overly complicated actions even when they have already discovered a simple and effective technique on their own. Second, children are not always receptive to a complicated technique—they will not reproduce it in the presence of someone who has shown them a simpler one.

Here is an interpretation of these somewhat discordant strands of evidence. Children are indeed receptive pupils but—unlike chimpanzees—their motives are not narrowly pragmatic. They are not simply on the lookout for causal information about how to solve practical problems. When they enter a new setting, they watch attentively to identify the norms that apply in that setting. They are looking primarily for cultural rather than causal rules. They regard what a person does as a demonstration of what one is supposed to do in that setting, rather than of what is effective from a purely causal standpoint. By implication, children think of a person who offers a demonstration as a cultural mentor—someone who shows you the right way to do things. If the mentor offers a complicated but seemingly inefficient demonstration, so be it—that is what you are supposed to do. If a mentor offers a simple and efficient demonstration, then that is what you should do instead. If two mentors offer different demonstrations, one complicated, the other simple, you should do what seems better suited to the context. For example, if one of the two mentors is watching you, you'd better do what he did. Finally, this hypothesis can explain why older children sometimes overimitate more than younger children (Nielsen & Tomaselli, 2010): we would expect older children to be more compliant with perceived norms.

If children overimitate because they try to copy what they believe they are supposed to do, rather than what they think is causally effective, this ought to be apparent when they are asked to explain their actions. To examine this prediction, Ben Kenward and his colleagues put various questions to children after showing them a demonstration of how to extract marbles from a container. As usual, the demonstration included both necessary and unnecessary elements (Kenward, Karlsson, & Persson, 2010). The children were asked what actions they planned to include when it was their turn to obtain a marble; they were asked to say why they would include those actions, and also whether the actions were needed or not. Not surprisingly, children explained the necessary actions in terms of their causal impact and confirmed that they were needed to obtain the marble. In the case of the unnecessary actions, they often admitted to not knowing why they would carry out them out, and expressed doubt about whether they were needed. Nonetheless, they went on to include them. By implication, the elaborate demonstration had not distorted children's analysis of what was causally effective—it had simply led them to think they, too, should use an elaborate technique.

Norms generally have a double aspect. They tell you what you are supposed to do in a given setting, but they also tell you what not to do. In certain circumstances, therefore, we can expect cultural learners to underimitate rather than overimitate—to omit components that are included by the demonstrator but apparently by accident. Two findings support this prediction.

Even infants will faithfully copy an overly complicated demonstration. For example, if an adult leans forward to press a lamp button with his forehead, infants will copy that technique rather than using their hands (Meltzoff, 1988). However, if there are clear indications that the demonstrator's inept technique is not freely chosen but dictated by immediate circumstances—for example, his arm movements are constrained because he is wrapped in a blanket—infants adopt the more efficient technique of using their hands (Gergely, Bekkering, & Király, 2002). Lyons and his colleagues uncovered a similar differentiation between the intentional and the involuntary components of a demonstration among 3- to 5-year-olds. They showed the children how to open a puzzle box, and, as usual, the demonstration included a useless action: the movement of an arm protruding from the box (Lyons, Damrosch, Lin, Macris, & Keil, 2011). One group of children watched the experimenter deliberately strike the protruding arm with a wand so that it swung from side to side before he proceeded to open the box. Another group saw the experimenter accidentally knock the arm. In mid-demonstration, he received a phone call, apparently from his mother looking for some lost object in the yard. Waving the wand back and forth as if indicating some location in imagined space, he said to her, "Well, you know I really feel like I saw it over by the dog house," and accidentally knocked the arm. As expected, overimitation was widespread in the intentional case but minimal in the unintentional case, even though, when quizzed afterward, children could remember the experimenter accidentally knocking the arm.

Some accidental actions are not just unnecessary—they are positively inappropriate and should be avoided. If children are cultural learners, then a demonstrator who makes mistakes—and marks them as mistakes—is likely to be especially instructive about what not to do. Children will be alerted to actions that should be avoided. Stephen Want and I found evidence for such active avoidance using the trap-tube task (see Figure 3.2), initially developed for testing capuchin monkeys (Want & Harris, 2001).

A toy man was marooned in the middle of the horizontal tube, but a stick could be inserted at either end to push him out. However, push-ing from right to left meant that the toy man would end up in the trap, whereas pushing from left to right meant that the toy would emerge from the right end of the tube (see Figure 3.2). Few 3-year-olds sponta-neously used the stick to extract the toy man. After an adult demon-stration, they did so—but with lots of mistakes. They successfully ejected the toy man on about half the trials and pushed him into the trap on the other half.

Some children saw the experimenter almost make a mistake during the demonstration. Inserting the stick into the wrong end, he pushed the toy man perilously close to the trap. Just as the toy man was about to plummet downward, the experimenter said "Oops," withdrew the stick, and reinserted it on the correct side. Now, instead of inserting the stick randomly into one side or the other (as they had done after watching a single correct insertion), 3-year-olds systematically chose the correct side and ejected the toy man without trapping him. The inclusion of the explicit marker—"Oops"—appears to be critical. Horner and Whiten (2007) omitted this marker and found that chil-dren no longer benefited from observing the experimenter's mistakes on the trap-tube task.

The same pattern emerged on a different task. Three-year-olds were given the apparatus illustrated in Figure 3.3. By dropping a marble into the correct arm of the tube, they could knock the toy man free of the magnet so that he would fall to the bottom of the apparatus and be re-

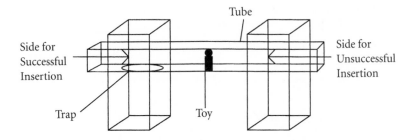

**Figure 3.2.** Illustration of the trap-tube apparatus, showing the location of the toy, the trap, and the sides for correct and incorrect insertion of the stick.

trieved. When dropped into the correct (right-hand) arm, the marble could fall unimpeded; but when dropped into the incorrect (left-hand) arm, it was impeded by a block (see Figure 3.3). With no demonstration to cue them, few children realized that the marble would be useful ammunition. Following a demonstration, most of them started to use it, but, as in the trap-tube task, they were indiscriminate in their choice of arm. However, if children watched the experimenter almost drop the marble into the wrong arm, heard him signal his mistake ("Oops"), and then saw him drop it in the correct arm, their accuracy rose dramatically to almost 90 percent correct, as opposed to about 50 percent correct.

If children think of a demonstration as showing you the "proper" way to do something, they should react negatively to any departure, even one that could be regarded as successful from a purely practical standpoint. Hannes Rakoczy and his colleagues confirmed this idea with 3-year-olds (Rakoczy, Warneken, & Tomasello, 2008). An adult showed the children that "daxing" involved pushing a block across a board with a stick, so that it fell into a gutter at one end of the board. The children also witnessed a different technique. At one point, the adult accidentally tilted the board, causing the block to slide into the

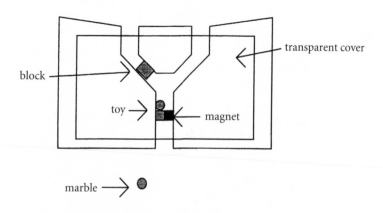

**Figure 3.3.** Illustration of the marble task, showing the location of the toy, the block, and the sides, for correct and incorrect insertion of the marble.

gutter. Looking startled, the adult said: "Oh no! That's not how daxing goes!" When a puppet appeared on the scene and improperly daxed by tilting the board, many of the 3-year-olds spontaneously protested at his "misdemeanor": "No, not like that!" or "Use the stick!" As in the two tube studies, children used the adult's signal to infer what was *not* supposed to be done—as well as what was supposed to be done. Note that in this case, however, both of the demonstrated techniques—pushing with the stick and tilting the board—were equally effective in casting the block into the gutter. Yet children regarded tilting as illicit. Apparently, after a brief demonstration, children can be sticklers for convention—even when convention dictates a relatively arbitrary way of doing things.

## Conclusions

Children are not only more curious than chimpanzees—they are also more deferential. Whereas chimpanzees copy selectively, leaving out a demonstrator's evident inefficiencies, children copy more faithfully and include inefficiencies. But this is not because children politely "go along" with an instructor, nor is it because they are looking for purely causal information. Instead, children assume that a demonstration tells you what you are supposed to do and not do in that social setting. This explains why children act differently in the presence of different models. It explains why they sometimes overimitate and why they sometimes underimitate. Children faithfully reproduce an action if it appears to be deliberately executed by the demonstrator, but they avoid reproducing an action that is obviously accidental or marked as a faux pas.

The deeper implication is that children and chimpanzees watch a demonstration with different assumptions and objectives. Chimpanzees do engage in imitation, but they do not appear to conceive of a demonstrator as a cultural mentor. Recall Kanzi, the bonobo discussed in the previous chapter. Despite having been raised in a technologically rich human environment, and despite his relative mastery of a symbolic keyboard, Kanzi asked no questions. He did not think of his human interlocutors as teachers who could offer guidance. The findings on chimpanzee imitation point to the same conclusion. The demonstrator is watched and imitated, but not as a teacher who might know better than the pupil. Chimpanzees abandon faithful copying if they have a more efficient strategy at their disposal.

Children, by contrast, appear to view a demonstrator as a repository of cultural knowledge—someone from whom they can learn the culturally appropriate way to do things. Again, this analysis fits the evidence presented in the previous chapter. Young children look to their interlocutors for guidance by asking questions. Moreover, their questions are not confined to simple matters of fact—for example, the location of an object. They also pose questions about cultural practices—the way things are referred to and the functions that they serve. Similarly, children use demonstrations to figure out what to do and what not to do—and this mode of cultural learning overrides considerations of efficiency. If the instructor deliberately does something that, from a practical perspective, seems overly complicated, children do the same thing. Conversely, if the instructor does something—tilts the board—that is effective but signals that such a technique is not the way to do things, children chide someone for using that improper technique.

How wide is the scope of overimitation—and its cousin, underimitation? Most investigators have conceived of the phenomenon primarily in terms of how children learn to manipulate objects and tools. Lyons and his colleagues, for example, explicitly refer to overimitation as a mechanism for the transmission of "artifact culture" (Lyons et al., 2011). In the same spirit, Whiten and his colleagues point out that overimitation is likely to be a useful strategy for children because, given their lengthy immaturity—as compared to the development of other primates—what they have learned can be refined. Unnecessary or superstitious elements can "later be corrected by children's direct interaction with reality" (Whiten et al., 2009, p. 2425).

My guess is that this characterization underestimates the scope of cultural learning from demonstration, as well as its persistence into adulthood. Watching others in order to figure out what you are supposed to do is not just a strategy for coming to grips with artifacts, or even with reality. Consider the various ritualized cultural behaviors that children are expected to reproduce when they play a new game, greet an adult, or eat a meal. Viewed in this light, learning from demonstrations is better seen as a pervasive lifelong strategy for cultural adaptation. Novices everywhere use this strategy to identify and blend in with local norms.

Finally, we may return to the question raised at the beginning of the chapter. Can this shift from practical, efficiency-oriented imitation to normative imitation account for the differences between the use of tools by nonhuman apes and the more elaborate tool-culture of humans? In particular, can it offer any help in explaining the onset of the ratchet effect in human history? Here is a speculative proposal. If children watch a demonstrator not for self-interested, pragmatic reasons, but in order to master local cultural norms, then more complex practices, those that go beyond the constraints imposed by immediate efficiency, can be faithfully transmitted from one generation to the next. In particular, opaque procedures that are valued and performed by the older generation will be reproduced and maintained by the next generation. Children can be led to imitate procedures and techniques whose purpose and value they may not understand or appreciate. An elaborate procedure will be imitated even though children cannot see it as having any tangible or immediate value. This means that a given cultural procedure, even one that is mysterious, can be preserved and passed on to the next generation. For example, the rationale for the selection and preparation of certain plants and the taboo against others—either for food or for medicinal purposes—is often not transparent to an observer. Yet such practices can be faithfully copied by children. Assuming such practices are adaptive for their adherents, they can be perpetuated across many successive generations. Chimpanzees, by contrast, can be led to imitate only if they see some immediate, tangible, practical advantage in doing so. A ratchet effect is short-circuited because they are reluctant to do anything with no self-evident payoff.

An important implication of this interpretation of children's normative imitation is that a variety of cultural practices will be transmitted and subject to a ratchet effect—including those that do not, in fact, have any practical or technological impact. For example, religious or supernatural rituals, decorative techniques, and cultural practices concerning food preparation and consumption will all increasingly be transmitted from one generation to the next and can increase in complexity across generations. As it happens, this is what we see the course of human history.

# CHAPTER 4

# Moroccan Birds and Twisted Tubes

⋆

$F$aced with a choice between copying an adult's demonstration and doing it their way, children are surprising deferential. Even when they know of an efficient procedure, they faithfully copy an adult's more ornate and inefficient demonstration. What happens when children face similar conflicts between what an adult tells them and what they can see for themselves? Here too, children might stick to their own judgment or they might be deferential.

Guided by how confident they are, children steer between these two possibilities. They do query the answers that they receive to their questions, when those answers are obviously discrepant from their own past knowledge and past experience. But if the conclusions that they have reached are more tentative, children accept what other people tell them—even if it does not fit what they think themselves. I describe this pattern in two domains: the classification of objects, and predictions about the physical world. These are not the only domains in which conflicts between firsthand observation and testimony can occur;[1] but because of their obvious importance for children's early cognitive development, they provide a good starting point.

## The Classification of Objects

It is tempting to think that our classification of the various objects and creatures in the world is something that we do on our own. We look at a snake—or an apple—and we classify it on the basis of its visible properties with no help from anyone else. Yet even as adults, we are likely to refine our judgment in the light of feedback from other people. If we go to the fruit stall at the market, we have no difficulty telling an apple from a pear. But in a New England orchard in mid-September, we probably need some help to decide whether the apple we have picked is a McIntosh or a Macoun and which is better for baking. We defer to experts. More generally, many of the classifications that we make ultimately depend on the testimony of other people. Whether the entity is a palpable object such as a fruit or a tool, or something more abstract such as a neighborhood or a college, we often turn to others to learn how to classify it and what its properties are. How do young children handle this issue? Do they stubbornly classify objects for themselves, or do they routinely follow the advice of other people? Overall, the evidence suggests that children are judicious: they display a mix of autonomy and deference.

Even infants are good at using the perceptual features of a set of objects to classify them into categories. Shown a series of objects in the same category—for example, various pictures of cats—young infants notice the underlying similarity and repetitiveness of certain perceptual features across successive instances. As a result, they gradually habituate or lose interest, but they stare with renewed curiosity if unexpectedly shown a picture of a member of a different category, such as a dog (Quinn, Eimas, & Rosenkrantz, 1993). Infants can also build up a representation of a new category quite quickly. If they are shown various examples of a hitherto unfamiliar category—for example, a set of Identikit, schematic faces, each with a family resemblance to Richard Nixon—they rapidly start to differentiate between faces that look as if they fall into that category, as compared to those that do not. Indeed, when shown a new member of the now familiar category—one that they have never actually seen before—they show signs of "recognizing" it, provided it has a sufficient number of Nixonian features (Cohen, 2009; Strauss, 1979).

By implication, the infant brain is well equipped to operate in an independent fashion when learning how to classify objects. Across a variety of category members, it can spot recurrent or characteristic features and compose a mental prototype of the category. The fact that this type of perceptual classification is possible for preverbal infants should be no surprise: nonhuman primates and even pigeons can do much the same (Herrnstein, Loveland, & Cable, 1976).

If preverbal infants can rapidly construct their own categories based on the detection of perceptual similarity, names would generally distinguish categories that infants have already constructed for themselves. On this view, language would rarely help children to classify or reclassify particular exemplars. When children first hear a particular member of a category named—"That's a horse"—they should appropriately apply the name to other horses but avoid extending it to creatures lying outside the category, such as cows and sheep. Moreover, if they hear someone naming an object in a way that violates their classification system, they should balk. Indeed, there is evidence for such resistance early in children's language-learning career. When 16-month-olds were shown a picture of a cup, and a speaker called it a cup, they behaved as might be expected: they turned to look at the named object. However, if the speaker misnamed the object—for example, called the cup a shoe—infants were likely to turn and stare at the speaker, as if puzzled by her mistake. Remarks made by the infants also suggested that they had registered the mistake. After a misnaming, they often named the object themselves but with the correct name. So if the speaker had referred to a cup as a shoe, they insisted that it was a cup. Some children even tried to correct the speaker via pointing. For example, one resourceful child pointed to her shoe, as if to say: "No, *this* is a shoe!" (Koenig & Echols, 2003).

More evidence for children's ability to reject an adult's incorrect claims emerged in a study of older infants aged 18–30 months (Pea, 1982). When a speaker said something that children knew to be wrong—for example, "That's a cat" with reference to a dog—children often produced a denial ("No"), something they rarely did if the speaker had named the object correctly. Figure 4.1 shows the proportion of such denials issued by toddlers ranging from 18 to 36 months, in response to false as compared to true claims. Evidently, from 30 months, if not earlier, toddlers say "No" to false claims much more often than to true ones.

If we turn to slightly older children, the evidence for skepticism toward a speaker's false or unexpected claims is very systematic. In sev-

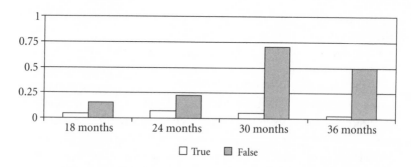

**Figure 4.1.** Proportion of true and false claims by the adult speaker that provoked a denial from the child, as a function of age.

eral studies, we presented 3- and 4-year-olds with two speakers at a time: one who named various familiar objects correctly, and one who named them incorrectly. Afterward, when children were asked to say what they thought the object was called, they almost always agreed with the correct speaker and were rarely swayed by the incorrect speaker (Pasquini, Corriveau, Koenig, & Harris, 2007). In a more challenging test of their skepticism, 3- and 4-year-olds were given an opportunity to look at an object and note its color before it was concealed in a box. Next, two different speakers—one who had described objects correctly up until that point and one who had described them incorrectly—each looked in the box and each produced a misleading claim. For example, if the toy inside was actually red, the hitherto reliable speaker might say it was green and the hitherto unreliable speaker might say it was blue. Children were then asked what they thought. Faced with this three-way choice of colors, the majority stuck to their own perceptual judgment. They said that the toy was red—in line with what they had seen a minute or so earlier (Clément, Koenig & Harris, 2004).

Not only do preschoolers generally deny claims that they judge to be false, but they are reluctant to use them as a basis for inference. For example, if they are presented with a claim that they regard as absurd—"All fishes live in trees"—they are unwilling to draw any further conclusion from it. When told about Tot the fish and asked whether he lives in a tree, they typically resort to their own knowledge of where fishes live, not to what they have just been told. "No—he lives in the water," they declare, and back that up with reference to their own past experience: "I know—I've seen where fishes live" (Dias & Harris, 1988; 1990; Harris & Leevers, 2000).

In short, infants and young children can be stubbornly autonomous. At 16 months, they stare at a speaker who misclassifies an object and offer corrections. By the age of 30 months, they produce explicit denials of an adult's mistakes. Three- and 4-year-olds concur with a speaker who produces a name or a description that matches what they themselves would say—but disagree with a speaker who contradicts a name that they have learned or a visual property that they have just seen. Finally, preschoolers resist using claims they believe to be false as a basis for reasoning: they show what has been described as an "empirical bias" by reasoning from their own past experience and not from a speaker's implausible assertions (Harris, 2000; Scribner, 1977). The autonomy that we might be inclined to associate with mature judgment is built into the foundations of children's early communication system.

But children do not invariably resist assertions that conflict with their own beliefs. Blanket skepticism is no more satisfactory for learning than blanket credulity. It would mean that once children had established a given belief, any subsequent assertions querying that belief would be rejected. The door would be shut to any revision of belief. Such deep and pervasive inflexibility seems unlikely. Indeed, a variety of experiments show that the door is left ajar.

Consider the hybrid creature depicted in Figure 4.2. It has some bird-like features, but most of us would probably say that it is a fish. When shown this picture, most 2-year-olds said the same (Jaswal &

**Figure 4.2.** A fish-bird hybrid (based on Jaswal, 2004).

Markman, 2007). In addition, they said that it lived in a lake. However, children who heard an adult describe the creature as a bird reached a different conclusion. Most children now said that it lived in a nest. A similar pattern emerged for various other hybrids. Shown a picture of a key-like object, most 2-year-olds looked at it and said that it could be used to start a car. On the other hand, after hearing the adult describe it as a spoon, they said it was for eating. Overall, when left to their own devices, these very young children made appropriate judgments based on the object's perceptual features. They attributed properties to the hybrid—such as its habitat or function—that were consistent with its overall appearance. Yet when an adult categorized it differently—children accepted that categorization and used it to infer a different set of properties.

One explanation for 2-year-olds' deference in these experiments is that they are unsure of the exact boundaries to a category. They have a reasonably good idea of what a fish looks like, but they do not know exactly how far the category of "fish" extends. Presumably, it includes goldfish and trout—but does it include stingrays and dolphins? It's difficult for young children to figure this out for themselves, because visible perceptual features are not much help. The similarities between goldfish and stingrays—as opposed to dolphins—may not be obvious to the naked eye. Children who are at the very beginning of their linguistic career might be unsure—and appropriately so—about which category some unfamiliar creature or object belongs to, and might be appropriately deferential toward people who appear to have more expertise. However, when Jaswal (2007) compared 2-year-olds who had an above-average vocabulary with children the same age who had a below-average vocabulary, it was the large-vocabulary group who deferred the most when the hybrid was labeled unexpectedly by an adult. By implication, early deference is not due to shaky lexical boundaries. Even when their vocabulary grows, children do not stop listening to experts.

Here, then, we have evidence that young children are not autonomous. They yield to adults who make claims that contradict their own judgment. Why do children defer in these studies, yet did not defer in those described earlier? Figure 4.2 suggests a plausible answer. This hybrid does look mostly like a fish but it has some bird-like features. It might conceivably be a bird, even if that appears to be somewhat improbable. Consider now the study by Koenig and Echols (2003) where infants did not defer. In that study, the speaker looked at a cup and called it a shoe. The cup was a regular cup—it looked nothing like a shoe. By implication, toddlers use some kind of implausibility metric when they weigh the unexpected claims of an adult. Completely implausible claims—those that are markedly discrepant from the conclusion that children would reach by themselves—are rejected. In contrast, those that call for an unexpected but not altogether outrageous reassessment—given the perceptual clues available—are accepted.

Older children might be more stubborn defenders of their own perceptual judgment. Alternatively, they might increasingly recognize the scope of adult authority and the possibility of their own error. To examine this question, Jaswal (2004) presented pictures of hybrids, such as the fish-like bird depicted in Figure 4.2, to 3- and 4-year-olds. When told that it was a bird, some children resisted—"No, this is a fish"—but many accepted the unexpected label and drew inferences accordingly. How did the two age groups compare? If anything, the 3-year-olds were more inclined to accept the unexpected classification than the 4-year-olds. However, this was not necessarily due to any greater autonomy on their part. Rather, they simply needed some indication that the experimenter was not just making a mistake. When the experimenter implied that the unexpected name was deliberately chosen ("You're not going to believe this, but this is actually a bird"), 4-year-olds generally responded in the same way that 3-year-olds did: they drew conclusions based on the experimenter's categorization. Similarly, if the experimenter tacitly signaled that the choice of name was no accident—for example, by mentioning a distinctive subgroup ("This is a *Moroccan* bird"), 4-year-olds, like 3-year-olds, mostly accepted the unexpected classification. Note that this finding fits the pattern described in the previous chapter. Children are sensitive to the ongoing, pedagogic signals that an informant provides, and they are especially receptive to information that is marked as deliberate.[2]

Summing up the story so far, children can and do make firm, perceptually based classifications right from the beginning of language acquisition. Faced with an informant who makes claims that run directly counter to their perceptual intuitions, they stand firm. "If it looks like a fish," they seem to be saying, "well, then, it *is* a fish—and it has the properties of a fish!" Nevertheless, children are far from adamant—especially when the perceptual evidence is less than overwhelming. If there are clues suggesting that the informant is not flat-out wrong, preschoolers accept the unexpected classification, and draw inferences based upon it. Older preschoolers are especially likely to acquiesce if the informant implies that the classification is indeed unexpected. In line with the speculation set out earlier, children leave the door open to counter-claims. So even if young children are autonomous, in the sense that they are fully capable of sorting objects into classes on the basis of the objects' visible features, they are not stubborn autodidacts. They realize—particularly when some of the available evidence does not square with their own convictions—that other people can tell them what is actually the case. Here, then, we have a judicious mix of autonomy and deference.

The classification of objects might be a domain in which children are especially inclined to accept information from other people. After all, many of children's early questions are precisely about what something is and what it should be called (Chouinard, 2007). But are they less deferential in domains where they can be self-sufficient?

## Naïve Physics

A long tradition of research shows that infants—before they can speak fluently or learn from what other people tell them—construct firm ideas about physical objects and the objects' movements. For example, one-year-old infants realize that an object that disappears from sight continues to exist and can be retrieved. If they watch an object being hidden in a particular container, they will search for it there some 5 to 10 seconds later (Hunter, 1917). They also search correctly when an object is hidden at several successive hiding places, provided the delay between each hiding and the opportunity to search is brief (Diamond, 1985; Harris, 1973). In the second year, infants start to keep track of objects that are hidden and then moved. For example, if an object is put into a closed container and then carried inside that container to other potential hiding places, infants search at those potential hiding places (Haake & Somerville, 1985; Piaget, 1954).

Children's robust intuitions about moving objects persist into adulthood, but some of those intuitions are wrong. For example, asked to predict the path of a ball that is launched from a curved tube, children and adults often expect the ball to continue along its curvilinear trajectory, rather than to assume a straight trajectory once it is out of the tube (Kaiser, McCloskey, & Proffitt, 1986; McCloskey, Caramazza, & Green, 1980). Conversely, when asked to predict the path of an object that is dropped from a flying plane, children and adults often mistakenly expect the object to drop straight down, rather than to fall forward in a curved (parabolic) arc. This error persists even among adults who have taken college-level classes in physics (Kaiser, Proffitt, & McCloskey, 1985; McCloskey, Washburn, & Felch, 1983).

If children readily form intuitions about the physical world that can be impervious to correction and formal education, they might ignore other people's advice in this domain and repeatedly act on the basis of their own naïve expectations. On the other hand, given their deference toward adults in the classification of objects—at least when the available evidence is equivocal—children might also defer in the domain of naïve physics, especially when they are unsure of their own judgment.

A task devised by Bruce Hood offers a way to examine these conflicting expectations (Hood, 1995). Preschoolers ranging in age from around 1½ to 3 were presented with an apparatus like the one illustrated in Figure 4.3. When a ball was dropped into one of the upper "chimneys" it rolled down the curved tube and ended up falling into the cup at its base. Having watched the experimenter drop a ball into a chimney, children were invited to search for it. Only a handful of the oldest children systematically searched in the correct cup. The majority searched in the cup directly underneath the chimney, even though such a direct drop was physically impossible, given the arrangement of the tubes.

This error proved difficult for children to suppress. If the opaque tubes were replaced by transparent tubes, so that the ball was visible as it traveled down them, children did manage to search in the correct

**Figure 4.3.** The chimney apparatus. Balls inserted into the upper chimneys roll down the tube, ending up in one of the cups below.

cup. However, when the opaque tubes were put back in position, children again started making errors. Sustained training on a single opaque tube was equally ineffective (Hood, 1995).

Why do children make errors so persistently? The most plausible interpretation is that they have undue respect for the power of gravity. From infancy, children have lots of experience with objects that fall straight down. Even if the entire trajectory of a falling object cannot be easily seen—either because of visual obstacles or because it falls too quickly—it will typically be found at a location directly below where it was dropped. Children appear to be applying this rule-of-thumb to the tubes task: they ignore the fact that, in this setup, the solid walls of the opaque tube cannot be breached by the ball, and they fail to realize that the ball will drop down the tube into the cup positioned at its base even when that cup is not directly underneath the point of departure. Consistent with this hypothesis, children make fewer errors if gravity is neutralized as a misleading force—for example, if the apparatus is rotated to the horizontal so that the ball rolls along a tube, rather than down it—or if the balls are pulled up through a tube, rather than dropped down into one (Hood, 1998; Hood, Santos, & Fieselman, 2000).

It is tempting to think that children will correct themselves once they have empirical experience of where the ball does end up. However, if they are encouraged to search among the cups until they eventually find it, or if they are shown where it has landed, children still display no improvement on subsequent trials (Bascandziev & Harris, 2010; Hood, 1995). Apparently, firsthand evidence that their gravity-based intuition is wrong does not help toddlers to abandon it.

Are there experiences that *do* help? In particular, do children heed verbal advice? Vikram Jaswal explored this possibility with 2-year-olds. When they watched a ball being dropped into one of the opaque tubes, and made their prediction about where it had landed—typically in the "gravity cup" (the one directly beneath the point of departure)—he promptly told them where it had actually landed. Most children followed this advice and searched for the ball in the correct cup, not the gravity cup (Jaswal, 2010, Experiment 1).[3] Yet repeated trials like this also led to no improvement in the accuracy of children's later predictions. Apparently, even when children are immediately told the correct location and obtain firsthand evidence that it is indeed correct, they still hold on to their mistaken, gravity-based intuition.

However, telling children which cup is correct does not offer them a strategy for figuring out the correct cup for themselves. Can a more elaborate verbal explanation help in this regard? To explore this possibility, Igor Bascandziev and I compared various kinds of verbal advice (Bascandziev & Harris, 2010). First, 3-year-olds were given four pretest trials in which they received no particular guidance. Figure 4.4 shows, as expected, that gravity errors predominated in all three of the groups that were tested.

Next, children received two advice trials in which the nature of the advice differed for each of three groups of children. For children in the "No Escape" group, the advice focused on the constraints imposed by the tube: "The ball could not escape from that tube. It rolled inside that tube." The advice to children in the "Eye Movement" group focused on what they needed to do: "What you need to do is to watch which tube the ball goes in and then you need to follow that tube with your eyes.

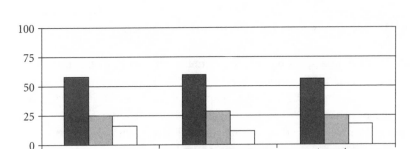

**Figure 4.4.** Percentage of gravity, correct, and other responses in pretest trials, as a function of group.

Okay?" Finally, the advice to children in the "Attention" group was more generic: "You have to pay attention to the tubes in order to find the ball immediately." Children in all three conditions then received four post-test trials in which, once again, they received no guidance about what to do.

The percentage of gravity, correct, and other responses made by each group is shown in Figure 4.5. Children in the "No Escape" and "Eye Movement" conditions showed a sharp improvement. The percentage of gravity errors declined and the proportion of correct searches increased, relative to performance in the pretest. Clearly the gravity error is not impervious to correction. Verbal instruction from an adult helps children to overcome it. Two different explanations of the beneficial effect of instruction are plausible. Each suggests that instruction helps to generate a kind of mental proxy or stand-in for seeing the ball traveling inside the tube. One possibility is that, when reminded that the ball cannot escape from the tube or when told to follow the tube with their eyes, children are sensitized to the causal constraints that the tube imposes on the movement of the ball. More specifically, they are reminded that the ball cannot drop vertically into the gravity cup, because it is prevented from doing so by the walls of the tube. On this hypothesis, the adult's instruction alerts children to something they already know—namely, that one solid object cannot pass through an-

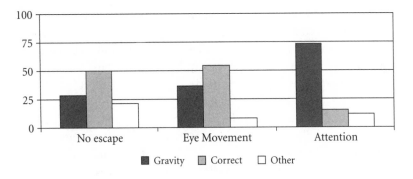

**Figure 4.5.** Percentage of gravity, correct, and other responses in post-test trials, as a function of group.

other. Hence, they end up correctly visualizing its passage down the curved tube. A second possibility is that instruction is vital precisely because it prompts children to engage in a thought experiment: to visualize the ball traveling inside the tube. Once they begin to do that, children realize for themselves the important constraint imposed by the walls of the tube.[4]

Further work is needed to sort out which of these two interpretations is more plausible. Does testimony activate children's latent knowledge or their latent imagination? Whichever interpretation proves correct, both imply that children learn from what adults tell them because it helps them to accurately visualize the invisible movement of the ball inside the tube. More generally, we can conclude that the naïve physics of young children is not a discipline that they study oblivious to instruction from adults. Verbal guidance helps them to suppress an error that they produce endlessly when left to their own devices, despite repeated empirical feedback that their expectations are wrong. Here, we see that verbal testimony is not *as effective* as empirical experience. It is actually *more effective*.

## Conclusions

Infants and young children have the capacity to independently classify objects. But this capacity does not stop them learning from expert advice. Admittedly, when they are sure about the perceptual evidence, children resist counter-claims. Looking at a cup, they correct an informant who calls it a shoe. Nevertheless, when an adult informant assigns the object to a different category, and the object has some features consistent with that alternative classification, children accept what they are told.

Young children are also self-taught physicists. They figure out how to keep track of a moving object, even when those movements are not fully visible. When an object is dropped, they expect it to follow the laws of gravity and to land directly below the place where it was dropped. They make that prediction when it is correct (for example, when the object is released in midair), but they persistently make that prediction when it is false (when the object is dropped into a curved, opaque tube). Nevertheless, despite making such gravity-based errors, children defer to an adult who tells them where the object has actually landed.[5] Apparently, even in the domain of naïve physics, where children autonomously develop strong intuitions—incorrect as well as correct—they are still open to guidance from an adult. Indeed, not only can verbal advice guide children's behavior with respect to their immediate search—it can also serve a more stable regulatory function. Having either been reminded that the ball cannot escape from the tube or told to track the ball's trajectory, 3-year-olds manage to suppress the gravity error—and, what is especially important, they manage do to so in later trials. Even when the advice is no longer being provided, children continue to benefit from it.

Overall, the evidence shows that children are flexible in their response to adult input. If the perceptual evidence is clear-cut, they typically ignore advice and rely on their own intuitions. On the other hand, if the relevant perceptual information is equivocal or hidden, children appear to see adults as offering guidance that is intended to be helpful. Indeed, when an adult concedes the unexpectedness of what the advice proposes, children are all the more willing to accept that adult guidance. As discussed in the previous chapter, they are well disposed to the role of pupil—often giving an informant the benefit of the doubt. In this respect, they are much more receptive to instruction than their primate cousins—who watch and emulate, but show little inclination toward trust or deference.

In the next chapter, we will explore the scope of such deference. Are children equally willing to learn from anyone—or do they invest greater trust in some people more than others? There is a long-standing idea that young children are all too credulous. But for a species so dependent upon others for information, indiscriminate trust in all comers would seem perilous and maladaptive.

# CHAPTER 5

# Trusting Those You Know?

Children accept information that runs counter to their own ideas. They revise their classification of an object if an adult proposes an alternative, and they set aside robust intuitions about an object's movement in light of what they are told. These deferential reactions are consistent with a long-standing philosophical conception of young children as credulous. Thomas Reid, the Scottish Enlightenment philosopher, proposed that we human beings have "a disposition to confide in the veracity of others and to believe what they tell us. . . . It is unlimited in children" (Reid, 1764/2000). In the twentieth century, Bertrand Russell claimed that "doubt, suspense of judgment and disbelief all seem later and more complex than a wholly unreflecting assent" (Russell, 1921). Ludwig Wittgenstein reached a similar conclusion: "A child learns there are reliable and unreliable informants much later than it learns the facts which are told it" (Wittgenstein, 1969).

On the other hand, indiscriminate credulity is not biologically plausible. Children who trusted anyone, including strangers, would be unlikely to survive in a competitive and hostile world. In thinking about this issue, we can usefully distinguish between two types of doubt. When offered information by one person, especially someone who is familiar, children may be disposed to accept it—in line with the philosophical tradition just sketched. However, young children do not grow up with one single informant. As members of a family, of a group, and of a culture, they have access to many potential informants—parents, siblings, and peers, as well as various other children and adults in the extended family or the larger community. Evolutionary approaches to the transmission of information within a species, or indeed within a culture, have led to the conclusion that various selection principles are likely to improve fitness (Cavalli-Sforza & Feldman, 1981; Richerson & Boyd, 2005).[1] It will be to children's advantage if they learn from people who offer good-quality information and who provide it with the children's interests at heart. If children are willing to learn from fools or knaves, they will not prosper. In short, from an evolutionary perspective, children should be biased to learn from some informants rather than others.

In fact, many experiments—as well as evolutionary reasoning—show that children are indeed biased, both when deciding which person to ask for advice and when deciding whose advice to accept. In this chapter, I describe how children choose among the informants they know, depending on their prior history of interaction with them. In the next chapter, I ask how children select among relatively unfamiliar informants. Taken together, the findings show that even if children are ignorant, weak, and credulous, they are smart at navigating their social network.

## Trusting People Who Take Care of You

Faced with uncertainty or danger, human infants do not seek help or reassurance indiscriminately—they turn to someone familiar, someone who has taken care of them in the past (Bowlby, 1969). This type of early selectivity is all but universal among children growing up under normal rearing conditions. Only after extreme social deprivation is such selectivity compromised. For example, many children who spent a prolonged period during early childhood in Romanian orphanages under the Ceauşescu regime received minimal care and affection from a variety of caregivers. Despite subsequent adoption, many of these children have continued to show indiscriminate and inappropriate trust in strangers (Rutter et al., 2010). But such grossly mechanical and impersonal care is exceedingly rare under normal rearing conditions.

The selectivity that emerges in the course of normal development might operate not just when young children seek emotional reassurance or a safe haven, but also when they are looking for information.

Clearly, if familiar caregivers have an investment in providing trust-worthy information to those in their care, children's inclination to seek and accept information from them would be adaptive.

As a first step in examining this possibility, we tested 3-, 4-, and 5-year-olds in two different daycare centers with the help of two care-givers, one from each center (Corriveau & Harris, 2009a). Children were shown a series of unfamiliar objects that we had obtained from the hardware store. They could ask for information about the name or function of the object from either caregiver. Irrespective of which care-giver children asked, both volunteered information by either supplying a name for the object or demonstrating how to use it. However, the names or functions that the caregivers proposed were different, so that children were asked to decide who they thought was right. For exam-ple, one caregiver might call an unfamiliar metal bathroom hook a "linz," whereas the other might call it a "slod." One caregiver might look though a plastic sprinkler attachment as if it were a telescope, whereas the other might hold it to her mouth and blow into it.

Children in Center 1 were familiar with Caregiver 1 but not with Caregiver 2, whereas the reverse was true for children in Center 2. Fig-ures 5.1 and 5.2 show the findings from the two centers. In Center 1, all three age groups clearly preferred to seek and accept guidance from the caregiver who worked there—who was familiar to them—rather than the caregiver from Center 2 who was a relative stranger.

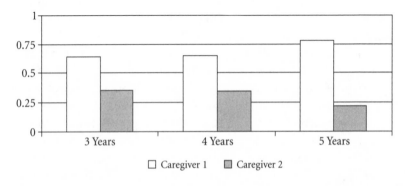

**Figure 5.1.** Proportion of choices directed at each caregiver by 3-, 4-, and 5-year-olds in Center 1.

The results obtained in Center 2 were the mirror image of those obtained in Center 1. All three age groups showed an equally strong preference for Caregiver 2—the person they were familiar with.

Placing these findings in the framework of attachment theory invites us to rethink the relationship between cognitive and emotional development. If we think of children's early cognitive development as primarily based on their active exploration and observation of the physical world, it is easy to suppose that the main function of an attachment figure is to offer emotional support—a secure base from which those exploratory sorties into the larger world can be conducted. Note that this metaphor of the secure base is not too different from the figure of the teacher as described by Rousseau, Piaget, and Montessori. The adult figure may be present, but he or she is not represented as someone who engages in active dialogue with the child. Rather, the child is left to engage in independent exploration, confident that someone remains available in the background.

However, contrary to this classic conception of cognitive development as involving hands-on, autonomous exploration of the physical world, a central theme of this book is that such exploration is inadequate in many domains of cognition. The relevant observational evidence may be simply unavailable or equivocal. Children need other people's testimony to make sense of and interpret the world. Children themselves recognize that need, and that is why they ply their attach-

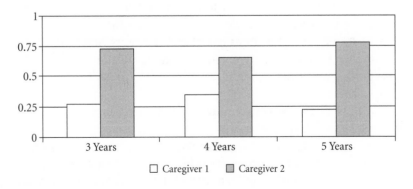

**Figure 5.2.** Proportion of choices directed at each caregiver by 3-, 4-, and 5-year-olds in Center 2.

ment figures with questions, sometimes with great tenacity. Viewed in this light, attachment figures do not simply provide an emotional safe haven—a place for children to retreat when the exploratory system is temporarily on hold or shut down. They also supply key information; and that information is likely to be trusted to varying degrees, depending on the nature of the attachment relationship.

With these theoretical considerations in mind, we asked if the type of attachment relationship that children have with a caregiver moderates their confidence in the information that she offers. To answer this question, we tested a large group of children with their mothers (Corriveau, Harris, Meins, et al., 2009). Each mother was obviously very familiar to her own child. Nevertheless, the quality of the relationship between mother and child, as assessed when children were approximately 15 months, varied. Children had been categorized as *secure, ambivalent,* or *avoidant* in their attachment, based on their behavior in the "Strange Situation" devised by Mary Ainsworth and her colleagues (Ainsworth, Blehar, Waters, & Wall, 1978).[2] In accordance with attachment theory, secure children were able to cope well with their mother's brief absence and were positive toward her when she returned. Ambivalent children coped less well with her absence and were less easily reassured by her return. Avoidant children showed few signs of missing their mother when she was absent and tended to ignore her on her return.

We revisited the children just after their fourth birthday, and tested them using a procedure similar to the one just described for the two daycare centers. Children could choose to seek and accept information about the names or functions of unfamiliar objects either from their mother or from a relatively unfamiliar stranger. Figure 5.3 shows the proportion of choices that children in the three attachment groups directed at each person.

In all three groups, children invested more trust in their mother— they asked more questions of her than of the stranger, and they accepted information from her rather than from the stranger. However, the strength of that preference varied from group to group: it was an unreliable trend among children with an avoidant relationship; it was much more evident among children with a secure relationship; and to our surprise, it was especially marked among children with an ambivalent relationship.

How should we interpret these findings? Important clues can be gathered from attachment theory, which has focused on the way that children vary in the expectations that they have formed about their mother. Avoidant and ambivalent children—who are both regarded as having an insecure relationship with their mother—differ sharply in this respect. Avoidant children are thought to have become pessimistic about their mother's responsiveness and availability. As a result, they tend to deliberately ignore her, disregarding the signals that she might express. At the other extreme, ambivalent children want their mother to respond to them but they are not always confident that she will do so. As a result, they monitor her frequently and with some anxiety. Between these two extremes, secure children are confident that their mother will make herself available for them. They check on her presence from time to time, but not in an anxious or hypervigilant fashion.

The results, displayed in Figure 5.3, point to the interesting possibility that children's trust in the information offered by their mother might vary along the same lines. At one extreme, avoidant children are relatively indifferent to their mother, displaying no systematic confidence in the information that she offers, as compared to that offered by

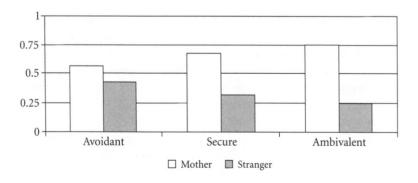

**Figure 5.3.** Proportion of choices directed at the mother versus a stranger, by attachment classification.

a complete stranger. By implication, they have learned not to invest any special trust in what she has to say. At the other extreme, ambivalent children are quite dependent on their mother's guidance. Conceivably, they would accept her statements even in circumstances when the available evidence suggests that she is wrong. If this speculation is correct, we might think of secure children as occupying a well-judged middle ground—turning to their mother when the evidence is equivocal, but otherwise confident about their own judgment if they think their mother is mistaken.

To test this idea, we returned one year later, when the children were close to their fifth birthday. This time, their mother and a stranger provided conflicting names for a series of hybrid creatures of two different types. The asymmetrical hybrids were like the fish-bird depicted in the previous chapter (Figure 4.2). They mostly resembled one creature (e.g., a fish) even if they had some features of another creature (e.g., a bird). In order to probe children's pattern of trust, the mother always categorized the creature with the less likely name ("That's a bird"), whereas the stranger categorized the creature with the more likely name ("That's a fish"). If children opted for the category proposed by their mother rather than the one suggested by the stranger, they would be setting aside most of the perceptual evidence and trusting their mother instead. Recall from the previous chapter that 4-year-olds are willing to do that, particularly if the person who makes the unexpected claim signals its apparent implausibility ("You're not going to believe this . . ."). However, mothers did not include this signal. Moreover, children heard the stranger offer a name that was more appropriate because it fit most of the perceptual evidence. In short, children faced a dilemma. They could go along with their mother even though most of the evidence was against her. Alternatively, they could ignore their mother and side with the stranger—since the stranger's proposal was more plausible. As a point of comparison, children were also given a series of symmetrical hybrids. These were composed so that they resembled two different animals to the same degree—for example, a cow and a horse, as shown in Figure 5.4.

In this case, opting for the mother's category name over the stranger's was likely to generate less of a conflict, because the available evidence did not favor the stranger. We will first look at how children responded to the identification of these symmetrical hybrids. Figure 5.5 shows the proportion of choices in which children sided with their mother, rather than with the stranger. The pattern of results was very similar to the pattern that had emerged for the novel hardware objects presented a year earlier—compare Figure 5.5 with Figure 5.3. Avoidant children showed no reliable preference for their mother; secure children showed a strong preference for her; and ambivalent children showed an especially strong preference for her.

The clear parallel between the findings with the unfamiliar objects

**Figure 5.4.** Example of a symmetrical hybrid: a cow-horse (based on Jaswal, 2004).

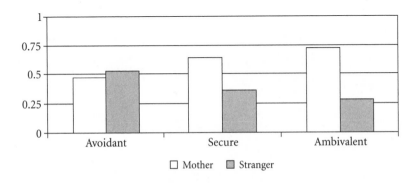

**Figure 5.5.** Proportion of choices directed at the mother versus a stranger, by attachment classification (symmetrical creatures).

from the hardware store and the findings with the hybrid animals makes sense. In each case, the perceptual evidence was effectively neutral as between the names proposed by the mother and those offered by the stranger. Faced with this equivocal evidence, two groups—the secure children and especially the ambivalent children—went along with their mother, but the avoidant children showed no such preference. Note that the avoidant children's lack of preference for their mother is very striking when we compare it to the findings obtained in the two daycare centers. As shown in Figures 5.1 and 5.2, a strong inclination to trust the familiar caregiver rather than a stranger emerged in both centers. The indifference shown by the avoidant children toward the information supplied by their own mother highlights the fact that familiarity in itself does not guarantee or maintain a child's selective trust. Even in relation to a very familiar attachment figure—their mother—children can be cautiously neutral, if an avoidant relationship has been established.[3]

The pattern of results for the asymmetrical hybrids—shown in Figure 5.6—offers a striking contrast to the pattern for the symmetrical hybrids. The avoidant and the secure children now displayed a preference for the stranger's claims. By contrast, the ambivalent children showed no such shift in trust toward the stranger—if anything, they continued to rely more on their mother than on the stranger.

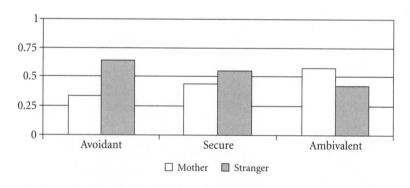

**Figure 5.6.** Proportion of choices directed at the mother versus a stranger, by attachment classification (asymmetrical creatures).

These results were in line with our earlier speculation. Ambivalent children appeared to be overly dependent on their mother's guidance, often accepting what she said even when countervailing information was available. For example, although the hybrid looked like a fish, and although the stranger had called it a fish, ambivalent children agreed with their mother. Despite the match between the perceptual evidence and the name supplied by the stranger, ambivalent children were loath to reject the mother's claim that it was a bird. The avoidant and secure children, by contrast, tended to favor the stranger's claim—consistent with what they could see for themselves.

In sum, looking at the results across the various probes, we may speculate that children adopt one of three strategies: *balanced, self-reliant,* or *dependent.* Secure children adopt a balanced strategy. With regard to their mother, they alternate between trust and skepticism, depending on the available evidence. When the perceptual evidence is ambiguous, they trust their mother. When the perceptual evidence runs counter to her claims, they are skeptical. Avoidant children are inclined to self-reliance rather than trust. When the perceptual evidence is ambiguous, they show no special trust in what their mother says, and when the evidence runs counter to her claims, they are firmly skeptical. Ambivalent children are dependent, rather than self-reliant. When the perceptual evidence is ambiguous, they firmly trust their mother. Yet even when the evidence runs counter to her claims, they are not inclined to doubt her.

As I have argued, children learn about the world in two different ways. They can make their own observations and form their own judgments, or they can look to other people for guidance. The findings just described offer a way to think about how children navigate between these two sources of information. Secure children are flexible. They turn to a familiar attachment figure when the perceptual evidence is uncertain or equivocal, but they may affirm a different conclusion when the perceptual evidence points elsewhere. The other two groups are more inflexible, but in dramatically different ways. Note that, in research on attachment, avoidant and ambivalent children are often lumped together as "insecure." Our findings show, however, that the nature of their insecurity and the ways in which they look for information are quite different. Both groups of children are inflexible, but not in the same way. Avoidant children show no definite inclination to trust their mother's judgment, even when perceptual sources of evidence are equivocal. By contrast, ambivalent children show the opposing tendency. They invest considerable trust in their mother's assertions. They are reluctant to draw conclusions that differ from her statements, even when much of the perceptual evidence goes against what she has said.

Again, this means that caregivers offer much more than a secure base for autonomous exploration. What they say about the world may or may not be internalized and become part of the child's conception of the way things are. Children listen to what they are told by an attachment figure and then weigh this against conclusions that they may reach for themselves, and also against conclusions that may be proposed by another adult, including a less familiar adult. The evidence indicates important individual differences in that process, differences that can be traced back to a core aspect of children's emotional development—namely, their attachment to their mother as assessed early in the second year of life.[4]

## Trusting People Who Are Accurate

Children's tendency to gather and accept information from someone depending on their emotional relationship with that person is likely to serve them well in early childhood, when one or more familiar caregivers are routinely available. However, as children get older and move into a wider world, they will interact with people they have known for only a short time. In such cases, children cannot use a long-standing emotional relationship to help them decide whether to accept what the person says. How do children assess the claims of people they do not know well?

Recall from Chapter 4 that even toddlers noticed and reacted when someone said something they regarded as wrong. When an adult blatantly misnamed an object—for example, called a cup a shoe—they stared at the speaker and issued denials or corrections. When an adult made a claim that was obviously false—"All fishes live in trees"—they balked at reasoning from such a premise. Suppose that young children not only register inaccuracies, but also keep track of who has been more or less wrong. They might use this accuracy-monitoring strategy in subsequent encounters, placing more trust in someone who has just proven accurate as compared with someone who has not. Even if they cannot check the claims made in those subsequent encounters, they can place more trust in someone who has been right before.

There is now a wealth of evidence showing that 3- and 4-year-olds engage in exactly this type of accuracy monitoring (Harris, 2007). For example, in one study, children were first shown a video of two unfamiliar adults. They watched and listened as one of the adults named various well-known objects correctly, whereas the other named them incorrectly (Corriveau & Harris, 2009b; Experiment 2). If children were monitoring for accurate naming, they had evidence during this brief introduction that one informant was accurate but the other was not. Next, children were shown several unfamiliar objects. This part of the procedure was similar to that used with the preschool caregivers in the study described at the beginning of this chapter. When shown each unfamiliar object, children were invited to ask its name. The two adults offered a different name. For example, when an unfamiliar object was presented, one adult might say, "That's a roke," whereas the other might say, "That's a cham." Having heard both claims, children were asked to say which they thought was correct.

In addition to this immediate test, half the children received a delayed test four days later and the remaining children received a delayed test one week later. On these delayed tests, children were again shown unfamiliar objects and given an opportunity to seek and endorse information from the two adults. Figure 5.7 shows the proportion of test trials on which children selected the previously accurate or inaccurate speaker on the immediate test, four days later, and one week later. Three- and 4-year-olds responded in much the same way, and so their choices are combined.

These findings show that 3- and 4-year-olds form an impression of a speaker's accuracy very quickly—over the course of a few minutes. Having done so, they hold on to that impression. Not only do they favor the more accurate speaker immediately afterward, but they show the same selective trust up to one week later. Children's selectivity is all

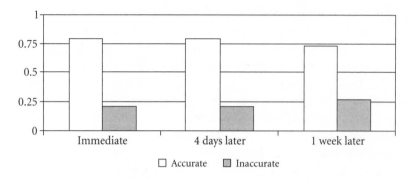

**Figure 5.7.** Proportion of test trials in which children selected the accurate and the inaccurate speaker, across three tests (immediate; 4 days later; 1 week later).

the more impressive in that they were not explicitly asked about the accuracy or inaccuracy of the two speakers in the course of the experiment. Yet despite the absence of any leading questions from the experimenter about the two speakers, children spontaneously made use of what they had observed for themselves and invested more trust in the accurate speaker.

Children were finally quizzed about the two speakers at the very end of the study (i.e., after the four-day test for half the children and the one-week test for the remaining children). At this point, both age groups could still remember and report on the differences between the speakers—saying, for example, that the accurate speaker was "very good" at naming things, whereas the inaccurate speaker was "not very good" at it. These results consolidate a broader pattern of findings. When observing two informants who differ in the accuracy of their claims, whether it is with respect to the names or to the properties of objects, preschoolers subsequently invest trust in the more accurate informant (Birch, Vauthier, & Bloom, 2008; Clément et al., 2004; Jaswal & Neely, 2006; Koenig, Clément, & Harris, 2004; Koenig & Harris, 2005).[5]

Admittedly, in the course of their everyday lives, children do not often meet someone who produces a string of blatantly false claims. In that respect, the experiments just described offer children a relatively artificial choice between a consistently accurate and a consistently inaccurate speaker. Are young children alert to less dramatic, more natural variations between two speakers? Across several studies, the following conclusions have emerged. Four-year-olds are indeed sensitive to less extreme differences between informants. If one informant occasionally makes mistakes, whereas another often does so, 4-year-olds—but not 3-year-olds—invest more trust in the relatively more accurate informant (Pasquini et al., 2007). Second, if one informant proves to be accurate in naming several objects but the other makes only noncommittal remarks ("Oh, look at that"), 4-year-olds—but not 3-year-olds—subsequently prefer the more evidently accurate informant. Apparently, 4-year-olds keep a fairly precise, cumulative record of their informants, building up trust in those who have proven accurate or mostly accurate. Three-year-olds, by contrast, appear to focus in a narrower fashion on inaccuracy. If an informant makes a mistake—even a single mistake—they become mistrustful. If both informants make mistakes even with differential frequency, or if one informant is accurate and the other noncommittal, 3-year-olds invest no more trust in the one than the other. By implication, 3-year-olds are on the lookout for mistakes. Whether they are confronted by a single mistake or by several, their reservoir of trust in that person is depleted (Corriveau, Meints, & Harris, 2009).[6]

A likely underpinning for this increasing recognition of accuracy is the improvement in children's understanding of belief, an improvement that has been widely observed in children of 3 and 4 (Wellman, Cross, & Watson, 2001). When asked to predict how a person might act, or what a person might say, 4-year-olds are better able than 3-year-olds to keep in mind the fact that a person might hold a false belief. So we may speculate that children who grasp the potential for false beliefs—typically children of 4 and older—not only withdraw credit in the case of inaccurate claims, but also tender credit in the case of accurate claims. They realize that accurate claims are not automatic; such claims typically reflect the beliefs of the speaker, and those beliefs might be true or false. By contrast, most three-year-olds, being less alert to the potential for false beliefs, withdraw credit in the case of inaccurate claims but take accurate claims for granted.

## Familiarity versus Accuracy

At this point, we have identified two heuristics that children use. The first is to trust familiar informants rather than strangers. Faced with a choice between trusting information from someone who looks after them—their mother or a preschool teacher—versus trusting information from a stranger, children favor the person they know. This familiarity heuristic is widely displayed, but not toward every familiar person—children who have an avoidant relationship with a familiar caregiver show no bias toward that caregiver. The second heuristic that children use is to monitor informants for the type of information they offer. Four-year-olds monitor for accuracy as well as inaccuracy, but even 3-year-olds look out for inaccuracy.

So far we have considered these two heuristics separately, but children may sometimes have to choose between them. What if a familiar informant starts making mistakes? Do children show signs of mistrust, or do they continue to trust her just because she is familiar? As adults, we also face this dilemma. Should we continue to listen to a familiar advisor—a hitherto trusted physician, teacher, or financial expert—or should we take note of their track record and switch when it proves less reliable than that of someone we know less well?

To examine this issue, we asked the caregivers at the two daycare centers discussed earlier to help us again (Corriveau & Harris, 2009a). After the tests with unfamiliar objects described earlier (see Figures 5.1 and 5.2), in which children had shown a marked preference for the familiar caregiver, half the children in each center watched as the familiar caregiver named some well-known objects accurately, whereas the unfamiliar caregiver named them inaccurately. The remaining children saw the reverse arrangement: the familiar caregiver named the objects inaccurately, whereas the unfamiliar caregiver named them accurately. Children then received test trials similar to those described earlier, in which the two caregivers provided conflicting names for unfamiliar objects.

Three-year-olds were scarcely affected by this differential feedback (see Figure 5.8). Whether the familiar caregiver had just proven accurate or inaccurate, they were inclined to direct the majority of their choices to her, rather than the unfamiliar caregiver. By contrast, 4-year-olds were affected. Their preference for the familiar caregiver was quite marked if she had been accurate, but it disappeared if she had been inaccurate. Finally, 5-year-olds displayed the sharpest reaction of all. Like 4-year-olds, their preference for the familiar caregiver was very evident if she had been accurate, but it was reversed if she had been inaccurate. Few of their choices were directed at the familiar caregiver; instead, they were mostly directed at the unfamiliar—but accurate—caregiver.

Apparently, there is a major shift in the basis for children's trust in the preschool years. Younger children are primarily influenced by their relationship to a familiar person. Older children, by contrast, look at the person's track record and prefer to learn from someone who has been accurate, no matter what their relationship with the person. In broad terms, this shift seems sensible. The older they get, the more children will have to deal with people they do not know well. Still, it is one thing to say that the shift is sensible; it is another thing to come up with an explanation at the psychological level for how it occurs. What exactly goes on in children's minds as they weigh familiarity as compared to accuracy?

We can begin by asking why the 3-year-olds failed to react to the familiar caregiver's mistakes. Several possibilities come to mind. Maybe 3-year-olds are simply less alert to mistakes and inaccuracies than older

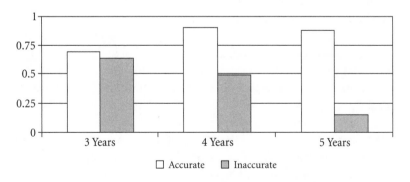

**Figure 5.8.** Proportion of choices directed at the familiar caregiver, depending on whether she had previously been accurate or inaccurate in naming well-known objects.

children are. However, looking back at the findings discussed earlier, there is plenty of evidence that 3-year-olds notice, remember, and use past inaccuracy as a guide to trustworthiness. Recall that when they met an unfamiliar person who made mistakes, they mistrusted the information provided by that person up to one week later (Corriveau & Harris, 2009b). We can safely conclude that 3-year-olds are able to notice mistakes and take them into account when selecting an informant.

Another possibility is that 3-year-olds register the mistakes of a familiar person, but weigh those mistakes against the overall record of their relationship with the person. Because the preschool caregiver was familiar to the 3-year-olds, she would presumably have had quite a long history of communication with the children in her care. Most of that communication would have been accurate, or at least not obviously mistaken. Perhaps 3-year-olds blithely discount a few mistakes—treating them as uncharacteristic of the person they have come to know. However, despite its initial plausibility, this interpretation ignores an important point. Five-year-olds did not overlook the errors of the familiar caregiver. They ended up preferring the less familiar but more accurate caregiver. Yet their interaction with the familiar caregiver would probably have been over a longer period than that of 3-year-olds, because they were more likely to have been daycare veterans. Moreover, their interaction with her was probably more frequent and intense, given their greater verbal skill. Accordingly, if we think of children as building up a reservoir of trust that an occasional error does not deplete, we might expect 5-year-olds to have a deeper and less exhaustible reservoir than 3-year-olds. Yet the results plainly do not fit this interpretation. Five-year-olds abandoned trust in the familiar caregiver quite ruthlessly, as compared to 3-year-olds.

We are led, therefore, to a different explanation for the insouciance of the 3-year-olds. They are not blind to a caregiver's mistakes. Nor do they draw on a huge reservoir of prior accuracy to offset recent errors. Rather, they are less likely to conceive of a caregiver's mistakes as an index of trustworthiness. Three-year-olds are inclined to say, "So you made a few mistakes—I know and like you and that's what counts," whereas 5-year-olds are inclined to say, "Look, we have a good relationship—but it does bother me when you make mistakes." It is too early to be sure of the exact explanation for this change of attitude, but three different lines of explanation are plausible.

One possibility is that cultural learning is so critical for the survival of the human species that nature has built a maturational shift into the conduct of such learning. Just as toddlers increasingly locomote by walking rather than crawling, so young children may increasingly navigate among sources of information by opting for the person who is accurate and knowledgeable, rather than the person who is familiar. In most human societies, as children get older, their social circle widens beyond known caregivers. Perhaps nature has ensured that children become increasingly judgmental about their nearest and dearest, comparing them for better or worse with other potential informants in terms of relative accuracy. After all, those other informants will have access to information about situations and practices that lie beyond the home. Someone from outside the family may prove to be a more knowledgeable and accurate source of information about what to do and say when away from home.

A second possibility is that the shift is experientially rather than maturationally driven. More specifically, the children tested in all the experiments reviewed in this chapter were attending preschool. They were spending several hours each week in the company of caregivers and children from outside their immediate family circle. Conceivably, it is such an expansion of children's social horizon that triggers greater attentiveness to the geography of human knowledge. As their horizon widens, children may realize that the distribution of knowledge is in many respects uneven and localized. Their mother knows what's what at home, but in the preschool you'll need to consult the teacher. More generally, individuals have particular domains of expertise that depend on where they live, their activities, their work, and the people that they meet (Keil, Stein, Webb, Billings, & Rozenblit, 2008; VanderBorght & Jaswal, 2009). In future research, it will be important to compare children who vary in the breadth of their social networks. According to the maturational hypothesis, a stable shift will be found somewhere between three and five years, whether their network is big or small. According to the experiential hypothesis, by contrast, the focus on accuracy will take place earlier among children who have often traveled beyond a narrow circle of familiar caregivers and learned more about the distribution of knowledge.

A third possibility is that the shift has a conceptual basis. Children's understanding of knowledge changes during the preschool years. Their increasing sensitivity to accuracy and inaccuracy might be part of a wider conceptual change in their understanding of knowledge and how it is acquired. More specifically, older preschoolers might be increasingly alert to the fallibility of knowledge and more attentive to indices of epistemic reliability. We can test this idea by looking for connections between children's developing conception of knowledge and their pattern of trust in accurate as opposed to familiar caregivers.

## Conclusions

Despite a long-standing assumption, especially within philosophy, that young children don't doubt what they are told, it is clear that children can be more or less skeptical. They are willing to put their questions to someone they know, and they often (but not always) accept what that person says. Yet they hesitate to place their trust in a stranger. Indeed, even their trust in someone they know is not automatic. Its strength varies, depending on the type of emotional relationship that the child has to the person in question.[7]

Children are also remarkably quick to "profile" the various people they meet. They come to think of some people as reliable informants and of other people as unreliable, depending on their past history. Moreover, such profiles are not easily set aside. Having met someone briefly and having spotted the person making mistakes, children remember this on subsequent encounters.

The weight that children give to the particular characteristics of an informant shifts in early childhood. At first, children appraise an informant's trustworthiness mostly in terms of socioemotional factors—their familiarity with, and attachment to, the person. But in the course of the preschool years, they give more weight to the reliability or accuracy of the informant.

A major implication of this developmental pattern is that ideas borrowed from attachment theory can help us to conceptualize young children's selective trust. Attachment figures do not simply serve as a secure base to which children can retreat after a solo expedition. Attachment figures also serve as privileged sources of information. Nevertheless, attachment theory falls short as an explanation of the entire developmental pattern. Children keep track of a person's epistemic profile; and in the case of older children, it is that epistemic profile rather than their attachment to the person that ultimately decides whose information they trust.

From the perspective of cultural learning, such a shift is likely to be adaptive. In most human societies—modern societies, as well as hunter-gatherer societies—children learn about their culture by looking "vertically" up to their primary caregivers: their mother and father, and others within their immediate family circle. However, children can also profit by looking "horizontally." Family members are not omniscient—neighbors, elders, and playmates likely know things that family members do not. Not surprisingly, children are willing to optimize their acquisition of skills and information by looking outside the circle of familiar caregivers—especially if the outsiders prove more reliable in the information they offer.

CHAPTER 6

# Consensus and Dissent

✦

$A$s adults, we often seek help from people we scarcely know. Suppose that you've just arrived at the main station of an unfamiliar city. Your hotel is in the neighborhood, but you're not exactly sure where. Two helpful passers-by offer conflicting advice. One gives directions for walking to the hotel, but the other recommends a taxi. A nearby couple join the debate. They look skeptical when the walking route is described, but nod when the taxi is proposed. You thank them, gather your belongings, and head toward the taxi rank. Without really thinking about it, you are inclined to trust the majority view.

We asked if 4-year-olds show the same inclination. Each child watched as two women they had never met before named a set of unfamiliar objects. Standing behind these two women, but easily visible, were two bystanders, listening to what was being said. When one of the women named an unfamiliar object—"That's a feppin"—the two bystanders smiled and nodded their heads in approval. By contrast, when the other woman named it differently—"That's a merval"—the two bystanders frowned and shook their heads in disapproval. When asked for their view, 4-year-olds generally endorsed the name supplied by the woman who had attracted bystander approval—they did so on about 90 percent of the trials (Fusaro & Harris, 2008).

It looks as if preschoolers—like adults—also trust the majority view, but there are other possibilities. Maybe they're just susceptible to social pressure. After all, they saw the two bystanders react with approval to some names and with disapproval to others. In the wake of these reactions, children may have sensed that they, too, would attract disapproval—in the form of frowns and headshakes—if they endorsed the "wrong" name. Another explanation is also plausible. Children may have interpreted the bystanders' reactions as comments on the two women themselves. Perhaps they took the bystanders to be expressing approval of one woman and disapproval of the other, and so they sided with the one gaining approval.

We compared these two interpretations in the next phase of the experiment. The two bystanders left, but in all other respects testing continued as before: more unfamiliar objects were placed on the table, the two women named them differently, and a group of children were again asked for their view. If they had thought of the bystanders as commenting only on the names, the children should now have regarded each name as equally acceptable because the bystanders were no longer present to pressure them. On the other hand, if children had thought of the bystanders as commenting on the two informants, they should have continued to agree with the informant who had attracted approval rather than disapproval. Whatever traits the bystanders were reacting to would presumably still have differentiated the two informants.

In fact, most children continued to agree with the informant who had received bystander approval. This bias was not as strong as in the initial phase, but it was still clear and systematic. By implication, some—perhaps all—of the 4-year-olds had come to think about the two informants differently in light of the bystanders' reactions. They saw one in a positive light and the other in a more negative light, even after the two bystanders had left.[1]

In the next study, we tried to figure out how exactly children had interpreted the reactions of the two bystanders. Did children think along the following lines? "These bystanders must obviously like one of these women and dislike the other one. I guess I'll go along with their opinion. I'll agree with the woman who seems more likable." Alternatively, did the children think of the bystanders' reactions as expressions of agreement or disagreement? Preschoolers use nods and headshakes to express agreement and disagreement themselves (Fusaro, Harris, & Pan, in press; Guidetti, 2005). So maybe they said to themselves: "These bystanders agree with one of these women and disagree with the other one. I guess the woman they agree with gets things right, but the other one keeps making mistakes. I'll agree with the woman who gets things right."

To examine these two possibilities, we changed the procedure (Corriveau, Fusaro, & Harris, 2009). Three- and 4-year-olds were introduced to a group of four adult women. Several unfamiliar objects were laid out on the table and, using an unfamiliar name (for example, "Show me the modi"), the experimenter asked the women to point to one of the objects. Three women promptly pointed to one and the same object, but the fourth—a lone dissenter—pointed to a different object. Children were then asked to indicate which object they thought was the modi.

Note that this experiment was structurally similar to the previous one. Four adults were present. Three formed a consensus, whereas the fourth was marginalized. However, in this new procedure, the adults could not easily be construed as either liking or disliking one another. At most, by pointing to a given object, they conveyed agreement or disagreement with each other. This meant that if children were sensitive to the pattern of pointing, they were making sense of it in terms of agreement and disagreement, not in terms of liking and disliking. Indeed, when children were asked to say which object they thought was (for example) the modi, both age groups agreed with the consensus, not with the lone dissenter.

The next phase of the experiment resembled what had happened in the earlier study. Two members of the consensus left. This meant that one member of the consensus remained, together with the lone dissenter, and they continued to serve as informants. Several more unfamiliar objects were presented, and the children were given various opportunities to indicate which person, if any, they preferred to learn from. Both 3- and 4-year-olds displayed a clear preference for the former member of the consensus, not the lone dissenter. They were likely to ask her for the names of the unfamiliar objects, to agree with the names that she supplied, and to eventually say that she was better at answering questions than the lone dissenter. Similar results emerged in a follow-up study in which the total number of adult informants present at the start was reduced to three, with the consensus involving only two adults—versus a lone dissenter. Finally, children's behavior in the two phases of the experiment was consistent. Children who showed a strong preference for the consensus claims in the first phase, when all the informants were present, displayed a strong bias in the second phase, when only the consensus member and the lone dissenter were present.

Apparently, preschoolers "go with the flow"—in two related but distinct ways. First, when several potential informants are present, children agree with the claims of a person who is endorsed by other people—endorsed via nods and smiles or via parallel claims. Conversely, children disagree with the claims of a person who is out of step with other people—a person whose claims are met with frowns and headshakes or simply with conflicting claims. Children's sensitivity to whether an informant belongs to a consensus does not depend on whether other people express emotion. Even when informants respond unemotionally—for example, by simply pointing to the same object or a different object—children notice. They are drawn to consensus and flee dissent.

Preschoolers also remain selective when the initial sources of their differentiation between the two informants—namely, other people and their reactions—have quit the scene. When everyone has exited except for one consensus member and the dissenter, children still prefer to learn from the consensus member. Apparently, children think of an informant's group status as something that characterizes that person even when the group has dispersed.

Before starting to think about the best way to interpret these findings, it is worth describing one final study of children's sensitivity to a consensus. In the experiments described so far, children were introduced to several women from their own cultural and racial group. All the women looked—and sounded—European American. We wondered if this was important. Were children being influenced simply by the fact that several women had formed a numerical consensus, or was it important that the consensus was composed of women from their own group—namely, European Americans?

To explore this issue, we tested 3- and 4-year-olds in Boston and Taiwan (Chen, Corriveau, & Harris, 2011; in press). In each location, some of the children were tested in the same way as before: in Boston, all the women looked European American, whereas in Taiwan they all looked East Asian. The results were as expected. In the first phase of the study, children favored the consensus, and in the second phase, when they could choose between a consensus member and the dissenter, they preferred the consensus member. This familiar pattern emerged both in Boston and in Taiwan.

For the other children, we altered the cultural identity of the women —substituting East Asian women in Boston and European American women in Taiwan. Under this condition, children still preferred the consensus member over the lone dissenter but less strongly, and they showed no preference for the consensus member in the test phase. By implication, children register when there is a consensus no matter what its composition, but they are especially prone to do that if its members belong to the same group as themselves. They are less swayed by a consensus of people belonging to an outgroup and invest no special trust in its members.

### The Trustworthy Informant: Purveyor of Truth or Respectable Conformist?

Children's sensitivity to a group consensus—both when the group is present and even after the group has disbanded—might reflect two radically different learning strategies. On the one hand, children might think that someone who is endorsed by the majority gets things right. Consider what happens when several people offer an eyewitness report. We are inclined to assume that a witness whose testimony is backed up by other people is telling the truth. Ultimately, of course, we cannot be completely sure who is right. Especially in domains where only a few people have expertise, one particular informant may have better powers of discrimination and diagnosis than everyone else. A lone art expert may be right when he insists, contrary to everyone else, that a given painting is a forgery. Still, in unproblematic domains, where everyone can be regarded as a competent witness and where people ordinarily agree, it is sensible to pay attention to how the claims of a given informant stand in relation to those of other people, and to accept information from someone whose claims are endorsed by others, rather than from someone whose claims are out of line. To the extent that children are offered testimony about everyday issues—issues that most people are competent to report on—and not about matters calling for specialized expertise, it would be appropriate for them to be wary of dissenters and to seek out informants whom other people agree with. In short, according to this line of thinking, children seek the truth from competent and accurate informants, and their sensitivity to the group standing of an informant is part of that truth-seeking enterprise.

An attractive feature of this interpretation is that it implies that, depending on the circumstances, children can use two quite different indicators of trustworthiness for the same purpose. In some cases, notably when they can check on the accuracy of an informant's claims for themselves (as described in the previous chapter), children can assess an informant's competence without looking to other people for guidance. In other cases, when they are unable to judge the accuracy of an informant's claims for themselves, they can monitor bystander assent and dissent. Whichever strategy they use, they effectively feed their observations into the same metric: an assessment of an informant's competence at reporting the truth.

But consider a different line of argument. Perhaps children are not interested in the truth, or have, at best, an incidental interest in it. When they turn to other people for guidance, perhaps they are trying to find out what counts as the "proper" way to behave or think. Their goals may be normative, rather than epistemic. In support of this argument, consider the fact that children are members of a highly social species, with a plethora of cultural practices involving tools and symbols. In learning how to use a tool by watching a demonstration, children readily take a normative stance, as we saw in Chapter 3. They chide those who deviate from what they regard as the appropriate way to do things. Similarly, when children acquire language, there is little doubt that most of them eventually honor the linguistic norms of their own community. Most of those norms have no particular truth-value. As a Briton living in New England, I may sometimes have to repeat my request for water, but my nonstandard accent is not violating the truth. Similarly, if I have trouble understanding French as spoken in Quebec,

I cannot accuse the Québécois of distorting the way things really are. I am simply not attuned to their accent.

So young children's overriding goal when they look to informants for guidance may be to learn about the norms and practices of their community. To the extent that they seek such normative information, children might be especially inclined to trust informants who honor rather than breach those group norms. This hypothesis, like the first, posits that children are vigilant sociologists, noticing where there is a consensus and where there is dissent. Yet the motive for their vigilance is not to discover the truth, but to gather information that will enable them to fit into their own cultural group. Notice that this hypothesis neatly explains the findings obtained in Boston and Taiwan. If children aim to fit into their own cultural group, they will be especially attentive to a consensus that is composed of people from their own social group but will be less attentive to an outgroup consensus.

Initially, some of the results described in the previous chapter seem to provide convincing evidence that the first hypothesis—the truth-seeking hypothesis—is correct. Recall that in the experiments on accuracy monitoring, children were presented with two informants, one who named objects accurately and one who named them inaccurately. It seems plausible that the children were judging whether the informants' claims were true or false. In other words, when one informant said that a spoon was a spoon, they tacitly assented—"Right you are!" —but when the other informant said that a spoon was a duck, they mentally expostulated: "What? That's no duck! It's a spoon" (Corriveau & Harris, 2009b). Following these accuracy judgments, children went on to construe the two informants as more or less likely to provide reliable and truthful information in the future.

However, there is another way to think about children's reactions to the accurate and inaccurate informants. Maybe they thought of them as more or less respectful of local conventions. So when one informant named objects correctly, children thought of it as unexceptional, normal behavior; but when the other informant named objects incorrectly, they thought of it as weird and unacceptable: "Hey! Nobody calls *that* a duck around here. They call it a spoon." On this interpretation, children are thinking of the two informants not as more or less truthful, but as more or less representative of the appropriate way to do things.

It is difficult to think of ways that an informant could say something false—for example, misname an object—without also violating a norm (not least the conversational norm that when information is provided it should be true). On the other hand, an informant can violate a linguistic norm without saying something false—recall the earlier examples of variation among speakers in their accent. So we can ask if children trust a speaker who sticks to local linguistic conventions, as compared to one who departs from them—even though neither speaker says anything false or untrue.

In one experiment of this type, preschoolers were introduced to two speakers who differed in their use of morphological markers (Corriveau, Pickard, & Harris, 2011). One speaker produced singular and plural nouns in the conventional fashion—for example, "This is a shoe" and "These are some shoes." But the other speaker did so in a deviant fashion: "This is a shoes" or "These are some shoe." These modest deviations were sufficient to elicit mistrust. The 4-year-olds preferred to learn from the morphologically conventional speaker, whether the learning involved new object names or new forms of the past tense.[2]

Further evidence that children are sensitive to the conventionality of a speaker, independent of his or her truth-telling, emerged in a study of children's sensitivity to accent (Kinzler, Corriveau, & Harris, 2011). Four- and 5-year-olds listened to two informants, one who spoke English with a standard American accent and one who spoke English with a Spanish accent. Some children listened to the speakers read a passage that made sense, from *Curious George,* whereas others listened to them read a nonsense passage from "Jabberwocky," by Lewis Carroll. The two speakers then showed the children how to use various unfamiliar tools, but offered conflicting demonstrations for any given tool. Children preferred to emulate the informant with a native accent, and this preference was equally obvious whether the familiarization period had involved the passage from *Curious George* that children could understand or the nonsense extract from "Jabberwocky." This study provides especially strong evidence that children are swayed by an informant's conformity to local norms. Even when children listened to the two in-formants read the nonsense passage from "Jabberwocky"—so they were clearly in no position to decide whether the speakers had said anything true or false—children were sensitive to their accent. They preferred to learn from someone who conformed to their own sense of standard speech, and that preference persisted even when the two speakers offered silent demonstrations.

Summarizing across these experiments, they show that young children are sticklers for convention. When a speaker is mildly ungrammatical (e.g., says "some shoe" instead of "some shoes") or speaks with a foreign accent, they are less willing to learn from that speaker. Their mistrust of an unconventional speaker goes beyond the information that he or she supplies about linguistic matters, such as the names for objects or the way to form the past tense. Children are also less willing to learn how to use a novel tool from such a speaker.[3] This does not mean that children ignore a speaker's accuracy and attend only to his or her conventionality. After all, none of the experiments mentioned above asked children to choose between an accurate but unconventional informant and an inaccurate but conventional one. Faced with that choice, children would probably drop their sensitivity to conventionality and opt for the accurate informant; and to judge by the developmental pattern described in the previous chapter, that switch is likely to be especially evident among older preschoolers.[4] Still, the experiments make the point that in the absence of any clues as to whether an informant is saying something true or false, an informant's way of speaking makes him or her more or less trustworthy as a source of information for young children.

## Testimony and Simple Perceptual Judgments

In certain ways, the evidence reviewed so far is reassuring. It makes good sense for children to keep an eye out for consensus, and to go along both with that consensus and with the recommendations and claims of any given member of that consensus. One could also make the case that when children are sticklers for convention, they are learning to act in accord with the proprieties of their culture. If they prefer to learn from people who do things the way they should be done, they will end up doing them the right way, at least so far as their own culture and community are concerned.

However, there is a classic set of studies in social psychology showing that adults can, under certain circumstances, go with the flow in a way that is thoroughly disconcerting. When there is a clash between the opinions of other people and their own simple perceptual judgments, adults can be surprisingly deferential—particularly if all the other people are unanimous in their judgment. For example, if adults are shown three lines, clearly different in length, and invited to pick out the one that matches a fourth, they do so accurately and without hesitation. But if they are invited to make that judgment in the wake of several other people, who have all pointed to a different line, doubt appears to seep in. Adults ignore what their eyes tell them and defer to the consensus about one-third of the time (Asch, 1956).

Are young children similarly deferential? We might expect them to defer to a consensus even more than adults do. On the other hand, young children might not be as acutely aware as adults that people generally agree on simple perceptual judgments. In that case, children would be less disturbed to find themselves making a perceptual judgment that's different from everyone else's. In any case, as discussed in Chapter 3, young children do not ordinarily give way when someone says something that flatly contradicts what they have observed for themselves. Do they also resist when several people contradict them?

To answer this question, we placed 3- and 4-year-olds in a situation similar to the one devised by Asch (Corriveau & Harris, 2010). Children were shown three strips that were clearly different in length, and we asked them to pick out the biggest one. They did this without any difficulty—no mistakes were ever made. Next, they watched a video in which three adults were also asked to point to the biggest strip. Instead of pointing correctly, all three adults pointed to the medium strip or even, on some trials, to the smallest strip. Children were then invited once again to point to the biggest one. Most of the time, they stuck to their original, correct judgment. However, on about one-quarter of the trials they changed their judgment; and when they did so, it was to pick out the strip that the adults had chosen.

We checked whether such shifts in judgment affected children's practical behavior. They were invited to complete a bridge with one of the strips, so that a toy bunny could cross a river to retrieve a valuable sticker. Only the biggest strip was long enough to span the river. Children invariably picked the biggest strip, showing that the influence of the adults was circumscribed: it affected children's immediate judgment, but not their pragmatic behavior. But why exactly had the children deferred at all—even briefly? Close analysis showed that something more interesting and complicated than mere conformity was taking place—what we came to think of as "respectful" deference toward the adult consensus. Four pieces of evidence pointed to this intriguing pattern of behavior.

First, children became increasingly less likely to agree with the adult consensus with repeated trials. Yet if children were simply prone to conformity, they should conform just as often across all trials. Second, we rounded off the experiment by asking children to say how good the adults had been at making length judgments. For the most part, children said—quite reasonably—that the adults had not been very good. However, those children who had deferred at least once were likely to say that the adults had been good, whereas children who never deferred said that the adults had not been very good. Third, when asked to say which strip the adult consensus had pointed to, children mostly indicated the incorrect selection that the adults had indeed made—but deferential children were likely to claim that the adults had pointed to the biggest strip. They mistakenly "remembered" the adults as being correct. Finally, we noticed an unexpected but provocative variation among the children that depended on their cultural background: across two studies, Asian American children deferred more often than European American children. Indeed, when we looked back at the large body of findings using the Asch paradigm, we belatedly discovered that exactly the same pattern had been found with adults (Bond & Smith, 1996).

Our interpretation of this cluster of findings was that children have two judgment modes that ordinarily yield the same conclusion. First, they can make an autonomous judgment. In the case of line judgments, children's own perceptual system will easily enable them to pick out the biggest line. Recall that children always did this accurately before they were swayed by the adult consensus. Second, as we have repeatedly seen throughout this chapter and the previous one, children make socially guided judgments. Children defer to other people's opinions, and they are especially prone to defer when those other people form a consensus. Ordinarily, especially in commonsense matters and in the formation of simple perceptual judgments, the conclusions that children arrive at via either judgment mode will be equivalent. Children's own judgment will coincide with those of other people, and no conflict will ensue.

When these two modes conflict, however, which one wins? As noted in Chapter 4, children do not ordinarily revise simple perceptual judgments—for example, judgments about color—in deference to another informant, even one who has proven reliable in the past (Clément et al., 2004). However, when there is a consensus among several informants, as in the line judgment task, children may be conflicted. On the one hand, they may conclude that their perceptual judgment is right, that the consensus is wrong; and they may become, as a result, increasingly skeptical about the judgments made by the adult consensus. This would explain the gradual decline in deference in the course of the test trials. On the other hand, they may conclude that the consensus is correct and has identified the longest line. In that case, we might reasonably expect three interrelated behaviors: children will defer; they will think of the consensus as being good at making judgments; and they might even misremember the line identified by the consensus as the longest line. This is, of course, exactly the pattern that was displayed by children who did sometimes defer. In other words, the data suggest that children occasionally set aside their own perceptual judgment and agreed with the consensus, not because they were prone to mindless conformity but because they were disposed to respectful deference: they concluded that the consensus had made the right judgment.

What about the difference between European American and Asian American children? A speculative but plausible interpretation is that it reflects a broad difference in the way that cultures weigh the merits of relying on one's own autonomous judgment versus those of respectful deference to the group. As noted above, private judgments and the judgments of a social consensus often coincide. When they conflict, however, children may be socialized to go in one of two different directions: to respect the social consensus or to prioritize their own private judgment. It is plausible that early child-rearing practices nurture one or the other orientation. In East Asian cultures, young children are encouraged to respect the expectations and judgments of other people. In European American cultures, they are encouraged to rely more on their own independent judgments (Rothbaum, Weisz, Pott, Miyake, & Morelli, 2000).

To probe this cultural variation further, we subsequently compared three groups living in the United States: European American children, second-generation East Asian children, and first-generation East Asian children. Respectful deference was greatest among the first-generation East Asian children, and least frequent among the European American children; the second-generation East Asian children were in between (Corriveau, Kim, Song, & Harris, 2011; Kim, Song, Corriveau, & Harris, 2011).[5] By implication, following migration, East Asian families shed their traditional child-rearing practices and shift toward those common in the United States, although more research is needed to identify which particular practices are modified in the wake of migration and increasing assimilation.

In the future, it will also be fascinating to explore the distribution of these two orientations. One possibility is that they reflect a broad difference between East and West—between the cultures of East Asia on the one hand and the cultures of North America and Western Europe on the other. This interpretation is consistent with a large body of research with adults (Nisbett, Peng, Choi, & Norenzayan, 2001). However, an equally plausible interpretation is that the pattern of respectful deference found among Asian American children is quite common in the world's cultures, not just in Asia but beyond. On this hypothesis, it is the relatively autonomous pattern of judgment displayed by European American children that might prove to be atypical when placed in global perspective (Henrich, Heine, & Norenzayan, 2010).

## Conclusions

Young children are receptive to the judgments of individuals who agree with one another. Several findings show that they regard a consensus as a trustworthy source of information. Particularly when conflicting claims are made by a consensus on the one hand and a lone dissenter on the other, children endorse the consensus. In addition, the influence of a consensus is persistent. Even when the group disbands, individual members are still trusted more than a dissenter.

Children might think that consensual judgments have a good chance of being true. This would be consistent with standard notions of cognitive development that portray young children as truth-seekers. However, an equally plausible hypothesis is that children think of consensual judgments—and the people who supply them—as a reliable guide to the norms of their culture, rather than as an index of truth. So when faced with a choice, they do not endorse or emulate a deviant; rather, they follow the lead of someone who fits in with the group.

The evidence also shows that children are not interested in conformity to just any group. They are especially swayed by people who fit in with the norms and conventions of their own group. They are prone to trust someone who looks and sounds like them. These findings are nicely consistent with the conformist bias emphasized by Richerson and Boyd (2005) as a key component of cultural learning, but they add an important twist. They show that children do not simply assess the frequency of a given behavior, endorsing and adopting behaviors that are widespread. They also prefer to emulate a new—and hence, from their perspective, rare—variant, provided it is modeled by someone who has elicited agreement rather than dissent from members of their group. Thus, children do not simply conform to frequently modeled behaviors; they conform to the judgments of people who have shown themselves to be conformists.

Occasionally, children will agree with a consensus even when it flatly contradicts their own accurate, perceptual judgments. Such "respectful deference" is especially noticeable among Asian American children. More research is needed in order to figure out how frequent this stance is across the world's cultures. The more deferential stance taken by Asian American children might be atypical, or it might be characteristic of many young children around the globe. Whatever the outcome of further research, it is likely to show that children's repertoire of cultural learning strategies is shaped by the culture that they grow up in.

When we think about young children's social behavior, especially in a new and unfamiliar environment—the first few days at preschool, for example—we may be inclined to focus on their lack of conformity to the prevailing norms. However, as preschool teachers know, it will not be long before various group habits and rituals are accepted by almost every child—whether these concern how to behave during story time or where to put one's lunch box. An intriguing implication of this chapter is that children have a built-in tendency to gravitate toward members of the group whose behavior is representative of prevailing norms. Provided that the classroom has several veterans who know how things are done, the novices will fall into line pretty soon.

In the next chapter, we will examine the judgments that children make in the moral domain, taking another look at a question that has often surfaced in this chapter: How far do children rely on their own judgment, and how far do they look toward other people for guidance?

# CHAPTER 7

# Moral Judgment and Testimony

·✦·

The idea that other people's testimony might play a critical role in children's moral judgment has rarely been considered. The classic question in developmental psychology has concerned when and how children arrive at their own moral decisions, independent of other people's guidance. I will argue for a somewhat paradoxical conclusion. Children can be surprisingly autonomous in their moral judgment. They may even reach moral conclusions that their families do not share. At the same time, in reaching their independent conclusions, children make use of the testimony that other people provide. Indeed, their thoughtfulness underlines the point that complete autonomy in making moral judgments is no more attainable—or desirable—than is complete autonomy in the making of factual or epistemic judgments.

## Autonomous Moral Judgments

Young children are able to make autonomous moral decisions. When they are asked to think about a hypothetical environment in which there are no rules or authority figures, they claim that certain actions would still be wrong. For example, if preschoolers are invited to think about a school with no rules and no punishments, they insist that hitting or stealing in such a school would still be very bad. By contrast, they acknowledge that deviations from convention—sitting in the wrong place, dressing in an odd fashion—would be rendered acceptable (Turiel, 2006). Various pieces of evidence suggest that the reason children differentiate between moral and conventional transgressions is that they are sensitive to the harm and distress that moral transgressions cause other people (Harris, 1989). Hitting another child will be painful for the victim; coming to school in pajamas, by contrast, is not likely to upset anyone—even if it is funny and surprising.

The striking implication of these findings is that explicit adult instruction may not be essential for children's moral education. Children can be moral autodidacts—they can figure out what is right and wrong for themselves. Consistent with this speculation, children who are neglected or abused by their parents still come to recognize that actions like hitting and stealing are wrong (Smetana, Kelly, & Twentyman, 1984). Despite the way they are treated by their parents, such children have opportunities to learn right from wrong. If they play with other children or attend a daycare center, they can observe what actions cause distress. For example, squabbles about who owns what—which happen frequently among preschoolers—often involve a "thief" and a distressed owner (Strayer & Strayer, 1976). Provided children recognize that it is bad to make another child upset, they do not necessarily need parental commentary to help them figure out, for example, that it is wrong to take something that does not belong to you. They can judge for themselves that certain actions are right and wrong, because they know what emotional impact those actions have.

Still, in making these judgments, children's autonomy may be shallow rather than deep. Even if they can imagine a school with no rules, one in which hitting and stealing would be permitted, children may realize that such a school would be a dramatic departure from the norms that are widespread. At best, then, children may be endorsing what they have observed to be the status quo. In any case, whatever their capacity for autonomous moral judgments about theft and violence, preschoolers are not very good at practicing what they preach. Filching, grabbing, and hitting are common in preschool environments. Later in this chapter, I will discuss a group of children who seem to have a much stronger claim to moral autonomy: self-elected vegetarians. First, however, it is helpful to discuss the role of testimony in moral judgment.

## Learning via Testimony

An emphasis on the role of autonomous judgment is plausible, provided that children can make the relevant observations. In the domain of moral judgment, as we have just seen, it seems likely that children can make those observations: they can discover—both in their own case and in the case of other children—that hitting someone causes pain and discomfort. Similarly, they can observe that having one's belongings taken without permission is upsetting. They need no help in registering the emotional consequences of these misdemeanors. Indeed, it is plausible that children are especially likely to learn right from wrong when they have such firsthand experience. Certainly, immediate and visible evidence of suffering provokes moral qualms among adults. In Stanley Milgram's classic studies of obedience, for example, adults were instructed by an authority figure—a scientist in a white coat—to administer what they thought were painful electric shocks to a learner, allegedly to study of the effects of punishment on learning (Milgram, 1969). The willingness of adults to obey the instructions was dramatically affected by direct observation of the suffering that they were inflicting on the learner. If the victim was seated beside them so that his facial and vocal expressions of pain were observable, most adults (70 percent) disobeyed the scientist's instructions at some point. On the other hand, if the victim was seated in another room so that his suffering could not be directly observed, but could be inferred from the warnings beside the various switches on the shock apparatus and from the muffled sound of his beating on the walls, then a much smaller percentage (35 percent) disobeyed at any point in the experiment. In fact, most adults were willing to go beyond voltage levels that were clearly marked as "Danger: Severe Shock," and they administered what they were led to believe was the maximum possible voltage.

If children can see a victim's suffering and distress, what effect does that visual evidence have on their moral judgment? This was studied in an ingenious experiment by Judith Smetana (1985). She told preschoolers several stories in which the protagonist engaged in novel actions. These were referred to only by means of unfamiliar words—

"mibbing" or "fepping"—and so it was not immediately clear whether the actions were good, bad, or neutral. However, some children were presented with stories in which they could see that another child was upset when these actions occurred. For example, they heard about Sally, who got mad when she could not find her favorite doll and then "mibbed"—whereupon her baby brother, Michael, began to cry. Children could observe the effect on Michael for themselves, because they were shown a picture of him in tears.[1] Having listened to these illustrated stories, children systematically judged that the unfamiliar actions were very bad, whether they were carried out in school or elsewhere, and the children justified their judgments by referring to the pain and distress that the actions evidently caused. Apparently, preschoolers can indeed learn that an unfamiliar action is wrong simply from seeing its emotional impact on a victim.

We can now ask about the role of testimony. Given the developmental findings just described, as well as the findings of Milgram's studies with adults, it would be reasonable to think that children might easily learn from being able to see a victim's distress, but not from hearing verbal reports. Still, it is possible to think of cases in which adults and children might benefit from such testimony. Suppose that a person is committed to treating people equally, but is not very good at noticing the emotional impact of sexist or racist remarks. Or suppose that the targets of those remarks routinely hide their anger and distress. In each case, other people's testimony might be instructive in highlighting the emotional impact of such remarks (Jones, 1999). This type of learning seems especially likely in the case of children. Other people might alert them to the fact that certain actions cause harm and distress in ways that children do not immediately realize for themselves.

As an initial exploration of this possibility, Angie Kim and I adapted Smetana's story procedure (Kim & Harris, 2009). Children again listened to stories in which the main protagonist engaged in unfamiliar actions such as "mibbing." However, the stories were presented in one of three ways. Control stories provided no information about any harm or suffering that these novel actions caused. Picture stories included a picture of the victim, Amy, crying as a result of Sally's mibbing. Thus, as in the study by Smetana (1985), children could see the suffering for

themselves. Finally, orally conveyed stories included only verbal information about the suffering caused. Children were told, for example,
about an interchange between Sally and her teacher: "Ms. White, the
teacher, walked by and said: "When you mibbed Amy, you hurt her." As
expected, children judged that the unfamiliar action of mibbing was
bad when they saw a picture of the victim crying just as Smetana (1985)
had found, but they also said that mibbing was bad when they learned
about its impact only via the teacher's oral comment. Moreover, in
both cases, they explained their judgments by reference to Amy's distress—"Because she got hurt" or "Because Amy cried."

So we have three initial conclusions. First, children recognize from
an early age that actions causing distress are wrong—and indeed remain wrong whether or not anyone forbids them. Second, if children
see that an unfamiliar action causes distress, they judge it to be wrong.
Finally, children do not need to see visible signs of distress. If they learn
via testimony from other people that an action causes distress, that information is enough for them to judge the action as being wrong.

Putting these three conclusions together, we can make the following
unexpected prediction. If young children are told that something that
they do on a routine basis actually causes a good deal of suffering, they
will likely conclude that it is wrong. Indeed, they might decide that it is
wrong even when obvious authority figures such as parents and teachers allow or encourage the action in question. In the next section, we
take a close look at children who fit this intriguing prediction.

## Independent Vegetarians

Although the case is far from common, some children choose to become vegetarian even though they are being raised in meat-eating families. Discussion with these unusual children reveals that their decision
is, in certain key respects, autonomous. It runs counter to the expectations and practices of their immediate family. On the other hand, they
have not arrived at their decision in a social vacuum. It appears to be
based on the testimony of other people. More specifically, although
children are not ordinarily reminded within their own family of what
meat-eating entails, they do learn about it from people outside the

family circle, including other children. They are told about the suffering and slaughter of animals, and this information leads them to decide that eating meat is wrong.

Karen Hussar and I studied a small group of these "independent" vegetarians—"independent" in the sense that they were growing up in meat-eating families but had decided to stop eating meat (Hussar & Harris, 2010). The children—five boys and eleven girls—ranged in age from 6 to 10, with an average age of 8. The families were supportive— they catered as best they could to their children's decision not to eat meat. We talked to the children to find out whether they framed their decision in terms of moral considerations—rather than, for example, taste or health considerations. We also asked the children how they viewed the meat-eating world. Did they condemn meat-eating by other people, or did they withhold judgment? If the children avoided eating meat on moral grounds, they might reasonably be expected to criticize other people—and, logically, that would have to include members of their family—who did eat meat.

To highlight the distinctive way in which these independent vegetarians framed their decisions about eating meat, we compared them to two other groups of the same age and background. One group comprised so-called "family" vegetarians—children who likewise avoided meat but who did so because they were being raised in vegetarian families, not because they had reached a decision independent of their family. The other group comprised children who were regular meat-eaters being raised in ordinary, nonvegetarian families. All the children, including the meat-eaters, were asked to name a particular meat that they did not ordinarily eat. They were then asked to give their reasons for not eating it. Children offered a variety of reasons for their decision: animal welfare (for example, "I don't like the idea of killing animals"); family practices ("If my parents weren't vegetarian, I wouldn't be vegetarian either"); religious considerations ("In my religion, you don't eat meat"); health considerations ("I think they [corn and carrots] are healthy [as compared to chicken]"); and finally the taste of the meat in question ("It tastes kind of . . . like, weird"). Figure 7.1 shows the percentage of children in each of the three groups who gave replies of each type.

Figure 7.1 shows that all the independent vegetarians mentioned animal welfare as a consideration, whereas fewer than half of the family vegetarians did so. Among meat-eaters, taste and health considerations predominated, and none of them referred to animal welfare. Hence, children's answers to this simple question suggested that the independent vegetarians based their decision to avoid meat on moral grounds—they explained it by saying that eating meat involves the suffering and death of animals. Unlike the family vegetarians, they made no mention of religion or family practices; and unlike the meat-eaters, they rarely mentioned benefits to themselves by way of health or taste.

How ardent were the independent vegetarians about not eating meat? To probe any tendencies toward zealotry, we asked all the children about four different types of potentially transgressive action: moral transgressions, such as hitting and stealing; transgressions of social convention, such as eating salad with the fingers; somewhat unusual but essentially personal decisions, such as reading alone during recess; and finally, meat-eating. Our aim was twofold. We wanted to compare the independent vegetarians with the other two groups on various potential transgressions that had nothing to do with eating

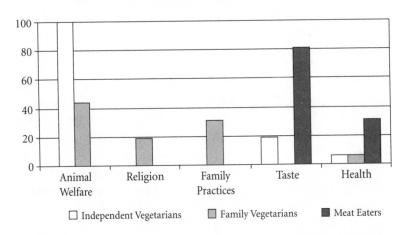

**Figure 7.1.** Percentage of children who offered each of five types of explanation. Note that some children offered more than one explanation.

meat. Our hunch was that all three groups would come to similar con-clusions outside the domain of meat-eating. Second, we wanted to compare the three groups with respect to eating meat. Here, we ex-pected the independent vegetarians to be much more condemnatory.

As expected, all three groups came to similar conclusions outside the domain of meat-eating. They all judged moral misdemeanors to be very bad; they were also negative—but considerably less so—about de-partures from social convention; and they were not at all condemna-tory of essentially personal decisions. This essentially replicated the classic pattern that has emerged in studies of children's normative judgments (Turiel, 2006). However, to our surprise, all three groups were equally nonjudgmental about eating meat. Even the independent vegetarians said that it was acceptable. All the children appeared to view meat-eating as a personal decision, on a par with reading alone during recess.

Arguably, the tolerance displayed by the independent vegetarians to-ward other people's meat-eating is not surprising. After all, for most of the population the decision to eat or not eat a particular type of meat is indeed a matter of taste or personal preference. It has no moral freight. However, putting the overall set of replies together, we were puzzled. On the one hand, the independent vegetarians framed their own deci-sion in moral terms. In explaining why they did not eat meat, they in-voked the same type of considerations that children mention with re-spect to hitting and stealing: concerns for the suffering of the victim. Of course, in this case, the independent vegetarians were focusing on the suffering of animals, not of human beings. Still, their tendency to "expand the circle" (Singer, 1981) so as to include animals was compel-ling as a moral argument. At the same time, if these children thought of eating meat as causing animals to suffer, why didn't they condemn other people for doing so?[2]

We speculated that independent vegetarians, and possibly all chil-dren, think of the decision to avoid meat as a kind of promise or com-mitment. If you have made such a commitment, it would be wrong to break it; but if you have made no such commitment, then it's okay to eat meat. Children might even recognize that commitments can have different bases. Someone might pledge to avoid meat in order not to hurt animals. Alternatively, someone might pledge to avoid meat for taste reasons. Perhaps children assess not just whether a person has re-neged on a commitment, but also the initial basis for that commit-ment. They may be mildly disapproving of someone who has reneged on a personal commitment to abstain from eating meat, but especially critical of someone who has reneged on a morally based commitment.

To assess this idea, we asked children to think about four different individuals—a morally committed vegetarian who had "made a prom-ise not to eat meat because she thinks of animals as her friends and doesn't want to hurt them"; a personally committed vegetarian who had "made a promise not to eat meat because she doesn't like the taste of meat"; an uncommitted individual who had "never made a promise not to eat meat"; and the participant him- or herself. We wanted to find out if children differentiated among these various types of com-mitment, and also if they saw themselves as akin to one or another of the various types.

As before, we interviewed three groups of children—independent vegetarians, family vegetarians, and meat-eaters. The children were asked to consider how bad it would be for each of the four individuals to eat various types of meat. The results are shown in Figure 7.2. Every-one agreed that it would be bad for the morally committed person to

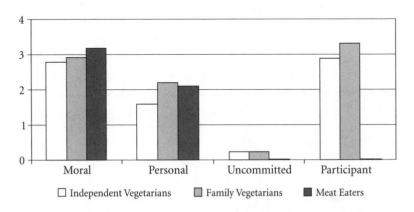

**Figure 7.2.** Average levels of condemnation by independent vegetarians, family vegetarians, and nonvegetarians of four individuals: a morally committed vegetarian, a personally committed vegetarian, an uncommitted individual, and the participant him- or herself. Scale ranged from 0 ("OK") to 4 ("very, very bad").

eat meat, not so bad for the personally committed person, and just fine for the uncommitted person. In sum, children in all three groups were highly sensitive to whether or not the agent had made a commitment, and more precisely to the type of commitment that he or she had made—whether it was a moral commitment based on concern for animal welfare, or a personal commitment based on taste considerations. How did children judge themselves? Their judgments varied sharply, driven by the kind of commitment that they had made. Both independent and family vegetarians judged that it would be wrong for them to eat meat, whereas meat-eaters said it would be okay.

These results begin to clarify the paradoxical finding that independent vegetarians do not condemn meat-eaters, despite framing their own abstinence in moral terms. They do condemn the eating of meat, but only if the person doing so has made a commitment not to eat meat—and they are especially condemnatory if that commitment is based on issues of animal welfare. By implication, even if independent vegetarians are tolerant of other people who eat meat, it would be a mistake to construe their tolerance as moral laxity. They condemn meat-eating by people who have made a moral commitment not to, and they condemn their own potential meat-eating for the same reason. At the same time, they accept that some people may not have made a commitment—this would apply to members of their own family, for example—and they do not criticize them.

A further interesting point that emerges from Figure 7.2 is that all the children, meat-eaters as well as vegetarians, agreed that someone who had made a moral commitment to avoid meat would be wrong to eat it. Similarly, all the children agreed that it would be fine for someone who had made no such commitment to eat meat. Stated differently, this means that independent vegetarians are not unusual in their views about moral commitment. They are unusual only in having made that commitment in the first place.[3]

Despite the clarity of the findings shown in Figure 7.2, they still leave us with a puzzle. The independent vegetarians see themselves as having made a commitment to avoid eating meat, and they judge any potential backsliding on their own part as bad. Why, then, do they accept the fact that other people have made no such commitment? Of course, it might seem eminently realistic of them to tolerate a lack of commitment, given that so few people make such a commitment. But why exactly are they so tolerant in this respect? After all, in the case of other moral obligations, we do not exonerate the uncommitted. Confronted by an inveterate liar who protests, "I never said I would tell the truth in the first place," we would not relent and condone their lies. Some moral obligations weigh on us, irrespective of any promise or commitment that we have made. So why do independent vegetarians condone inveterate meat-eaters?

Perhaps independent vegetarians think of their own abstinence from meat as an action that goes beyond the call of duty. Philosophers refer to such actions as "supererogatory." They are good actions, but they are not obligatory for everyone. Consider blood donation, for example. We typically approve of the generosity of blood donors, but we would be unlikely to argue that everyone has a duty to donate blood; even blood donors are unlikely to condemn those who fail to give blood. Vegetarianism, like blood donation, can be seen as supererogatory. Perhaps independent vegetarians applaud the decision not to eat meat, but they do not think that everyone is obliged to make that decision. For them, it is something worthy of extra moral credit, like blood donation, but not a universal obligation.

This interpretation of the independent vegetarians' stance makes good sense. On the one hand, it is consistent with the idea that such vegetarians think of abstinence as a worthwhile commitment, because it reduces animal suffering. On the other hand, it is consistent with the puzzling finding that they do not condemn meat-eating in general. They condemn meat-eating only by those who are committed vegetarians. Still, there are other considerations that do not fit this line of explanation so easily. First, prototypical examples of supererogation, such as blood donation, appear to turn on the notion of the replaceable volunteer. If any particular individual does not donate blood, no great harm is done, because in normal circumstances other people will volunteer instead. However, in the case of vegetarianism, especially vegetarianism that is aimed at the reduction of animal suffering, the notion that one vegetarian might replace another seems feeble and inadequate. Presumably, the goal of independent vegetarians is to eliminate all unnecessary animal suffering as far as possible, not to achieve some minimal or fixed reduction in suffering. To state this differently: it is only when everyone opts to become vegetarian that independent vegetarians might rest easy. If so, the proposal that independent vegetarians think avoiding meat is creditable, but ultimately a matter of personal choice, seems to ignore something of the dedication and concern that drives their decision and commitment.

A further, related consideration is that independent vegetarians, as we have seen, are inclined to explain their own abstinence in utilitarian terms. They justify their decision to avoid meat in terms of the ensuing benefits for animals. Some philosophers, notably Peter Singer, have claimed, precisely on utilitarian grounds, that vegetarianism is not just a desirable and laudatory extra—it is incumbent on everyone, given the animal suffering that might be avoided (Singer, 1975). From this perspective, vegetarianism should be seen not as a supererogatory action, but as an imperative for everyone. So if independent vegetarians think of vegetarianism not as a universal obligation but as a supererogatory choice, we still need to explain why they think that way.

Admittedly, children do not think through their moral decisions with the same degree of explicitness and self-reflection that philosophers do. Perhaps, like Singer, they base their decision on utilitarian considerations, but—unlike him—fail to draw the seemingly rational conclusion that such considerations ought to be incumbent on everyone. On this argument, independent vegetarians suffer from a kind of benign egocentricity in their moral reasoning. They make their own dietary decisions in the light of enlightened moral concerns, but they have difficulty imagining themselves in the shoes of other people, who actually face, or should face, exactly equivalent concerns.

Summing up this somewhat meandering exploration of how to explain the stance adopted by independent vegetarians, one is tempted to argue that independent vegetarians think of vegetarianism as desirable, yet not obligatory; but their self-proclaimed reasons for not eating meat should, strictly speaking, lead them to the more bracing conclusion that everyone ought to become vegetarian. Why don't they reach that conclusion? Benign egocentricity offers one plausible explanation, but there may be others. In the next section, I discuss what differentiates independent vegetarians from other children, and then return to their mysterious tolerance for meat-eaters.

## How Do Independent Vegetarians Come to Their Decision?

The two studies described so far illuminate the nature of the commitment that independent vegetarians make, and the consequences that they see as flowing from that commitment. However, the findings do not cast much light on why exactly they make that commitment in the first place. In particular, they give us no clue as to what distinguishes these children from the vast majority of children in meat-eating families. What are the distinctive thoughts and feelings of independent vegetarians that prompt them to stop eating meat? Presumably, most children have learned something about the way animals are farmed and slaughtered, even if they have little firsthand experience of that process. Why do independent vegetarians respond differently from most other children to this testimony?

As we have seen, independent vegetarians emphasize the harm and distress to animals that meat-eating causes. These considerations are similar to those that young children typically cite in claiming that an action is wrong. They judge that an action is bad if it causes distress— even when they know nothing more about the action in question. By implication, independent vegetarians are not unusual when they focus on harm and suffering. They are unusual only in their extension of those concerns to animals. There are—at least—three plausible explanations for this unusual expansion of the moral circle.

First, having been told about the harm and suffering that eating meat entails for animals, independent vegetarian children may have an especially strong emotional reaction to that information. In particular, they may have more empathy for animals than most children. Maybe they want to form, or do easily form, attachments to animals. If so, those feelings of attachment might lead them to react more strongly than typical children to any implication that eating meat causes harm and distress to animals. A second possibility is that independent vegetarians are unusual not so much in their strong feelings of attachment to animals, but in the way that they conceptualize the similarities between human beings and animals. Perhaps they are more prone to believe that animals can suffer. Finally, independent vegetarians might differ not in their feelings toward animals, or in the way that they conceive of animals' capacity for suffering, but rather in their sensitivity to the direct connection between eating meat and animal suffering. Having been told about the way animals are raised, captured, and slaughtered, independent vegetarians may bring that suffering to mind more actively and consistently than do most children. Perhaps they find it hard to forget.

To sum up: all three hypotheses suggest that independent vegetarians differ from typical children in the way they represent animals, but each hypothesis focuses on a different aspect of that representation. They may think of animals as their close companions; or they may think of them as having a human-like ability to suffer; or they may find it hard to suppress thoughts of animal suffering whenever they contemplate meat on their plate.

At present, there is no decisive evidence to help us choose among these hypotheses, but we can weigh their merits. First, the decision to become a vegetarian is rare among children being raised in meat-eating families. The vast majority of children have no qualms about the carnivorous practices of their families. On the other hand, survey data show that many children display an interest in, and affection toward, animals. They enjoy owning pets and they enjoy visiting farms and zoos (Melson, 2001). Children who are cruel to animals are quite unusual. Indeed, they are at risk for later criminality (Kellert & Felthouse, 1985). So the first hypothesis is questionable because attachment to animals, and empathy toward them, is widespread among children, whereas self-elected vegetarianism is rare. Further grounds for skepticism toward this hypothesis have been reported by Tjeert Olthof (2009). Independent vegetarians and typical, meat-eating children were compared on various measures of empathy, both toward other children and toward animals. For example, they were asked: "When an animal is locked up without being able to get into the open air, some children try to imagine how that is like for the animal. Is that true for you?" The two groups proved similar in the extent to which they reported trying to imagine both how other children feel and how animals feel.

Are independent vegetarians more likely than typical children to think of animals as capable of suffering? Various considerations also weigh against this hypothesis. First, most children judge it to be wrong to cause suffering to animals. For example, Olthof and his colleagues asked children and young adults to judge whether it was wrong for someone to cause unintended—but foreseeable—harm to hypothetical creatures with varying mental capacities. Nine- and 11-year-olds judged that such acts were much worse if the creatures in question could feel pain. They also said that the perpetrator would feel more guilt if the creature was capable of feeling pain (Olthof, Rieffe, Meerum Terwogt, Lalay-Cederburg, Reijntjes, & Hagenaar, 2008). In two follow-up studies involving stories about familiar animals, such as a monkey, a hare, a bird, and a lizard (rather than hypothetical creatures), a similar pattern emerged. Across all children, there was a greater tendency to condemn the deliberate killing of animals (even in order to save human life) the more the animal in question was deemed capable of suffering (Olthof, Postma, & Kasperts, 2008). In view of these findings, it appears that even typical, meat-eating children think that it is wrong to make animals suffer. Still, independent vegetarians might be more likely to think that animals have a human-like capacity for suffering. Olthof (2009) obtained some support for this conclusion. Independent vegetarians were more likely than typical, meat-eating children to judge various types of animals—pets, nonedible creatures such as squirrels and foxes, and edible animals such as cows and sheep—to be similar to human beings, particularly with respect to their ability to suffer, rather than their ability to think. However, the differences between the two groups were not dramatic. Like the vegetarians, the meat-eating children also recognized some capacity for animal suffering even if, for them, it was not so human-like.

What about the third hypothesis? This hypothesis proposes that independent vegetarians are more sensitive not toward animal suffering in general, but toward the animal suffering that the practice of meat consumption entails. In evaluating this possibility, it is useful to consider not just the information about animal suffering that clearly has an impact on independent vegetarians, but also the much larger pattern of countervailing information (regarding the positive aspects of meat-eating) that most children receive. As Pallotta (2008) has underlined, children growing up in the United States and in Europe are given countless indications that eating meat is acceptable. The suffering that animals endure is not ordinarily brought to children's awareness by their families or by society at large. Indeed, the eating of meat is cast as a pleasurable, healthy, social activity, often linked to holidays and celebrations. It is not cast as a moral transgression.

By implication, independent vegetarians may be distinctive in that when they contemplate eating meat, despite the positive testimony that normally frames that activity, they dwell on the fact that it entails the death and suffering of animals. Intriguing evidence in support of this idea was obtained by Olthof (2009). When independent vegetarians were asked about their emotional reactions to suffering, including animal suffering, they differed from meat-eaters in two ways: they reported feeling more distress, and they also reported fewer attempts to stop thinking about the distressing situation in question. Many of the interviews that Karen Hussar conducted with independent vegetarians highlight a similar pattern of rumination. In particular, the children's comments suggest the intimate connection in their minds between eating meat and the death of animals.

"I really don't believe in killing animals for their meat and I think so many animals have been treated so, like, poorly when they are kind of caged for meat."

"I love animals. I don't think it's right that people kill animals just to eat meat and then like throw away like half of it . . . like people just throw away stuff and that's like an animal that was killed. Like I don't like the way they treat animals like in the slaughterhouses."

"I don't believe in killing animals. Well, I know what happens to the animals when they get like [turned] into meat. . . . I think it's really horrible."

"There are a lot of companies that make hot dogs that are very cruel to the animals that they're made from, so that's why I choose not to eat them. . . . I still don't believe that animals should be killed. Since I like animals, it would kind of be hypocritical by liking them but not really doing anything."

A plausible interpretation of these various remarks is that when independent vegetarians contemplate the eating of meat, they think more vividly about the slaughter and suffering that it entails. By contrast, even if meat-eaters know about that killing and suffering, they do not frame the act of eating meat in such terms. In line with the pattern of testimony that is offered by the broader community, they think of meat-eating as a pleasurable, sociable, and healthy activity.

Returning once more to the earlier question of why vegetarians—both independent vegetarians and family vegetarians—are tolerant of people who have made no commitment to vegetarianism, it is likely that vegetarian children, and indeed all children whether they are vegetarians or meat-eaters, are aware of public opinion. They realize that the overwhelming majority of the population has not made such a commitment. It is true that we condemn liars even if they have made no commitment to telling the truth. However, people who profess no commitment to telling the truth and who make a daily habit of lying are rare. By contrast, people who have made no commitment to vegetarianism and who make a daily habit of eating meat are ubiquitous. According to this speculative argument, vegetarians are tolerant because, like other children, they realize how few people are committed to vegetarianism.

Notice that this line of argument is consistent with the findings of the previous chapter. Children are highly sensitive to the presence of a consensus. They often endorse the claims made by a consensus over those made by a lone dissenter. The pattern of judgment displayed by the vegetarians suggests that they are reluctant to condemn the meat-eating majority because they themselves are isolated dissenters.

## Conclusions

Research on moral judgment has often focused on the question of when children become able to ignore the dictates of authority and make their own independent judgments. A plausible answer is that they can do so at a surprisingly early age. They observe for themselves that actions such as hitting and stealing cause harm and distress to the victim, and they conclude that such actions are wrong. However, some actions cause suffering that is difficult to observe firsthand. In such cases, children are prepared to learn from the testimony of other people. More specifically, if they are told that a particular action causes harm and distress, they are likely to conclude that the action is wrong, even in the absence of any direct experience of the victim's suffering.

Such learning via the testimony of other people appears to have an important impact on the attitudes of some children toward eating meat. When animals are raised and killed for meat, the suffering and slaughter of the animals is not generally observed by the meat-eater. Nevertheless, children who are independent vegetarians universally report that they avoid eating meat because of the harm and suffering it entails for animals. The plausible implication is that they have learned about such harm and suffering from the testimony of other people, and that this information has led them to stop eating meat—despite the habits and preferences of their family.

Yet the stance of such independent vegetarians is highly unusual. Most meat-eating children explain their refusal to eat certain types of meat in light of health and taste considerations, not in terms of any concern about the death or suffering of animals. Surprisingly, despite their own moral stance, vegetarian children do not condemn meat-eaters. They appear to keep in mind the fact that meat-eaters, unlike themselves, have made no commitment to vegetarianism. Indeed, such tolerance is part of a more general pattern displayed by vegetarian and nonvegetarian children alike. They refrain from condemning someone who eats meat if that person has made no moral commitment to vegetarianism. On the other hand, once someone has made such a moral commitment, children are quite critical of any backsliding.

How have independent vegetarians arrived at their unusual decision, and how do they sustain it? The most plausible explanation is that they keep in mind the fact that eating meat entails the suffering of animals. They differ from meat-eating children not in being especially attached to or empathic toward animals, nor in having a radically different conception of how much animals suffer, but in the relative weight that they attach to two conflicting representations of the act of eating meat. Eating meat is typically represented as enjoyable and acceptable. Yet it can also be represented as the cause of unacceptable suffering and slaughter. Judging by their informal comments, independent vegetarians dwell much more than their peers on that suffering and slaughter.

The findings highlight an intriguing paradox in moral development. As noted earlier, there is a long tradition, both in philosophy and psychology, emphasizing the importance of autonomous moral judgment. Indeed, recent research lends succor to that tradition by showing that young children are capable of deciding what is right and wrong, independent of the dictates of authority. They identify actions that lead to harm and suffering as morally wrong. At the same time, research on meat-eating and vegetarianism highlights the key role of testimony. The consequences of a given action are not always visible and evident. The consequences of eating meat, for example, can be framed in markedly different ways. They can be framed in terms of health and pleasure, but they can also be framed in terms of the suffering and slaughter of animals. By implication, despite the striking capacity displayed by young children for making autonomous moral judgments, all of them—even those children whom we have referred to as "independent" vegetarians—depend on the testimony of others to inform their judgments about actions that do and do not cause harm and suffering. In this respect, the ideal of the autonomous moral agent is no more attainable than the ideal of the autonomous epistemic agent. Both depend on others to inform their judgments, and there is nothing intrinsically wrong or immature in doing so.

# Knowing What Is Real

✦

The monster waiting in the closet and the imaginary companion who somehow gets "lost" at the shopping mall—both can make young children distraught, even if each is the work of their imagination. We might assume that children display these emotional reactions because they confuse fantasy with reality. But children are more sophisticated than that.

When preschoolers are invited to imagine an object or scene, whether it is a prosaic object such as a pair of scissors, or something more emotionally charged, such as a witch chasing after them, they realize that what they are imagining is not real and cannot be observed by other people (Harris et al., 1991; Wellman & Estes, 1986). This ability to differentiate fantasy from reality is found even among children with a rich, imaginative life. For example, children who create an imaginary friend and "play" with that friend for weeks or months remain lucid about the fact that the friend is just imaginary (Goy & Harris, 1990; Taylor, Cartwright, & Carlson, 1993). More generally, children's emotional reactions to the products of their imagination provide no convincing evidence of any early confusion between fantasy and reality. Adults also respond emotionally to imaginary events. They become quite involved with Elizabeth Bennet's initial rejection of Mr. Darcy in Jane Austen's *Pride and Prejudice,* or with Rick's sacrificial choice in the film *Casablanca*—but not because they confuse fiction with reality. Overall, the evidence suggests that children resemble adults. They become absorbed in—and moved by—imaginary events *despite* their realization that the events are only imaginary (Harris, 2000).

Nevertheless, the assumption that children confuse the products of their imagination with reality has preoccupied psychologists for a long time—ever since Freud and Piaget drew attention to the possibility. This preoccupation has meant that a different and arguably much more pervasive challenge for children's understanding of reality has been ignored. How do children decide on the status of the many creatures and events that they hear about but never encounter firsthand? They learn about dragons and dinosaurs, Voldemort and Stalin, Middle Earth and Antarctica, and they can conjure up all of them in their imagination. But do children think they all have the same ontological status?

These several examples show that the imagination can be used to contemplate real beings and real places, as well as imaginary beings and imaginary places. Although it is tempting to think that we use our imagination to think about the nonexistent or the fantastical, that conception of the imagination is far too narrow. As discussed in Chapter 1, even toddlers use their imagination to learn about reality. On the basis of what they are told, they can represent an object's new properties or location and act accordingly. The expansive scope of the imagination raises a fundamental question about how children decide on the status of entities that they contemplate within it. They cannot have a direct encounter with either a dragon or a dinosaur, but they can contemplate both via their imagination. Do they think of both as equally unreal? If they recognize that dinosaurs have a different status from dragons, how do they come to this realization?

Suppose that children adopt the following strategy for deciding whether something is real or purely imaginary: they ask themselves whether they have ever observed the entity in question. If they can answer "Yes" to that question, they conclude that the entity is real; and if not, they assume that it's only imaginary. This "empiricist" strategy could serve children quite well. It would enable them to differentiate between a real friend and an imaginary one, between places they have actually visited and imaginary places they can only conjure up in their mind's eye. Still, there is an obvious limitation to this strategy. It would lead children to dismiss all sorts of real entities as imaginary. Children living in the twenty-first century have never seen a real dinosaur or the emperor Napoleon; they have not witnessed the sack of Rome or a battle between men-of-war; they have never seen viruses or atoms. Yet they would be wrong to conclude that these various phenomena are simply imaginary, on the grounds that they have had no direct acquaintance with any of them.

Children might therefore adopt a different strategy. Arguably, they recognize that reality extends much beyond the narrow sphere of what they have personally observed. They hear people talk about a vast number of events, objects, and creatures that they themselves have never encountered. In the wake of all this talk, children might deferentially conclude that each of these various entities is real—even if they personally have never set eyes on them. This ecumenical strategy would certainly help children to realize that reality extends far beyond their ken. Still, if anything, this strategy is too inclusive. Children also hear people talk about Satan and Cinderella, Superman and Santa Claus. They would be wrong to conclude that all these various people enjoy the same type of reality status as a Roman emperor or an uncle in Australia, individuals whom they hear about but have never met.

In short, the empiricist and the talk-based strategies each have their shortcomings. The empiricist strategy is too conservative, and the talk-based strategy is too liberal. Still, either might be a reasonable starting point for children as they try to parse unobservable reality in all its heterogeneity. With this in mind, we asked 4-, 6-, and 8-year-olds to tell us about the status of various different creatures (Harris, Pasquini, Duke, Asscher, & Pons, 2006). We asked them about familiar animals, such as tigers and wolves—animals that they themselves had either encountered firsthand, or had likely seen with the help of some veridical representation such as a photograph or film. We also asked them about nonexistent, impossible creatures—flying pigs or red elephants. All three age groups agreed on the status of these two very different types of creature. Everyone, they said, believes that there are tigers and wolves, but nobody believes that there are flying pigs or red elephants.

This clear differentiation between entities whose existence is routinely accepted and those whose existence is routinely denied meant that we could probe children about a potentially more problematic category: entities that are normally completely invisible to young children—for example, germs and vitamins. We reasoned that if children adopt a strict empiricist strategy, they should claim that people do not believe in these entities. Most children have never seen germs and vitamins firsthand or even via a photograph or film. So on a strictly empiricist strategy, germs ought to be roughly equivalent to flying pigs or red elephants. On the other hand, if children rely on what other people talk about, they should claim that everyone believes in these normally invisible entities—children will almost certainly have heard people refer to them. For example, they will have heard about germs and vitamins in the context of conversations about everyday hygiene and health care. Indeed, if children adopt the talk-based strategy, they might conclude that germs and vitamins are as real as tigers and wolves.

The findings were clear-cut: children in all three age groups systematically claimed that everyone believes in germs and vitamins. They showed no signs of strict empiricism. Apparently, in thinking about what exists, children are heavily influenced by what other people say. One way to highlight the key role of testimony—even for adults—is to look back at the history of medicine. During the nineteenth century, Louis Pasteur's claims about germs and their implications for surgical practice were contested (Debré, 1998). Few doctors in North America accepted the critical role of microorganisms in the transmission of cholera, despite recurrent epidemics (Rosenberg, 1962). The situation is obviously quite different today. Doctors are not the only ones who accept the existence of germs—most parents take their existence for granted and warn children about the risks associated with their transmission. At the same time, children rarely, if ever, have an opportunity to look at germs in a microscope. Hence, the unequivocal assertions made by other people are children's main guarantee that germs really do exist. In sum, this experiment underlines the fact that children do not systematically rely on an empiricist strategy—they are also guided by what other people say: the talk-based strategy, or at least some version of that strategy.

In a follow-up study, we probed more deeply into children's ideas about invisible entities. Instead of asking children about other people's beliefs, we asked them about their own beliefs. We also asked about their confidence: Were they sure about the existence of a given entity— or not so sure? We also asked if they knew what the entity in question looked like. If children do not need to encounter something to believe in its existence, they should be willing to acknowledge, even when they are sure the entity does exist, that they do not know what it looks like.

As before, the children—ranging from 4 to 8 years of age—revealed their trust in what other people tell them. Not only did they claim that entities like germs and vitamins exist, but they expressed as much confidence in their existence as they did for tigers and giraffes, creatures that they had likely seen in one form or another. Moreover, despite their considerable confidence in the existence of germs and vitamins, children admitted to not knowing what they look like.

These findings provide strong evidence that children rely on what other people tell them in deciding what is real. In fact, that strategy serves them well. Children are right to think that germs and vitamins exist. But consider the variety of special beings that children hear people talk about: God, Santa Claus, witches, mermaids, giants, ghosts, dwarfs, and so on. Do children adopt an equally inclusive strategy when they hear people talk about these various special beings? Do they believe in the existence of all of them, or do they differentiate among them? If children listen closely to what people say, they might register not just whether other people talk about a given creature, but also the particular way in which they talk about it.

When adults talk about germs, for example, they generally take their existence for granted, and call attention to the causal processes in which germs play a role: "Be careful not to drink that water. It has germs and you could get sick!" Looking back at some of the special beings that children learn about, they might encounter a similar pattern of discourse. For example, in Christian communities, adults are likely to imply that God plays a causal role in various real-world outcomes. Children will be encouraged to pray and will hear people talk about God's power to intervene. Similarly, children will hear remarks about what will happen when Santa Claus or the Tooth Fairy pays a visit. Such remarks may take the existence of these special beings for granted and call attention to their causal powers. By contrast, few adults in Europe or North America are likely to suggest that witches, mermaids, giants, ghosts, or dwarfs are responsible for any real-world outcomes. These beings might be credited with extraordinary causal powers, but only in the context of fairy stories. They will not be represented as agents in the world that children actually inhabit.

If children are sensitive to this variation in the way that people talk about various invisible beings, they are likely to differentiate between two broad classes of special beings: (i) endorsed beings—for example, God, Santa Claus, and the Tooth Fairy—whose existence and causal powers are routinely invoked and connected to the real world; and (ii) equivocal beings—such as mermaids, ghosts, and witches—whose existence is invoked only in special contexts such as fiction or make-believe, and may even be explicitly denied.

With these considerations in mind, we asked if young children aged 5–6 years go beyond an undifferentiated talk-based strategy. We asked if they express more confidence in the existence of endorsed beings such as God and the Tooth Fairy, as compared to equivocal beings such as mermaids and ghosts. To check the findings from the two earlier studies, we also asked children about scientific entities such as germs and oxygen. As expected, children typically said they were "very sure" that germs and oxygen really exist, but they also differentiated sharply between endorsed and equivocal beings. They were quite confident about the existence of God and the Tooth Fairy, but they were dubious about the existence of mermaids and ghosts. As we anticipated, children appear to notice the pattern of testimony that surrounds a given entity and calibrate their confidence accordingly.

To sum up the findings: children realize that the unobservable entities they hear people talk about, but which they themselves can contemplate only via their imagination, are of two different kinds. Some of these entities do not exist—they belong to the world of make-believe. Others, according to the testimony of adults, exist and are not fictional. Children draw this conclusion about scientific entities such as germs, and also about special beings such as God. To the extent that children are confident about the existence of invisible, scientific entities, as well as about the existence of invisible, special beings such as God and the Tooth Fairy, do they think of them as having the same reality status? According to the line of argument set out above, they are likely to do so in certain key respects. If children attend to and learn from what other people tell them, they probably think of both types of entity as having causal powers that deliver consequences in the observable world. Indeed, support for this conclusion emerged when children were invited to explain why they were sure, for example, that germs exist or that

God exists. Children rarely claimed to have any direct encounter with either type of entity, lending support to the assumption that they do not rely on a simple empiricist strategy. Children also rarely mentioned a plausible source for their belief in those entities. For example, they rarely said that their parents or teachers had told them about germs or about God, a result consistent with various findings showing that children are quite poor at identifying and remembering the source of their knowledge (Esbensen, Taylor, & Stoess, 1997; Taylor, Esbensen, & Bennett, 1994). What children did more often was to justify their confidence by offering a generalization—by talking about the generic properties of the entity in question. In making these generalizations, they often referred to the causal powers of the entity. For example, they claimed to be sure that germs exist "because germs are little thingies and if you don't wash your hand they can make you sick," or that oxygen exists "because that's where you breathe from." They were confident that the Tooth Fairy exists "because who takes all your teeth if there's no Tooth Fairy?" and that God exists "because how would everybody be alive and how would our time have started and stuff?" Figure 8.1 shows how often children provided each type of justification (encounter; source; generalization) for endorsed, scientific. and equivocal entities.

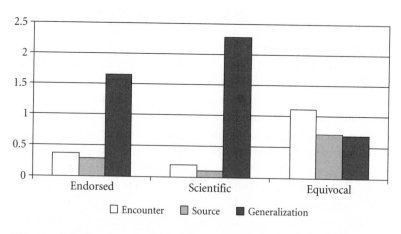

**Figure 8.1.** Mean frequency with which children offered three different types of justification for endorsed, scientific, and equivocal entities.

A glance at Figure 8.1 confirms that the pattern of justifications was quite similar for endorsed beings and scientific entities. In each case, children frequently offered generalizations about their hidden properties and their causal powers—something they rarely did for equivocal entities such as mermaids and ghosts.

## The Nature of Rationality

So far, we have established that children do not believe in the existence of every single invisible phenomenon that people talk about. They are confident about the existence of germs and vitamins; they believe in God; and, for a certain period of childhood, at any rate, they believe in special beings such as the Tooth Fairy or Santa Claus. Yet they are duly skeptical about the existence of mermaids and ghosts.

In thinking about children's belief in various types of invisible phenomena, it is worth backtracking a little to look at an important debate in anthropology. In a provocative essay, the anthropologist Robin Horton compared Western scientific thinking with traditional modes of thought in Africa (Horton, 1970). Rather than emphasizing some of the obvious contrasts between the two ways of thinking, he focused on overlooked similarities. He pointed out that in each case invisible causal agents are invoked to explain observable events. Horton acknowledged that the practices that accompany these beliefs in hidden causal powers are quite different in the two settings. Western scientists test competing claims about the nature of the atom, or the causes of cholera. By contrast, witch doctors do not critique or seek to refute one another's claims about the power of witchcraft. Nevertheless, in Horton's view, the fundamental explanatory strategy is similar. In each case, there is no hesitation in assuming that the world is not as it appears. Beneath—or behind—its surface, invisible agents are at work. Their operation can be used to predict and explain observable events, and those events can be forestalled or redirected by appropriate actions directed at the relevant invisible agents.

Horton's intriguing essay was part of a larger debate in anthropology about the nature of rationality. Partly because he could be interpreted as saying that magic, superstition, and witchcraft are no less rational than Western science—or at the very least that they have much in common—Horton's analysis provoked a good deal of commentary. In the next couple of decades, the larger debate about rationality and the standing of witchcraft as compared to science faded within anthropology. Yet, with modest adjustment, Horton's thesis opens up major empirical questions about the nature of cognitive development.

Suppose that you are a young child exposed to claims about various invisible beings or entities. Depending on your age and the particular community in which you are growing up, you might learn about God, about the everlasting soul, about the Ancestors, or about witchcraft. Because adults in your community endorse the existence of these invisible phenomena, you come to believe in the powers of such phenomena. You also hear about a variety of hidden agents acknowledged and investigated by Western science and medicine: the invisible but healthy substances in various foods, or the tiny organisms that make a stream unfit for drinking.

You also observe adults engaging in various observable behaviors that assume the existence of these invisible powers. Adults pray to God; they engage in ritual activities aimed at placating the Ancestors; they eat—and encourage you to eat—foods containing certain vitamins; and they avoid—and insist that you avoid—drinking from a contaminated water supply. Trusting what they say in each of these various domains, you construct a picture of the real world that is composed of two parts: the public domain and the invisible agents that can bring about observable consequences in that public domain.

According to the picture I have sketched so far, children acknowledge the difference between what is observable and what lies hidden, but they do not differentiate among the many inhabitants of the world of "invisibles." In particular, they do not assign a different ontological status to the various causal agents deployed behind the scenes. Thus, for a Christian child, there may be no obvious ontological distinction between the existence of germs and the existence of the soul. Similarly, for a child in Madagascar, there may be no obvious ontological distinction between invisible microscopic organisms that infest the water supply and invisible Ancestors that cause a particular family member to fall ill. Of course, this does not mean that children cannot differentiate between germs and souls, or between germs and Ancestors. They certainly realize that these entities have different properties and causal powers. What they may not acknowledge, however, is that there is any fundamental distinction between these entities in terms of their reality status.

The possibility of making a basic ontological distinction between the agents invoked in supernatural as compared to scientific modes of explanation was very much on the minds of those caught up in the original debate with Horton about the nature of rationality (Hollis & Lukes, 1982). The protagonists wanted to conceptualize the difference, as they saw it, between "irrational" causal explanations, couched in terms of witchcraft and the like, and rational causal explanations, couched in terms of allegedly scientific entities such as bacteria and viruses. None of the evidence presented so far suggests that the distinction between the two modes of explanation is either fundamental or self-evident from a psychological standpoint. In children's minds, the congregation of hidden, supernatural agents may mingle with a set of more secular and scientific agents. Children may simply think of each invisible agent as being invested with the power to bring about or alter a particular course of events in the perceptible world.

## Separating Science from the Supernatural

With the debate in anthropology as a backdrop, the findings with young children turn out—in the end—to offer an unexpected twist. As we have just seen, and just as Horton might have expected, children can readily conceive of hidden agents, whether they are the type of entities that belong to modern science or those that belong to traditional belief systems. Nevertheless, the data also contain a surprise: children display a budding distinction between these two different types of agent. To put this baldly, they express *more* confidence in scientific claims as compared to supernatural claims. In terms of the debate about rationality, children appear to cast their vote for science and for modernity, at least when pressed to express their confidence. I'll first review the evidence for this claim and then discuss its interpretation.

Recall that in the experiments described earlier, children were confident about scientific entities such as germs and oxygen, as well as about special beings such as God and the Tooth Fairy. The pattern of justifications—the frequent mention of characteristic properties, especially causal properties—was also similar in the two cases. However, close scrutiny of the findings showed that children did not conceive of the existence of those entities in exactly the same way. There were three noticeable differences. First, children expressed greater confidence in the existence of germs and oxygen—and this despite their more frequent acknowledgment that they did not know what these scientific entities look like. Second, when they were asked about other people's beliefs, children claimed that they too were more likely to believe in germs and oxygen than in special beings. Finally, although as noted earlier children often justified their existence claims by offering a generalization about the entity in question, particularly a generalization about a causal property, these generalizations were more frequent for scientific entities—as can be seen in Figure 8.1.

Thus, children appeared to be making some kind of distinction, however tentative and preliminary, between invisible entities that belong to the world of science and invisible beings with extraordinary powers. How do they come to make that distinction? Before trying to answer this question, we would do well to examine a plausible objection. Maybe this type of differentiation is relatively uncommon. Maybe it is confined to children growing up in a cosmopolitan, urban community, where scientific or secular explanations might be privileged. Consistent with that objection, the children in the experiment described earlier were attending a private school in Boston that mainly served middle-class and professional families. The differentiation that these children made between scientific and nonscientific "invisibles" might not be found among children growing up in a less cosmopolitan community.

To check on this possibility, we conducted another study with children aged 10–12 years recruited from a Catholic school in the city of Cuenca, in central Spain. Most of the teachers at the school were nuns (Guerrero, Enesco, & Harris, 2010). The religious character of the school was further reinforced by the ubiquity of religious icons, including pictures of Jesus and the Virgin Mary, crucifixes, and inscriptions. Given the homogeneity of the symbols and beliefs that surrounded children in this school, we speculated that they—unlike the Boston children—would place as much credence in religious phenomena as in scientific phenomena. With this in mind, children were asked about the existence of God and the soul, on the one hand, and about the existence of oxygen and germs, on the other. As expected, children proved to be quite confident about the existence of each type of entity. Nevertheless, like the children in Boston, they expressed more confidence in the existence of the two scientific entities. In addition, although children often justified their existence claims by describing some property or causal power of the entity in question (as in the previous studies), they did this more frequently for scientific entities. In short, the differentiation that we had observed in Boston reemerged among children from a staunchly Catholic environment in Spain. Despite the homogeneity, and prevalence, of the religious representations that surrounded the children, their confidence in two central religious phenomena—God and the soul—fell short of their confidence in two equally unobservable scientific entities.

As a further check on the robustness of the distinction between scientific and nonscientific "invisibles," we carried out a third study with children of the Tseltal-speaking Mayan community of Tenejapa, Mexico (Harris, Abarbanell, Pasquini, & Duke, 2007). This highland Mayan community has developed alongside, and in interaction with, mainstream Mexican society, but continues to live in relative separation from the nearby Ladino, or Spanish-speaking, population. For the most part, such Mayan communities have retained their languages, dress, and subsistence agriculture, as well as many of their traditional beliefs and practices. Most adult Tenejapa villagers believe in the existence of *ijk'al*—small, black, cave-dwelling creatures that allegedly assault people at night and are often credited with special powers, such as the ability to fly and to father children overnight. They also believe in the existence of *ch'ulelal*—the spirits or souls of the dead. Encounters with the *ch'ulelal* of an ancestor are associated with illness.

We chose such a community in order to probe a common claim in social anthropology—namely, that in certain traditional communities a belief in the spirit world is unavoidable and pervasive. For example, in his striking account of child-rearing in the Kwaio community on the

Solomon Islands, the anthropologist Roger Keesing (1982) writes: "No child could escape constructing a cognitive world in which the spirits were ever-present participants in social life, on whom life and death, success or failure, depend." In light of Keesing's assertion, we wondered whether children growing up in a small-scale community, where there was considerable uniformity of belief in such invisible entities among adults, might fail to show the type of differentiation that we had observed in Boston and Spain. In other words, we wondered if children in this community would express unalloyed confidence in the spirit world—in the manner implied by Keesing.

We asked the children in Tenejapa—who ranged in age from 6 to 13 years—about the existence of the *ijk'al* and *ch'ulelal:* cave spirits and dead souls. We also asked the children about real creatures that were familiar to them (squirrels and chickens), about impossible creatures (flying pigs and barking cats), and about scientific entities (germs and oxygen). As expected, the children were insistent that squirrels and chickens really exist, but they were equally insistent that flying pigs and barking cats do not. As in our initial study, these sharply different patterns of responding meant that we could confidently proceed to ask children about the main items of interest: germs and oxygen on the one hand, and cave spirits and dead souls on the other. Most of the older children and some of the younger ones had heard about all of these various entities, and so we could compare their confidence in each.[1]

Despite the prevalence of adult beliefs in the spirit world, the Tenejapa children displayed the by now familiar ontological bias toward scientifically established entities: they expressed more confidence in the existence of germs and oxygen, as compared to cave spirits or dead souls. Apparently, children's intuition that there is something less than certain about the various special beings they hear about is not confined to children living in cosmopolitan cities such as Boston, where there is a variety of communities with different belief systems. That intuition is also found in a more homogeneous city such as Cuenca, Spain, where Catholicism is the predominant religion, and in a smaller, traditional community, such as Tenejapa, where beliefs in the spirit world are widespread.

Granted the ubiquity of this differentiation between scientific entities and special beings, how do children arrive at the distinction? Two radically different lines of explanation seem feasible, the first focusing on children's independent judgments of plausibility and the second on children's sensitivity to other people's views. Child might listen to the claims made by members of their community, but reflect on the plausibility of those claims for themselves. Alternatively, instead of conducting their own independent analysis of those claims, children might be sensitive to subtle indicators of confidence and doubt on the part of the people making them. According to this latter explanation, children pay more attention to the manner in which people talk about an invisible entity than to its inherent plausibility. These two lines of explanation are worth scrutinizing in detail.

## Children's Independent Reflections

In earlier chapters, we saw that children do not listen to adults' explanations and assertions uncritically. When they receive an answer to a question, they notice when the answer is inconsistent with their own expectations and judgments—even when it comes from a familiar person such as their mother. They may call explicit attention to counterinstances or invest more trust in the alternative proposal of a stranger. Given this reflective stance toward adult testimony, including that of their parents, children might register surprise at the claims that they hear about special beings. After all, these otherwise human-like creatures are often credited with extraordinary powers. For example, 5-year-olds are led to understand that, unlike human beings, God knows everything, is not constrained by mortality, was never a baby, does not get older, and will never die (Barrett, Richert, & Driesenga, 2001; Giménez-Dasi, Guerrero, & Harris, 2005; Lane, Wellman, & Evans, 2010 and in press). In all these respects, children can presumably register that God is dramatically different from mere mortals. Presumably, they can recognize that other special beings such as Santa Claus and the *ch'ulelal* also have extraordinary powers. Santa Claus knows where you live, and he often figures out what gift you would prefer—even without your telling him. And a mere encounter with the *ch'ulelal* can bring about illness and misfortune.

Insofar as children recognize that special beings such as God, Santa

Claus, and the spirits of the dead have unusual powers—powers that are likely to be salient and memorable, given their extraordinary nature (Boyer, 2001)—they might reasonably conclude that the existence of these special beings is less than certain. Children's prototype or standard for any agent is likely to be an ordinary human being, and human beings do not possess these special powers. They often don't know things; they get old and die; and they lack the power to will misfortune on other people.

Such existential doubts should be less likely for scientific entities because children have no obviously contrasting case or prototype with which germs, vitamins, or oxygen may be compared. To the extent that these scientific entities are credited with causal powers, they are less likely to jar with children's preexisting assumptions about what is possible. In sum, if children weigh adults' claims about invisible agents against their own knowledge, they might end up being less than certain about the existence of special beings but might acquiesce with more confidence to claims made about the existence of scientific entities.

There is, however, a problem with this proposal. As children get older, it is likely that they increasingly recognize the constraints that apply to human knowledge and the human life cycle. So as children get older, they ought to have an increasingly firm grip on the ways that special beings deviate from ordinary human beings. Moreover, if children's existential doubts are triggered by the attribution of superhuman powers to special beings, their doubts should be greater for God than for Santa Claus or the Tooth Fairy. God's extraordinary powers go well beyond those of Santa Claus and the Tooth Fairy. So children should come to think of God as especially improbable. Yet we observed no evidence of any such differentiation. Children's doubts did not seem to increase with the range of extraordinary powers attributed to the being in question.

Another way that children might exercise their own independent judgment would be to use their understanding of visibility and invisibility. By 5 years of age, children have a simple but robust understanding of the conditions under which something is invisible (Flavell, 1978). In particular, they realize that something can exist but be invisible not because it is hidden behind an obstacle or wall, but because it is too small to see. For example, Au, Sidle, and Rollins (1993) studied young children's grasp of the fact that matter consists of invisible particles. They found that some 6- and 7-year-olds spontaneously invoked the existence of tiny particles—too small to be seen—when asked to say how a drink might still remain contaminated after a contaminant (such as rotten lettuce) had been removed. In addition, when the idea of tiny particles was put to the children—"Do you think that tiny bits of rotten lettuce might have fallen off and stayed in the juice? Tiny bits of rotten lettuce which are too small for you or me to see?"—they all agreed with this idea, and the majority then invoked such tiny particles to explain why they would not like to taste the drink. By implication, young children can conceive of microscopic entities.

Children might come to think about invisible scientific entities within this framework. They might learn that even if germs are living creatures too small to be seen by the naked eye, they are regular, physical entities nonetheless. This might lead them to remain confident about the existence of germs, even as they harbor doubts about the existence of God, the Tooth Fairy, or cave-dwelling spirits. Children will hear people make remarks that imply the efficacy or existence of special beings, but presumably they will not be offered a ready explanation for the constant invisibility of such beings in terms of their microscopic size.

The strength of this interpretation is that it offers a plausible explanation of why children growing up in diverse communities—Boston, Cuenca, and Tenejapa—with such diverse belief systems, converge on a similar pattern of trust and doubt. Whatever their cultural circumstances, it is plausible that children acquire the notion of invisible particles and of the microscopic size of germs and vitamins. However, there are two objections to this interpretation. First, it is difficult to see how this analysis can be extended to oxygen. Yet in all three settings, children expressed confidence in its existence. Second, when children were asked to justify their belief in the existence of scientific entities, they did not raise the possibility of observing them with the aid of special instruments such as a microscope or magnifying glass. Instead, as noted earlier, they referred to the properties, and especially to the causal powers, of these invisible entities. Conversely, children never expressed doubts about special beings on the grounds that their constant invisibility was mysterious. In summary, two initially plausible candidates for explaining how children might assess the plausibility of existence claims do not stand up to close scrutiny. Children's confidence in an invisible entity does not appear to be swayed by the extent to which people credit it with extraordinary properties or a particular size.

## Analyzing the Pattern of Testimony

If children look to the testimony of other people for guidance—and the experiments and analyses presented in previous chapters have repeatedly shown that they do—then it is plausible that they are sensitive to variation in the pattern of testimony surrounding the existence of one type of invisible entity as compared to another. On this hypothesis, children are smart linguists. They listen for subtle signs of confidence and equivocation.

Consider the way that adults are likely to talk about germs to children. As described earlier, they tend to make statements *presupposing* that germs exist. A mother might warn her child: "Don't drink that—it has germs." On the other hand, children are unlikely to hear people either assert the existence of germs—"There really are germs"—or aver their faith in germs—"I believe in germs." Listening to this pattern of testimony, children might register the fact that adults take it for granted that germs exist.

Consider, by contrast, the way in which people talk about God. It is true that adults make remarks presupposing God's existence—"one Nation under God" or "Thanks be to God." However, they will also assert God's existence or their faith in God's existence—"There must be a God" or "I believe in God." Much the same can be said of special beings such as Santa Claus and the Tooth Fairy. Children will undoubtedly hear people taking their existence for granted—"Santa Claus lives at the North Pole" or "Look what the Tooth Fairy brought!"—but they are also likely to hear people making claims about their existence—"I think there's a Santa Claus" or "The Tooth Fairy is a real fairy." Children might reasonably draw the conclusion that—despite their attestations—people do harbor doubts about these special beings. At the very least, children will hear people entertaining the possibility that such special beings might not exist but claiming that they do. By contrast, the existence of germs and vitamins is so routinely taken for granted that nobody ever bothers to make explicit assertions about their existence.

This line of explanation offers a satisfactory account for the findings in Boston and Spain. Can it also be extended to Tenejapa? Many of the adults there routinely express their belief in the *ijk'al* and the *ch'ulelal*. Still, they sometimes hedge their claims. For example, having repeated the report of an encounter, they might add: "That's what they say, but I've never seen them." In summary, in all three communities it is plausible that special beings are not talked about in the same way that scientific entities are discussed. Even if people sometimes presuppose the existence of both, children may notice various subtle attestations of faith, doubt, or uncertainty regarding special beings.

There is a related feature of the pattern of testimony that children may be exposed to. Recall that children are sensitive to a consensus from an early age. The findings in Chapter 6 showed that children are likely to endorse claims that are shared, rather than those expressed by lone dissenters. That sensitivity to a consensus may play an important role when children weigh up their confidence in invisibles. For example, not only is the existence of germs ordinarily presupposed, but there is also virtually no disagreement about their existence—at least in the twenty-first century. More or less everyone takes their existence for granted. More generally, children in all three communities—Boston, Cuenca, and Tenejapa—will likely detect little variation among informants in their endorsement of scientific entities such as germs, vitamins, and oxygen. Admittedly, children might receive more elaborate accounts of these entities from their teachers than from their parents, but they are not likely to meet people who doubt their existence. To the extent that young children notice these sociological data, they are likely to conclude that there is more or less universal endorsement of scientific entities.

The situation is more variegated with respect to special beings. Despite parents' best efforts to shield children from the skepticism of older brothers and sisters, children will sometimes hear doubts voiced about the Tooth Fairy or meet someone who flatly denies the existence of Santa Claus. If children live in a diverse community such as Boston, they are also likely to meet or hear about people with various attitudes toward God. As one 7-year-old commented in reply to my question about whether there really is a God: "Well, some families believe in God." He was acknowledging—albeit indirectly—that not every family (including his own) believes in God. Even in Spain, children will become aware of the fact that religious schools have practices and beliefs that differ from those of secular schools. They will come to realize that some families regularly engage in acts of worship, whereas others do not. In Tenejapa, children are likely to hear about nearby Ladino communities in which Catholicism is practiced and a belief in the spirit world is discouraged. They may even encounter religious dissent within their own community, through the growing presence of various proselytizing Christian groups who seek to suppress traditional beliefs and practices. In summary, the pattern of testimony that children encounter is likely to differ for scientific as compared to religious entities. In the case of scientific entities, children will generally encounter presuppositions of their existence but not affirmations, and they will meet no skeptics or dissenters. In the case of special beings, by contrast, they will encounter both affirmation and doubt.[2]

## Conclusions

Children are far from being skeptical empiricists. They accept the existence of many phenomena that they learn about via the testimony of other people. In particular, they accept the existence of two different types of invisible entity: scientific entities such as germs, and nonscientific beings such as God or cave spirits. In key respects, children's conceptions of these two types of invisible entities are quite similar. Certainly, children argue for their existence on similar grounds. They refer to the properties, and often to the causal properties, that these entities possess, rather than to the possibility of any firsthand encounter or acquaintance. In this respect, the developmental evidence is consistent with the provocative argument of Robin Horton (1970) regarding parallels between scientific and supernatural beliefs.

Nonetheless, three different studies in different communities have yielded evidence that children differentiate between the scientific realm and the religious or supernatural realm. It is too early to reach any firm conclusions about the basis for that distinction but a plausible interpretation is that children are alert to the pattern of testimony that they hear. In particular, they differentiate between, on the one hand, scientific entities whose existence is taken for granted by more or less everyone, and, on the other, supernatural entities whose existence is either averred or called into question by particular groups. To consolidate this conclusion, more research is needed, particularly on the pattern of discourse that children encounter in different cultural settings. For the time being, however, it appears that children are astute listeners who register the tacit ontological signals that are embedded in what they are told.

Yet if this interpretation is correct, it means that children, and arguably adults, do not build the distinction between the scientific and the supernatural on any deep, ontological foundation. In particular, the locus of that distinction will vary, depending on shifting cultural and historical patterns. For example, children, and indeed adults, will continue to entertain doubts about well-established scientific phenomena—such as the evolution of species—so long as they perceive that there is no universal consensus. Conversely, in seventeenth-century Europe, a near universal belief in the devil and in witchcraft could have led people to a quasi-scientific conviction of their reality.

# CHAPTER 9

# Death and the Afterlife

.⋆.

Children are told that there is an afterlife. Depending on the particular culture, they might learn that the dead meet their Maker or join the Ancestors. Most children and indeed most adults accept this testimony even if, at first glance, it denies the biological facts. They construct two parallel ideas about death: a secular conception in which death is viewed as a biological event bringing living processes to an end, and a spiritual conception in which death is not final, especially for human beings, who live on in an altered form.

## Two Conceptions of Death

A long tradition of research has focused on children's emerging grasp of the biological life cycle. Investigators have asked when children come to realize that death is inevitable for all living things—an irreversible change implying the cessation of all living functions. There is disagreement about the exact timetable and sequence of development, but there is a broad consensus that somewhere between the ages of 4 and 10 children come to grasp these biological facts (Kenyon, 2001). During this same period, children realize that they too will die. A critical aspect of this biological understanding, one that almost certainly depends on the testimony provided by other people, is the realization that the body is a complex biological machine. Its external functioning can be observed by children, but its internal functioning involves a set of interconnected organs that are normally hidden from view—the heart, the lungs, the brain, the stomach, and so forth. Children gradually come to understand the functioning of these hidden organs and the fact that if they no longer work—whether because of illness, an accident, or old age—then death is likely to ensue, and at the point of death a host of concomitant processes, physical as well as mental, are brought to an end.

The importance of children's developing insight into these ordinarily invisible body parts has been highlighted by Virginia Slaughter and her colleagues. Jaakkola and Slaughter (2002) divided 4- and 5-year-olds into two groups, depending on their grasp of bodily functioning: life-theorizers and non–life-theorizers. Life-theorizers knew about the canonical function of particular body parts (knew, for example, that the lungs are for breathing) and referred to their life-maintaining function (for example, "If somebody didn't have any blood, they would die"). This knowledge of invisible functions appears to help children construct a broader conception of death as a biological terminus. When interviewed about death, these knowledgeable children were more accurate than non–life-theorizers in recognizing that death is inevitable, irreversible, and restricted to living things, and that it brings various functions, such as eating and breathing, to an end (Slaughter, Jaakkola, & Carey, 1999).

Strong evidence for the didactic role of information about these hidden bodily organs emerged in a training study. With the help of a human-body poster as a visual aid, Slaughter and Lyons (2003) told non–life-theorizers about the way in which the integrated functioning of various organs helps to maintain life. The lesson had a dramatic impact. Almost all of the children who had started off as non–life-theorizers before the instruction became life-theorizers afterward, whereas few children in an uninstructed control group made any gains. Even more important, the instructed children advanced not just in their understanding of body parts—which they had been explicitly told about—but also in grasping the inevitability, irreversibility, and universality of death.

In an accelerated fashion, this training study illustrates the steps that children typically take in understanding mortality. Insight into the role of invisible bodily organs can be deliberately and rapidly conveyed to children via explicit classroom-style teaching, but it will ordinarily be conveyed through the informal anatomy lessons that children receive when, for example, they hear about a fatal illness or discuss a dead animal. Whatever the exact vehicle, children acquire a quasi-theoretical body of knowledge that helps them to conceptualize death as the end of the life cycle—a comprehensive and inevitable cessation of living processes.

These findings offer a plausible account of children's conception of death as a biological event, but they almost certainly fail to capture the full developmental story. A belief in the afterlife is widespread among adults in the United States and Western Europe. Moreover, that belief shows no signs of declining over recent decades (Greeley & Hout, 1999). By implication, at some point older children or adolescents come to believe that a form of continued existence is possible after death, despite their grasp of the biological facts. In fact, scattered signs of this emerging belief are apparent even in studies that have targeted the development of children's biological ideas. For example, when Sandor Brent and his colleagues interviewed a large sample of American and Chinese children (Brent, Speece, Lin, Dong, & Yang, 1996) virtually all children by age 6 agreed that everybody will die someday, and that a dead person can neither come alive again nor do any of the things that he or she once did. Yet this consensus was *less* evident among adolescents. More than a third claimed that some form of continued existence was possible. Asked to explain how a dead person might continue to do certain things, they typically offered religious explanations, both in China and the United States, citing the continued existence of the soul, the possibility of reincarnation, or God's power.

What is the psychological relationship between these two conceptions of death, the biological and the religious? One possibility is that children first master the biological facts—the irreversibility and universality of death. Subsequently, when they begin to contemplate their disturbing implications, children are increasingly receptive to religious teaching, which effectively displaces those facts. Below, I describe a study that Marta Giménez and I conducted with Spanish children, showing that that this interpretation is on the right track but misses a key aspect of our trust in testimony: our willingness to entertain parallel or coexisting conceptions of the same phenomenon.

## Death in Spain

We interviewed 7- and 11-year-old children attending state schools in the metropolitan area of Madrid (Harris & Giménez, 2005). Despite Spain's strong Catholic tradition, state schools are secular institutions, so that the children were not receiving any explicit religious instruction in school. That said, many of them came from Catholic families, and they were growing up in a culture where some exposure to Christian beliefs and symbols is just about inevitable. Rather than asking children about the universality or inevitability of death in the abstract, we asked them about the consequences of two particular deaths, having first described each in the context of a separate story. The "doctor" story referred only to the medical aspects of death; it included no religious cues. Children were first shown a picture of an elderly man and told: "In this picture you see Guillermo's grandfather. At the end of his life, Guillermo's grandfather became very ill. He was taken to a hospital where they tried to help him, but he was too old and they could not cure him. The doctor came to talk to Guillermo about what had happened to his grandfather. He said to Guillermo: 'Your grandfather was very ill. There is nothing the doctors could do. Your grandfather is dead now.'"

The "priest" story included the same basic narrative, but the final conversation took place between the grandchild and a priest, rather than between the grandchild and a doctor. Children were shown a picture of an elderly woman and told: "In this picture you see Sara's grandmother. At the end of her life, Sara's grandmother became very ill. She was taken to a hospital where they tried to help her, but she was too old and they could not cure her. The priest came to talk to Sara about what had happened to her grandmother. He said to Sara: 'Your grandmother was very ill. There is nothing the doctors could do. Your grandmother is with God now.'"

By embedding each death in a different story, we aimed to give children a distinctive context for thinking about the consequences of death. We expected that the medical context of the doctor story would prompt children to think about death as the end of the biological life cycle, and that the religious context of the priest story would prompt them to think about death as a spiritual metamorphosis, not a terminus. To probe for these two different conceptions, we asked children to make judgments at the end of each story about the continued functioning of various processes. Some questions included the explicit mention of a body part, for example: "Do you think her eyes still work?" Others included the explicit mention of a mental state, for example: "Do you think she sees anything?" We wanted to know if children would claim that mental processes, such as seeing, continue after death, even if they deny that the associated body part—the eyes, in the case of seeing—can function. We also wanted to know if children would answer the same question differently, depending on the narrative context in which it was asked.

Overall, children were inclined to say that most processes cease at death. Nevertheless, this tendency was *less* frequent among the older children, echoing the earlier findings of Brent and his colleagues. Children's replies also varied with the type of process that they were asked about. They were more likely to claim that various body parts (for example, the eyes and ears) stop functioning than to claim that the mental processes associated with them (for example, seeing and hearing) stop functioning. Finally, both age groups were sensitive to the story context. After the doctor story, they were likely to say that most living processes had ceased at death; but after the priest story, they were likely to claim that some processes continued.

Later parts of the interview helped us to make sense of the overall pattern of replies. Children were asked to say whether the mind (in general) and the body (in general) still functioned after death, and we asked them for explanations of their replies—for example, "Why is it that his body doesn't work anymore?" or "Why is it that her mind is still working?" Most of the explanations were of two types—biological or religious. When they offered biological explanations, children referred to the breakdown of the biological machine in various ways: the absence of movement (for example, "Because he is dead and he can't move"), the loss of particular bodily functions ("The heart doesn't beat and it can't distribute blood through the body and the organs"), the overall cessation of functioning ("If he is dead, nothing can work"), or the burial and decay of the body ("Because she has decomposed—because when you die, worms eat what you have"). By contrast, when they offered a religious explanation, children focused either on God (for example, "In Heaven everything can work, even if she is dead. God is believed to give you all that") or on the survival of the soul or spirit ("Her soul is alive, even if her body is buried").

Looking at children's judgments about whether the mind and the body continue to function, and also at their explanations, we identified three different patterns of responding: a biological stance, in which children said that the body or the mind no longer worked and offered a biological explanation; a religious stance, in which children said that the body or the mind could still work and offered a religious explanation; and finally (and much less frequently) an inconsistent stance, in which children's judgment and their explanation did not fit together or they produced no explanation at all. The percentage of children adopting each stance is shown in Figure 9.1 as a function of the story that children had heard and whether they had been asked about the body or the mind. The upper panel shows the results for 7-year-olds, and the lower panel the results for 11-year-olds.

A glance at the two panels of Figure 9.1 immediately shows that the proportion of children adopting the religious stance—as indexed by the white bars—is more frequent among older children than younger children, more frequent for the priest story than the doctor story, and more frequent for the mind than the body.

Looking at the overall pattern of results, we might be tempted to conclude that children first understand the biological facts of death, and then, realizing their disturbing implications, come to deny those facts in light of religious teaching. For example, younger children answering questions about the body in the context of the doctor story (the leftmost bar in the upper panel) overwhelmingly adopt the biological stance. At the other extreme, older children answering questions about the mind in the context of the priest story (the rightmost bar in the lower panel) overwhelmingly adopt the religious stance.

In fact, however, such an interpretation misrepresents the nature of the developmental change. This became clear when we looked at the several replies made by individual children. Each child had produced a judgment, together with an explanation, on four different occasions—for the body and for the mind, following each of the two stories. So looking across their replies, we could ask if they consistently adopted a biological conception on all four occasions, consistently adopted a religious conception on all four occasions, or adopted both but on different occasions—for example, a biological conception when talking about the body in the context of the doctor story, and a religious conception when talking about the mind in the context of the priest story.

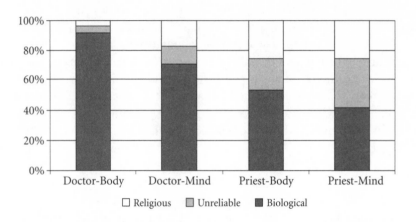

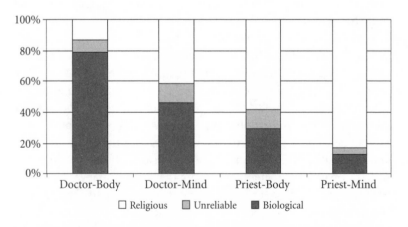

**Figure 9.1.** Percentage of younger children (upper panel) and older children (lower panel) who displayed a biological, a religious, or an unreliable stance, as a function of Story (Doctor versus Priest) and Process Type (Body versus Mind).

Figure 9.2 shows the percentage of children falling into each of these three categories. In line with the thrust of the discussion so far, the proportion of children consistently adopting a biological conception declines sharply with age. However, this is not because the proportion of them consistently adopting a religious conception increases—only a small minority of children do that at either age. Instead, it is the proportion of children displaying both conceptions that increases with age. Indeed, as Figure 9.2 shows, this mixed stance is the dominant pattern among the 11-year-olds.

By implication, children do not first construct a conception of death as a biological terminus and then proceed to dismantle it as they get older. Instead, they leave that early emerging biological conception intact, but on top of it they build a different, religious conception —one that is especially likely to be activated when they are asked to think about death in a religious rather than a medical context, or to think about the fate of the mind rather than the body. To state this differently, there is no evidence in these data that older children end up rejecting the biological facts. Rather, they construct an alternative or parallel conception of death—one that includes an afterlife—in the face of those facts. Especially in the minds of older children, the biological and religious conceptions of death appear to coexist along-

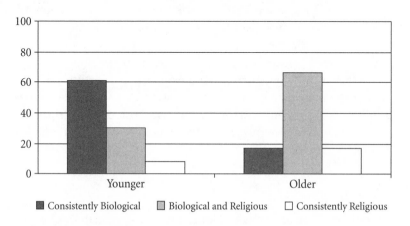

**Figure 9.2.** Percentage of younger and older children showing three answer patterns.

side each other. The religious conception does not displace the biological.

Yet there are several potential objections to this conclusion. First, if
we had tested adolescents or adults, maybe they would have displayed a
consistently religious stance, or at least would have moved further toward such consistency. This objection implies that the coexistence of
both conceptions, even if it is a genuine phenomenon among preado-
lescents—as suggested by the data of Figure 9.2—is only a transient
phenomenon. On this alternative account, the religious conception of
death should eventually displace the biological conception—in the
course of adolescence or adulthood. The oldest children we interviewed
in Madrid were only 11 years of age, and so this objection has some
force. We simply cannot tell how adults would have replied.

The second objection concerns the way that children may have interpreted the interviewer's questions. Children were given two stories,
each of which included a respected authority figure—a doctor and a
priest. Perhaps children thought they should offer different answers to
the two stories, and perhaps they took the presence of the doctor and
the priest as a clue to what exactly was expected for each story—secular
replies in the case of the doctor story, but religious or spiritual replies
in the case of the priest story.

Finally, it could be argued that the findings are at best parochial.
They may reflect the way that children elaborate two conceptions of
death when they grow up in a Christian community, and more specifically in a Catholic community, but they do not tell us if a biological
and a religious conception of death coexist in other cultural settings.
Given these various questions about the findings, Rita Astuti and I col-
laborated on a follow-up study (Astuti & Harris, 2008). We interviewed
a much wider age range; we presented a single story to each person;
and we conducted the study among the Vezo, a non-Christian community of Western Madagascar.

## Death in Madagascar

Betania, a village in Western Madagascar, has a population of about
1,000 Vezo people. The livelihood of the villagers depends on various

small-scale fishing activities, and on the daily trading of fish at the market of Morondava, a town that lies a few miles to the north. During several periods of fieldwork with the Vezo, Rita Astuti, an anthropologist, was able to observe how the village children have direct encounters with animal and human death. She offers a vivid description of how children wait for the return of the outrigger canoes that are used for line fishing. When a fish is cut open, children gather around to watch. They investigate the dead fish, poking it, examining its mouth and gills. Older children may tell the younger ones that the fish can no longer move by itself because it is dead. Smaller live fish, caught with fishing nets, are sometimes given to younger children to play with in the pools along the shore. When these fish eventually stop moving, younger children may again be told that this is because the fish are dead. Children will also be present on special occasions when an ox is slaughtered—partly because they may be given a few slivers of meat, but also because they seem to be fascinated by the process of dying: the slitting of the throat, the expulsion of excrement, and so forth.

Given these firsthand encounters with death and with the immobility that follows, it would be surprising if Vezo children did not grasp its implications at a fairly early age. Even if they receive little explicit teaching or instruction from adults, they hear comments and explanations from other children, and are likely to come to the realization that death means the cessation of a variety of functions, bodily as well as mental. To examine this possibility, Astuti gave young Vezo children two short interviews, one about a dead bird and the other about a dead person (Astuti & Harris, 2008). The bird was familiar to the children, being one that they often hunted and killed. Children were first shown colored drawings of the living bird and the living person. The bird was depicted diving into the sea, and the man was depicted standing up. Next, children were shown a picture of the bird lying flat on the sand with limp neck and wings, and a picture of the man lying prostrate on a bed with his eyes closed and, following Vezo custom, with a white cloth tied around his jaw. Then, with respect to both the dead bird and the dead man, children were asked a variety of questions about bodily processes (for example, "Does its heart beat or not?") as well as about mental processes ("Does he remember where his house is or not?") By the age of 6–7 years, children displayed a systematic understanding of the terminal effect of death. For both the bird and the man and for both body and mind, they generally claimed that all living processes stop at death. So, as expected, the children had mastered the biological conception of death and understood its implications. In a subsequent study, described below, both children and adults from a much wider age range were interviewed. The goal was to find out whether the Vezo—like children in Spain—construct two different conceptions of death in the course of development, rather than a single, biological conception.

Like many other groups in Madagascar (Middleton, 1999), the Vezo believe that the dead pass on to the world of the Ancestors. They also believe that, despite this passage, the Ancestors have an impact on the living. They can appear in dreams, demanding food, drink, and the maintenance of their tomb. If they become displeased with the treatment they receive, they may prevent women from bearing children, make people ill, and even cause people to die. Because of such anxieties about the Ancestors' displeasure, the Vezo seek to appease them by making ritual offerings and maintaining their tombs. These monumental tombs play a significant role in the culture. They serve to honor the Ancestors, but also to keep them safely apart from the community of the living.

Such beliefs and practices show that the Vezo do not subscribe to the Christian idea of Heaven. Yet they do believe in an afterlife. They think of the Ancestors as sentient beings with various mental states, including desires and beliefs: the Ancestors can be angry when a tomb is not tended properly; they want to hear about the plans and projects of the living; and they are proud when their descendants multiply. By implication, at some point in individuals' development, like most Europeans and Americans, members of the Vezo community come to question, or to think beyond, the biological finality of death, which ordinarily implies the complete cessation of all bodily and mental processes. Indeed, in some respects, the Vezo conceive of the afterlife in a more immediate fashion than do Christians: the Ancestors are regularly perceived as potential intruders into their everyday lives and well-being.

In view of this cultural background, we designed a replication and extension of the study in Madrid that could answer the various doubts and questions raised earlier (Astuti & Harris, 2008). First, individuals in a wide age range were interviewed: the children ranged from 8 to 17 years, and the adults ranged from 19 to 71 years. This meant that we could check whether the Vezo's conception of the afterlife does eventually displace their biological conception. Second, each person listened to only one story of two stories. In this context, especially since many of the adults had a long-standing acquaintance with Rita Astuti, the interviewer, and knew from past experience that she genuinely wanted to learn about Vezo beliefs and practices, it was unlikely they would think that they had to give an "appropriate" or "expected" answer to her questions. Rather, they were likely to offer a considered judgment in an effort to inform her. Finally, this study offered an opportunity to find out if the pattern observed in Spain was a local pattern, typical of a Christian (Catholic) community, or could also be found in a non-Christian community.

The interview presented to the Vezo was similar to the one used in Madrid, but various changes were made, to accord with the cultural setting. In place of the "doctor" story, a "hospital" story described the death of a man called Rampy from a serious malaria attack. Mention was made of his unsuccessful hospital treatment, but nothing was said about his funeral or his tomb. At the end of the story, participants were shown a picture of Rampy after he had died. Thus, the hospital story, like the doctor story in Madrid, focused on the medical and corporeal aspects of death. In place of the "priest" story, a "tomb" story described the death of a man named Rapeto. No mention was made of the cause of death. Instead, the story described how he was surrounded by many of his grandchildren when he died, and how his tomb had been properly prepared. At the end of the story, participants were shown a picture of his tomb. Thus, the tomb story, like the priest story in Madrid, focused on the nonbiological aspects of death.

The story context again had a marked effect on the pattern of replies. When presented with the "hospital" story, children and adults mostly insisted on the finality of death, claiming, for example, that the man's heart no longer worked, that his stomach no longer needed food, and that he could no longer see or hear things. This notion of death as an endpoint was much less evident among those who listened to the "tomb" story. They claimed that some processes continued even after death. As in Madrid, they were more likely to claim that mental processes—as opposed to bodily processes—continued after death; and this split emerged even when closely matched questions were asked—for example, about the experience of seeing, as compared to the functioning of the eyes.

Did their belief in the Ancestors eventually lead the Vezo to deny the biological facts of death? In particular, did Vezo adults show signs of denying its finality? Indeed, adults were more likely than children to claim that the dead man would know his wife's name, remember his house, and miss his children. These are the kinds of mental activities that are thought to be characteristic of the Ancestors: they serve to maintain a connection with the past and with the living. Nevertheless, evidence that Vezo adults do not abandon their understanding of the biological reality of death emerged when we looked at the overall set of replies made by individual participants. If a belief in the life of the Ancestors led to a denial of the biological facts, we would not expect any adult to claim that every single living process—mental as well as bodily—had ceased to function at death. Yet this "total cessation" pattern was shown by a considerable number of the Vezo adults who listened to the hospital story (Astuti, 2007). By implication, even if the Ancestors impinge on everyday life in all sorts of ways, the Vezo do not abandon their initial biological conception of death. Instead, as in Spain, a nonbiological conception of the afterlife is constructed "atop" the biological conception.

Summarizing across the two studies, one in Spain and the other in Madagascar, we find a surprisingly consistent pattern, despite important cultural differences between the two settings. In both studies, participants responded differently to the questions, depending on the story they had just heard. When led to think about death from a medical perspective, they were likely to say that most, or indeed all, living processes had come to an end. On the other hand, when led to think about death in relation to religious figures or symbols—a priest, a burial, or a monumental tomb—they were likely to say that some processes continued, especially those connected to the afterlife.

From a strictly logical standpoint, the effect of the story context is disconcerting. Recall that the same set of questions was asked after each story—for example, whether the eyes and brain still work, and whether seeing and thinking are still possible. In principle, one might have expected these various questions to be answered in the same way, independent of the story context. Admittedly, it could be argued that the Spanish children did not really subscribe to the inconsistent answers they gave, but simply made their best guess as to the "right" answer, depending on the particular cues in each story—the presence of the doctor in one story, and that of the priest in the other. Yet, as we have seen, that interpretation is much less plausible in Madagascar. Many of the participants were adolescents or adults, and they were questioned in the context of a single narrative by someone whom they knew to be keenly interested in their customs and practices. Yet they, too, were affected by the story context. They often insisted that all living processes had ceased in the context of the hospital story. Yet they rarely made that sweeping claim in the context of the tomb story. By implication, both in Spain and in Madagascar, children and adults sincerely thought that the two narrative contexts warranted different answers concerning the same processes.

How should we interpret this apparent inconsistency? Do the two conceptions peacefully coexist, or is there some tension between them? A classic tradition in American philosophy, reaching back to William James and Charles Sanders Pierce, argues that everyday thinking is less concerned with arriving at a coherent set of beliefs than with solving various pragmatic concerns about how to act in a given context. In a medical context involving a hospital or a doctor, the overarching goal is to ensure that the person remains a sentient living being as long as possible. Medical interventions are not aimed at a preparation for the afterlife. They are aimed at the prolongation of life on earth. If those efforts fail, and the person dies, the inevitable decay of the corpse means that some form of disposal is needed. Moreover, to the extent that the once-living person is now viewed as an immobile and insensate corpse, the stark conclusion that all living functions have come to an end imposes itself. By contrast, in a religious context involving a priest or funereal rites, a different set of concerns predominates. The focus is no longer on either the prolongation of living functions or the immediate aftermath of their cessation. Instead, it is on the way in which the person will take up his or her place in the afterlife. From this perspective, it is feasible that the dead person retains not just a social identity but also certain capacities.

According to this pragmatic analysis, neither children nor adults knowingly contradict themselves when they think about death in these different contexts. The two conceptions are tied to different goals and priorities. Hence, individuals rarely entertain both conceptions at the same time and rarely notice any tension between them, even if—examined dispassionately—the two conceptions lead to mutually inconsistent claims. It is true that individuals may claim—in the context of the doctor or hospital story—that the dead person is no longer able to see, whereas they may claim—in the context of the priest or tomb story— that the dead person is still able to see. Yet the pragmatic analysis implies that such a contradiction is more apparent than real. When a question is answered in these two narrative contexts, it is not exactly the same question that is being answered. Even if the wording remains unaltered, participants take it to be referring to two distinct entities. In the case of the doctor or hospital story, they take the question to be referring to the dead corpse. In the case of the priest or tomb story, they take the question to be referring to the person who has joined God or the Ancestors.

The context-bound nature of ideas about death is highlighted in the field notes of Rita Astuti. In the course of one visit to the Vezo, she participated in the rituals surrounding the death of a woman she knew well. This included helping other women in the village to prepare the body for entombment. In the course of these preparations—the ablution of the body in cold water and the struggle to disentangle her matted hair—the other women indulged in a certain amount of black humor, commenting on the fact that the dead woman could no longer feel the icy water on her body or the comb tugging at her hair. Apparently, their preparation of the corpse for its journey to the afterlife did not prevent them from making a clear-eyed assessment of what the corpse could and could not feel. Nevertheless, these same women were carrying out the preparations so that the dead woman could properly join the Ancestors. They believed that she would be mindful of her treatment by the living, the care devoted to her tomb, and the ritual sacrifices made on her behalf.[1] The head of one of the Vezo families regularly displayed a similar agility in his stance toward the Ancestors. He would call upon them, offer them food, request that they not make people ill, and so forth. Yet, at the end of this discourse, there would be a shift of tone and posture as he announced: "... and now it's over, and there is *not* going to be a reply!" At which point those present would laugh, get up, and help themselves to a drink (Astuti, 2007).

Despite the plausibility of there being two pragmatic, context-based conceptions of death, there are reasons for thinking that the two conceptions are not as separate as I have implied so far. Indeed, an appreciation of the tension between them might be an engine for children's cognitive development. Recall that the religious conception of death emerges later than the biological conception. One plausible interpretation of this developmental sequence is that a biological conception of death is a conceptual prerequisite for a religious conception. In that case, we ought not to think of the two conceptions as completely separate. In addition, even if people are not ordinarily aware of any inconsistency between the two conceptions, that lack of awareness may not always apply. When people contemplate both conceptions at once— rather than in different contexts—some tension may be generated. Each of these points warrants more discussion.

Looking across the two studies—one in Madagascar and one in Spain—we see a broad developmental change. Among younger children, it is the biological conception that predominates. In the course of middle childhood and beyond, children increasingly adopt a supernatural or religious conception alongside the biological conception. They claim that some processes, especially those linked to the mind or spirit, continue after death. Why is this double stance not found among young children? Thinking first about the Vezo, it could be argued that children first come to understand death in biological terms because they often deal with it in the context of animals, such as birds and fishes, where religious or supernatural beliefs are unlikely to be conveyed to them. Among the Vezo, a dead fish does not become an ancestral fish. In addition, although young children are likely to encounter human death at fairly close range—the death of a relative or neighbor—and also to attend burial rituals, adults typically provide them with little explicit instruction in the ways of the Ancestors, partly because such knowledge is regarded as dangerous for children (Astuti, 2011). On this account, the developmental pattern that is observed—a biological account at first, increasingly supplemented by a nonbiological, Ancestor-based account—is a simple reflection of the information that children have at their disposal at different points in their development.

However plausible for the Vezo, this account works less well for children growing up in Europe or in the United States. First, many children are likely to have some experience with human death by the age of 6 or 7 years. For example, in a survey of Midwestern children in the United States, parents reported that a fairly high proportion (38 percent) had experienced the death of a friend or relative—typically the grandparent or great-grandparent. Moreover, of these children, the majority had attended a funeral or memorial service (Rosengren, Miller, Gutiérrez, Chow, Schein, & Anderson, 2012). In addition, unlike their peers in Madagascar, children in Europe and the United States have many opportunities to learn about human death from books, television, and movies. Even if parents monitor their access to those media and seek to protect them from learning about death by violence, any child who is taught, however informally, a little history of Europe or the United States can scarcely avoid learning that it is more or less exclusively concerned with dead people. Whether they are Romans or Vikings, Native Americans or Founding Fathers, heroes or traitors, they are—by a large majority—dead.

Since the concept of death is so pervasive, even for young children in Europe and North America, it is feasible that parents will supply references to an afterlife—particularly if they themselves believe in an afterlife. Vezo adults may regard knowledge about the Ancestors as dangerous for young children, but many Christian parents are likely to think that it is reassuring for children to learn about Heaven. Indeed, this is what was found by Rosengren and his colleagues when they interviewed Midwestern parents—most of whom were Christian—about how they discussed death with their young children (Rosengren et al.,

2012). Although few of these young children spontaneously mentioned religious considerations in their questions about death, it was common for parents to answer them in religious terms. It seems plausible that parents will make similar references to the afterlife in Catholic Spain. Granted these two points—young children's almost inevitable awareness of human death, together with the likelihood that they are offered the comfort of religion by concerned parents—why does the consistently biological stance dominate the replies of young children during the early years? Why don't they adopt the mixed stance that is evident among older children? Even if the relative availability of religious as compared to biological information plays some role in this developmental pattern, another, internal factor is likely to be at work.

Arguably, it is only when children understand from a biological perspective that death leads to a comprehensive cessation of all living processes that the implications of the afterlife become meaningful. More specifically, only when they realize that death involves a total loss—the loss of all human contact and experience—for everyone, including themselves, do children understand that the afterlife is not just a continuation of mortality in some restricted or altered fashion. It is the beginning of a different form of life. Children who have not fully accepted or understood the biological dictates of death will be less able to appreciate the paradox of life after death. On this interpretation, for a belief in the afterlife to flourish, a preexisting host is needed—namely, the acceptance of biological constraints on mortality. In younger children, that host is likely to be missing or under construction. Notice that this analysis implies that at some level, however tacit, children and adults do conceive of the afterlife as a negation or denial of the biological facts. Contrary to the analysis set out earlier, the two conceptions might not ultimately enjoy an entirely separate and peaceful coexistence. Instead, when children come to believe in an afterlife, they assume that it somehow overrides or "trumps" biological reality.

One way to assess this claim is to bring the two conceptions of death into contact with each other. If they enjoy a peaceful coexistence, then children should comfortably endorse each of them, acknowledging that they are fit for different contexts. On the other hand, if at some intuitive level children believe that the afterlife triumphs over biological reality, they should be less evenhanded in their endorsement. More specifically, when the two conceptions are juxtaposed, children should opt for the religious conception rather than the biological conception.

We interviewed children aged 5–16 to explore these possibilities (Harris, 2011; Harris, Koepke, Jackson, Borisova, & Giménez, 2010). The children were told about two people—John and Susan—who made different claims about death. One person took a biological stance by claiming that all processes cease at death: "When a person dies, their mind and body stop working. The person is buried, and it's the end of life for that person." The other person took a religious stance: "When a person dies, their mind and body carry on working. The person goes to be with God, and it's the beginning of a new life for that person."

First, in order to determine if children understood these different claims and their implications, we asked them what each person would say about whether a dead person can see or remember. Almost all the children, irrespective of their age, realized that one person would say that people can see and remember things after death, whereas the other person would say that they cannot. In the next stage of the interview, we asked children for their opinion about the beliefs of each person. For example: "What do you think? Do you think that John is right when he says that people can't see and remember things after they have died? And do you think that Susan is right when she says that people can see and remember things after they have died?" In principle, children could adopt various positions—they could endorse both John and Susan, neither of them, or just one of them.

We found that the majority of children endorsed the religious stance and rejected the biological stance. Asked to explain their position, children typically gave a religious justification by referring to Heaven (for example, "I believe you go to Heaven"), to God ("We see God when we die"), to the soul or spirit ("As a spirit they can live"), or to their religious beliefs ("I'm Catholic—that's what we believe"). Some made a distinction between the mind and the body (for example, "They can see and remember things—their body stops working because they can't breathe any more") and some combined a religious reference with such dualist thinking ("You go to Heaven when you die. I don't think your body goes but your spirit does"; or "When you get buried that's the end of your body, but the spirit side of you goes up and lives with God forever and ever"). Overall, 80 percent of the children who had endorsed the religious stance and rejected the biological stance offered such religious explanations. Only a minority of children accepted the biological stance and rejected the religious stance. As one 11-year-old explained: "When you die your heart stops working, your body stops working. I don't think people go up to live with God. I'm not a very religious person." A 5-year-old was more cryptic: "They get buried. Teeth fall out. They can't talk. There's no God."

Overall, these findings temper the earlier conclusion. Children—and adults—do have two different conceptions of death. At the same time, when presented with these two conceptions, one beside the other, they are reluctant to endorse both. To state this differently, it looks as if the two belief systems coexist, but mostly because they keep out of each other's way. They are recruited in different contexts. Nevertheless, when the two conceptions are brought face to face, most children turn their back on the biological stance and embrace the religious stance. Few do the reverse. Why, exactly? We can only speculate, but a plausible answer is that in certain respects the religious conception of death is, from a conceptual standpoint, more elaborate and capacious: it concedes the biological facts, but it asserts that these should not be accepted at face value. This would fit the developmental account set out earlier. It implies that children think of the religious conception of death not as an alternative to the biological conception, but as somehow going beyond it.[2]

## Conclusions

Sociological surveys of religious belief have repeatedly shown that most adults in Europe and the United States believe in an afterlife. Even adults who do not attend church regularly deny that death brings an end to all living processes. No doubt, Vezo adults conceive of the afterlife differently from Western adults. They do not believe in the Christian God. Nor do they regard the afterlife as a happy reward for a life well lived. If anything, they think of the existence of the Ancestors as a continual and potentially threatening backdrop to normal everyday life. Nonetheless, the core belief in the survival of the person in some altered form is common to Vezo as well as Christian beliefs.

From a developmental perspective, the evidence suggests that children first construct a biological conception of death. They eventually elaborate a religious or supernatural conception in addition to that biological conception.[3] It seems likely that the later conception builds on the earlier one. When explicitly presented with both ideas of death, most children and adolescents endorse the religious conception and reject the biological. Nevertheless, there are various indications, ethnographic as well as experimental, that the biological conception is never truly abandoned. It remains crucial for understanding our mortality.

CHAPTER 10

# Magic and Miracles

.✦.

In this chapter, I ask how children conceive of the past. Do they think that anything could have happened there, or, on the contrary, that it was constrained by causal regularities? One way to approach this question is to look at children's ideas about stories. Because children cannot experience or revisit the past, they rely on the narratives of other people to learn about it. When do children start to distinguish between stories that are fictional and those that aim to describe what actually happened?

David Hume claimed that a sense of history as a genuinely factual narrative was slow to emerge: "The first page of Thucydides, in my opinion, is the commencement of real history" (Hume, 1742/1987). Subsequent scholarship has tended to support Hume's contention that writers before Thucydides did not make a clear differentiation between narratives with a fantastic story line that included interventions by the gods and those aiming at an accurate, factual history, shorn of superhuman elements. Hume's remark points to an interesting question about how children conceive of the unseen past. Like the writers of ancient Greece, young children might not distinguish between fantastic narratives with superhuman protagonists and historical narratives with ordinary human protagonists. Older children, by contrast, might be sensitive to the difference between fiction and history and use it to work out the status of a particular narrative and its protagonist.

Past research does indeed suggest that the distinction between fictional and real characters is not easy for young children to grasp. Yet the findings are not consistent. Some investigators report that young children are prone to think that various real figures are just fantasy figures. For example, Morison and Gardner (1978) found that children often judged real figures that were remote from their everyday experience—"knight," "Indian," and "dinosaur"—as pretend. Other investigators have found the opposite mistake—that children are prone to think of fantasy figures as real. For example, Applebee (1978) asked children, "Where does Cinderella live? Could we go for a visit?" Whereas 9-year-olds often looked quizzically at him, apparently recognizing that Cinderella is fictional, 6-year-olds were not so lucid. If they denied that a visit was possible, they typically offered pragmatic rather than ontological reasons: "She'll have to wash up the plates and all the dishes and wash the floor."

We revisited this question, taking various precautions to make sure that children understood what we were asking (Corriveau, Kim, Schwalen, & Harris, 2009). We gave them two easily distinguished boxes—a box for real people, soberly illustrated with a teacher standing at a blackboard, and a box for pretend people, more whimsically illustrated with a flamingo painting on a canvas—and asked children to allocate pictures of well-known people to the appropriate box. Among children aged 3–4 and children aged 5–7, individuals in both groups performed well. Figure 10.1 shows that they would put a picture of, say, Abraham Lincoln into the real box, whereas they would put

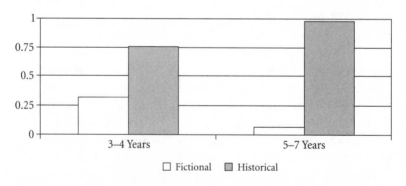

**Figure 10.1.** Proportion of times that younger and older children put familiar fictional and historical characters into the real box (as opposed to the pretend box).

a picture of Batman into the pretend box—although older children were more systematic than younger children.

We next asked if children would be able to use the events in a story to work out the status of an unfamiliar story protagonist. We replaced the pictures of familiar people with pictures of unfamiliar people, told a story about the person in each picture, and invited children to judge his or her status. For example, we showed children a picture of a young girl and told them either a fantasy story or a more factual, historical story about her. The fantasy story described the girl's special powers: "This is Sara Adams. She became a firefighter when she grew up. She had a secret blanket that protected her from any harm and made her invisible." The historical story, by contrast, represented the girl as an ordinary mortal: "This is Annie Paine. She became a doctor when she grew up. She was born in Washington, D.C., on the Fourth of July." Having listened to these brief stories, children were invited to allocate the picture of the protagonist to either the real or pretend box. Figure 10.2 shows that the children aged 5–7 did well, putting the protagonists embedded in historical stories into the real box and those embedded in fantasy stories into the pretend box. By contrast, the younger children were at a loss. None of them systematically grasped the difference between the real and pretend characters.[1]

The success of the older children implies that they understand a key

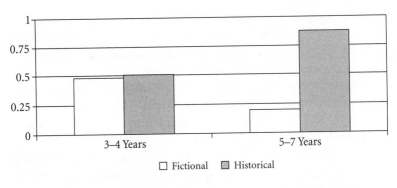

**Figure 10.2.** Proportion of times that younger and older children put unfamiliar fictional and historical characters into the real box (as opposed to the pretend box).

difference between history and fiction—the same difference that Hume had in mind with his comment on Thucydides. The magical or fantastic does not belong in a narrative about the actual past, so a story with such elements is likely to have a fictional protagonist. But how had younger children managed to sort the familiar characters correctly in our initial study if they lacked any appreciation of the distinction between history and fiction? The most plausible answer is that they sorted them on a piecemeal or rote basis. In everyday conversation, at home or in school, children might be told explicitly that George Washington "really" did cross the Delaware—or that Little Red Riding Hood's unhappy encounter with the wolf is "just a story." On this interpretation, younger children lack any principled way of assessing the status of an unfamiliar character. They rely on guidance from adults, and, in the absence of any explicit guidance, they are confused. Note that the difference between making a piecemeal distinction versus a principled distinction has wide application in cognitive development. Consider a child who is told that a banana is a fruit, whereas a carrot is a vegetable. Children might process and remember this specific piece of information, but we should not assume—when they subsequently echo it—that they understand the reasoning behind it or could apply the distinction to tomatoes. Similar considerations apply to children's differentiation between historical and fantasy characters. They might categorize familiar instances one by one, but lack a principled basis for distinguishing them.

More evidence for a conceptual shift emerged when children explained their judgments about the unfamiliar protagonists. Younger children mostly offered uninformative justifications: "She's doing something different" or "Just because," but older children were likely to offer a cogent rationale. Presented with a fictional story, they often referred to the impossibility of the story events ("There's no such thing as invisible sails"; "Seeds don't make you live forever"); but presented with a historical story, they alluded to the reality of events or people in the story ("He fought in the war"; "People are real"). This difference between the pattern of justifications for fictional stories and the pattern for historical stories is evident in Figure 10.3.

The older children appear to grasp that a genuinely historical narrative should include no impossible or magical outcomes. A story that has such elements is necessarily fictional, and so is its protagonist. To put this in somewhat hyperbolic terms, by approximately 6 years of age, contemporary children are on the modern side of the conceptual transition that Hume identified. They realize that some narratives describe what really happened, but that others describe events in a make-believe past.

How, then, do 3- and 4-year-olds conceive of the past when they listen to a narrative? Maybe they assume that all stories take place in one huge, undivided continent where all manner of events can occur: the travails of Peter Rabbit, their parents' own childhoods, the visit made by Little Red Riding Hood to her grandmother, and battles between dinosaurs. They recognize that different narratives involve different settings within that large continent. For example, they realize that Little Red Riding Hood will never come across Peter Rabbit as she walks through the forest (Skolnick & Bloom, 2006). Nonetheless, they locate both the real and the fantasy past within the same undivided mental space. Making no distinction between events that are ordinarily possible and those that are magical or miraculous, they regard the past as unconstrained. Anything and everything could have happened there.

A long line of research into children's developing ideas about causality can help to evaluate—and temper—this radical hypothesis. Piaget (1928) argued that young children do indeed have a very limited understanding of causality: they make no clear distinction between out-

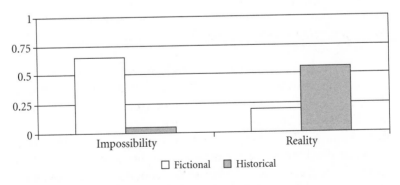

**Figure 10.3.** The proportion of justifications produced by older children that focused on impossibility and reality, for fictional and historical stories.

comes that are possible via ordinary causal processes, and outcomes that are impossible—except by magic. His thesis was later amplified by Bruno Bettelheim (1991), who claimed that fairy stories appeal to children precisely because the magical events that they include do not violate young children's own permissive causal expectations. For them, the extraordinary happenings in fairy tales are the stuff of real life.

However, Bettelheim ignored the fact that empirical research by Margaret Mead and the Chinese psychologist Huang Yi had cast doubt on Piaget's negative portrait. Even when asked to explain mishaps or mysteries, young children mostly invoke ordinary causal processes to explain them (Huang, 1930; Mead, 1932)—contrary to what Piaget would have expected (Harris, 2009). By implication, as they listen to a story, even preschoolers should be able to identify fantastic events that do not square with their understanding of ordinary causality. Later experimental work has consolidated this conclusion. If preschoolers listen to stories about either banal or causally impossible outcomes, they readily identify an ordinary human being as the likely agent of the banal and someone with magical powers as the likely agent of the impossible (Johnson & Harris, 1994).

Granted these findings, it may be that 3- and 4-year-olds can distinguish between possible and impossible events as they listen to a story, but do not yet realize that this is a vital tool for deciding what type of narrative they are dealing with. However, if such a tool is at their disposal, young children might figure out how to use it if they were suitably prompted. We tested this speculation by giving 3- and 4-year-olds such a prompt. The children listened to three sets of stories. The first set—a pretraining set—was presented in the same way as before. Children were asked to decide whether an unfamiliar character, embedded in either a realistic or fantasy story, was real or pretend. Just as expected, 3- and 4-year-olds sorted the characters in this first set of stories randomly, ignoring the clues provided by the surrounding story. The next set—the training stories—were presented in the same way, but children also received a simple prompt: immediately after listening to each story, we asked them whether the key event in the story could really happen or not. For example, after a story about a princess, we asked: "Could someone eat a magic cookie that allowed them to stay the same age forever?" Once they had answered this question, children went on to make a decision about whether the central character was real or pretend. Our hunch was that if children were asked to reflect on the plausibility of the story events, they might use that reflection to help them decide on the status of the protagonist. Finally, children received a set of post-training stories that included no prompt questions about the story events. Children were simply asked to judge the status of the main protagonist—just as they had done for the pretraining stories.

Some "systematic" children correctly answered all, or all but one, of the prompt questions. By contrast, "unsystematic" children answered more variably. This split highlighted a clear pattern. Those children who said, for example, that nobody could eat a magic cookie and live forever were likely to claim that the princess in the story was just a make-believe princess. These systematic children also went on to make correct judgments about the protagonists in the post-training stories. By implication, they no longer needed prompting—they spontaneously thought about the plausibility of the story events—and this helped them to figure out the status of the protagonist. By contrast, children who were unsystematic in assessing the plausibility of the story events remained poor at judging the status of the main character, in both the training and the post-training stories.

Figure 10.4 shows that, in the post-training stories, the systematic 3- and 4-year-olds produced a pattern of justifications like that of the 5- and 6-year-olds (compare Figure 10.3). They often referred to

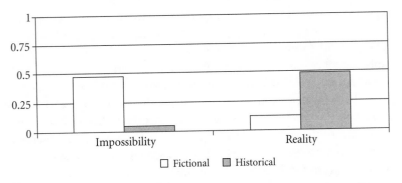

**Figure 10.4.** The proportion of justifications produced by younger children that focused on impossibility and reality, for fictional and historical stories.

the impossibility of the story events in the context of fictional stories, and to the reality of the story events in the context of historical stories. By contrast, children in the unsystematic group mostly offered uninformative justifications; the training did not "click" for them.

In sum, children who are starting school—and, with prompting, even some preschoolers—grasp that the historical past is not a place where regular and fantastic events jostle side by side. They deploy what we might describe as a "magic detector." Using their ideas about what is possible and what is not, they create a frontier between the historical past and the fictional past. They consign the impossible to the world of fiction. This is no mean achievement. Contrary to the claims of Bettelheim, children think of the entire canon of fairy stories as a genre that is distinct from real history.

Admittedly, the ability to grasp the difference between historical narratives and fictional narratives does not mean that young children's ontological troubles are over. There are at least two important ways in which they will continue to be challenged. First, although many children's stories include fantastic beings—giants, witches, elves, talking animals, sleeping beauties, toys that come alive, and so forth—there are also children's stories that aim for realism. Oliver Twist and Tom Sawyer live within the bounds of possibility, even if their lives are far from ordinary. If children divide up narratives into those that are fantastic and those that are historical, how do they categorize these realistic narratives? If they think that fiction necessarily includes fantastic or impossible elements, they might mistake such realistic narratives for historical narratives. They would think of Oliver and Tom as real children who lived in some bygone age, not as the inventions of authors Dickens and Twain. However, to offset this risk, children can presumably use other indications—the way a story is framed and introduced by its author, where it is located in the bookstore, and how it is categorized by the wider community—as reliable clues to its status. Such fictional narratives will be presented as fiction, even if they include accurate, historical detail. Conversely, historical narratives will be presented as a true record even if they suffer from exaggeration or omission. Once children grasp the fundamental distinction between history and fiction, they can probably deploy that distinction in conceptualizing the status of more opaque narratives. They may err along the way with particular exemplars of a given genre, but they need not fundamentally revise their ontological map.

The second challenge is much more complex. Religious narratives often include amazing departures from everyday causality. The dead are resurrected, seas are parted, water is turned into wine. On the strength of the findings discussed so far, children should realize that such events defy ordinary causal processes. They will recognize them as miracles. So how do young children respond to religious narratives? If the analysis so far is correct, they should spontaneously deploy their magic detector, note that such miracles cannot occur in the real world, and conclude that Bible stories are fairy stories—fantastic narratives about fictional events and characters. But we know that young children do not do that. Jacqui Woolley and Victoria Cox gave 3-, 4-, and 5-year-olds religious stories in which people interacted with God. For example, one story was about Jonah and the whale, and another was about David and Goliath (Woolley & Cox, 2007). Older children were increasingly likely to say that the events in the religious stories could really happen. A follow-up study produced similar results (Vaden & Woolley, 2011). When 6-year-olds heard stories involving God and characters from the Bible, they were likely to say that the characters were real and that the events had actually occurred.

What happened to the children's magic detector? Five- and 6-year-olds readily judge stories with implausible elements as fictional, so why don't they draw that conclusion for religious stories? Before we try to answer that question, it is worth emphasizing that this dual stance—a clear-eyed recognition of the miraculous, together with an acceptance of its reality—is not confined to children's reactions to Bible stories. This dual stance is also evident when we look closely at children's ideas about God. They recognize that his powers are extraordinary. Yet they also believe in his existence and in his capacity to exercise those powers.

Justin Barrett and his colleagues asked young children to say whether their mother would know what was inside a closed container without looking inside it, and also whether God would know. By 4–5 years of age, children differentiated between the constraints on their mother—

if she could not see inside the box, she would have to guess at its contents—and the lack of such constraints on God: he would invariably know what was inside (Barrett et al., 2001). Giménez-Dasí, Guerrero, and Harris (2005) obtained similar results. Five-year-olds claimed that God—unlike their best friend—would know what was inside a wrapped gift, and by way of explanation they invoked God's special powers (for example, "Because he is magic"; "Because he has very big eyes and can see everything"), something they never did in connection with their best friend. Children also distinguished between God and their best friend in terms of mortality. They acknowledged that their best friend had not existed in the age of the dinosaurs, had once been a baby, would get older as the years go by, and would eventually die. By contrast, they conceived of God as invariant, ageless, and immortal.

Given that young children are lucid about God's superhuman powers, how far do they believe in God? As discussed in Chapter 8, 5- and 6-year-olds living in Boston said that they were quite confident of God's existence—even if this confidence fell short of their confidence in the existence of germs and oxygen (Harris et al., 2006). Similarly, children growing up in Spain proved confident of God's existence and saw themselves as belonging to a community of believers, claiming that other people also believed in the existence of God (Guerrero et al., 2010).

Children not only believe in God and his extraordinary powers—they spontaneously invoke those powers. Margaret Evans (2001) asked children living in two different Midwestern communities about the origin of different species. In both communities, 6-year-olds made frequent reference to a divine creator. Woolley and Phelps (2001) studied children's developing conception of prayer. Among preschoolers aged 3–5 years, about half claimed that their prayers had been answered or would be answered. Faith in the efficacy of prayer was even more widespread among older children. Approximately three-quarters of children aged 6–8 years said that that their prayers had been or would be answered. God's perceived role in prayer clearly emerged when children were asked how they would teach someone to pray. They claimed it was important that the person believe in God. Finally, recall from Chapter 9 the evidence for children's belief in God's extraordinary powers: asked to explain how certain processes might continue after death, children claimed that God could accomplish that in Heaven.

In summary, young children understand key constraints on human beings: humans cannot know everything, and they are mortal. Children also realize that God is superhuman, in the sense that he is said to defy those constraints: he is omniscient and immortal. Yet despite their understanding of these extraordinary attributes, they believe in God's existence and invoke his superhuman powers—as divine creator, as someone who answers prayers, and as the being who presides over the afterlife. Although children grasp that God possesses quasi-magical powers, they do not think of him as a fictional character in some cosmic fairy tale. So we end up with a paradox. On the one hand, young children have their feet on the ground—they spot the magic in a fairy story and classify it as fiction. Yet they spot the miraculous in religious claims and accept it as fact.

## Believing in Magic

As mentioned in the introduction to this book, Hume emphasized that our everyday reasoning is highly dependent on testimony. At the same time, he cautioned against unthinking assent. Focusing on our belief in miracles, he argued that someone who claims to have witnessed a miracle should be believed if, and only if, the probability of that person's making a false claim is lower than the probability of the causal violation to which the person testifies. Hume's general conclusion was that it is almost invariably more likely that the testimony about a miracle is false—that the person is misinformed or seeking to misinform us—than that a law of nature has been violated. On Hume's argument, we should generally be skeptical about miracles—excellent advice from an epistemological standpoint, perhaps, but unsatisfactory as an account of the way that people ordinarily reason. As we have just seen, children—and indeed adults—routinely believe in the miraculous, whether the belief is in the extraordinary powers of God or the Ancestors, the efficacy of prayer or sacrifice, or the likelihood of a hereafter.

Before we analyze children's belief in the miraculous, it will be helpful to tackle something a bit less daunting: children's occasional credulity toward magic. Even if young children can appropriately identify magic as an outcome that defies ordinary causality, and can use their magic detector to pick out episodes that are fictional, there is nonetheless scattered evidence that they do not systematically rule out the possibility that magic can really happen. They seem to regard causal regularities as a rough and ready guide to the way the world works—but not one that is inviolable. In particular, when children are told about a device or a person with special or magical powers, they often come to believe what they are told.

Judy DeLoache and her colleagues introduced 2-year-olds to a machine and told them that it was able to shrink a full-size room to a scale replica, and, conversely, that it could expand a scale replica back into a full-size room (DeLoache, Miller, & Rosengren, 1997). Given an apparent demonstration of these "incredible" transformations, children appeared to accept them at face value. According to both their parents and other observers, most children firmly believed that the transformation had taken place. They reacted with interest and pleasure, rather than with astonishment or disbelief. They talked about the transformation as an actual change—claiming that the room was getting little or getting big—not as a pretense or a trick. Still, the children in this study were only toddlers, and their causal notions may have been fragile. Yet similar results have emerged with older children.

Eugene Subbotsky explored young children's reactions to a magic box and a magic potion. When he showed children aged 4–6 a "magic box" and told them it had the power to transform pictures of objects into real objects, most of them took advantage of an opportunity to try it out. Left alone with the box and several pictures, they would select a picture of an attractive object, place it in the box, and recite the "magic" spell, just as they had been told (Subbotsky, 1985). When the hoped-for magical transformation failed to materialize, they expressed puzzlement or surprise. Similarly, when they were presented with a potion that, allegedly, could "rejuvenate" an object—and indeed a person—by making it travel back in time, children were extremely reluctant to drink it, for fear they might end up younger than they really were (Subbotsky, 1994). In both of these cases, children acted with magic in mind, hoping—or fearing—to produce magical transformations.

Older children are, if anything, even more actively inclined to accept and discern the possibility of magic. Jesse Bering and Becky Parker told children aged 3–9 about an invisible agent named Princess Alice. They explained that she would somehow help them to avoid mistakes in a guessing game. When some untoward and unexpected event happened during the game—for example, a light suddenly went off—the older children were especially likely to treat it as a helpful signal from Princess Alice, telling them that their guess was wrong (Bering & Parker, 2006).

Apparently, even if children recognize magic for what it is—an extraordinary departure from everyday, causal regularities—they do not dismiss the possibility that it could happen. Told about magical possibilities—machines that can miniaturize or maximize, pictures that turn into the objects they depict, potions that rejuvenate, invisible advisors—they believe what they are told.

These findings can be plausibly interpreted in terms of the analysis set out in Chapters 3 and 4. When children bring their own clear-cut observations to a situation, they rarely defer to an adult who makes a counter-claim. On the other hand, when the situation is more opaque and children's own expectations are not so firm, they do defer, especially to a pedagogic or authoritative adult. Note that in the studies just described, children presumably brought their own nonmagical expectations to the situation: rooms do not ordinarily shrink, schoolchildren do not change back into toddlers, and so forth. Nevertheless, children were told by an adult to expect such magical outcomes. It is worth revisiting the studies briefly to highlight this key point.

In the study with the shrinking-expanding room, an adult showed toddlers an unfamiliar and impressive-looking machine and then "demonstrated" its capacity to miniaturize or inflate an entire room. In the "magic box" study, children first heard about the "magic box" in the context of a story about Masha, a young girl who was given the box as a present. They were told that Masha did not believe in its magical powers at first, but when she tried it out she discovered that it could, in fact, do magic. Some days after they had heard this story, children were interviewed again. This time, they were shown a box and told explicitly that it was "the same magic box that was given to Masha." The clear implication was that the box was real, not just a piece of fiction. Similarly, when children were offered the magic potion, the interviewer first demonstrated its restorative effect on an old, crumpled postage stamp and then issued the following invitation: "If you drink a little bit, you will probably turn into a little boy [girl]. Now you can try the water, if you want. I just want to see if it works. But if you don't want to try—it's up to you." The children who heard about Princess Alice were told that even if she was invisible, she was present in the room and would help them: "And guess what else: Princess Alice really likes you and she's going to help you play the game. She's going to tell you when you pick the *wrong* box. I don't know how she's going to tell you, but somehow she's going to tell you when you pick the wrong box." So in all these studies, an adult testified—with apparent sincerity—that an extraordinary event had occurred or would occur.

To review: children are aware of the regularities that constrain what can ordinarily happen. Shown or asked about an unexpected or puzzling outcome, they rarely explain it in terms of magic. Yet despite this ordinarily skeptical stance toward magical outcomes, they are also prone to credulity. Confronted by an extraordinary transformation and told by an adult that it has been produced, or could be produced, by magic—by a special machine, a box, a potion, or an invisible being—they accept such magical powers as feasible. Faced with a choice between trusting their own causal intuitions and accepting the testimony of adults, children defer.

## Believing in Miracles

We may now take this framework and apply it to the miraculous rather than the magical—to those extraordinary outcomes in which God or some divine power is said to have a hand. Consider the following conversation reported by the mother of a 4-year-old girl to Callanan and Oakes (1992). The child was intrigued by her mother's green eyes—a puzzling exception in her otherwise blue-eyed family—and she offered her mother the following creative suggestion about how to put an end to this anomaly: "I like Pee Wee Herman and I have blue eyes. Daddy likes Pee Wee Herman and he has blue eyes. James likes Pee Wee Herman and he has blue eyes. If you liked Pee Wee Herman, you could get blue eyes too." The mother explained her reply: "I told her it would take more than my liking Pee Wee Herman to make my eyes blue. I realized that she didn't understand me, so I explained that God gave me this color and they couldn't be changed."

To make sense of her mother's explanation, the daughter would need to entertain the notion of a world in which God exists and has the power to confer what no ordinary mortal can: a particular eye color. In conceiving of such a world, the daughter would not have to explicitly agree with her mother's explanation. But making sense of it would call for some mental representation of what her mother was implying: that God exists and has superhuman powers. Furthermore, the daughter would likely register at some level the fact that her mother was serious—she was not joking, wondering aloud, or recounting a fairy story. She was offering an explanation of why she was the only member of the family with green eyes.

Children growing up in a religious community are likely to hear many claims of this type, with respect to either the power of prayer, or the forgiveness of sins, or the divine origin of the world, or the nature of the afterlife. Each time they hear such affirmations, children will be cued to conceive of a world in which God exists and has extraordinary powers. To judge by children's reactions to magic, they will (as described earlier) likely entertain and even accept such extraordinary claims if those claims are sincerely expressed.

Cues implying the miraculous will not be confined to verbal explanations. Children growing up in a religious community will see its members engage in various practices that attest to their religious beliefs. When children go to church, they will see people kneeling, joining their hands in prayer, and addressing God. The demeanor of the adults will be serious, rather than playful. Such behavior may impress children as a departure from everyday pragmatic activity, but they are unlikely to conclude that it is an elaborate piece of theater in which God serves as an unseen but essentially fictional protagonist.[2] Instead, they are likely to interpret such actions as being directed at a God who exists, who hears the prayers that are uttered, and who has the power to grant them. In summary, whether they listen to religious claims or observe religious rituals, children are likely to adopt a simple, interpretive psychological strategy: they will recognize and entertain the guiding presupposition of such claims and rituals—namely, the existence of a divine being with superhuman powers.

## The Principle of Charity

Following usage in philosophy, we can refer to children's interpretive strategy as a "principle of charity" (Davidson, 1984). The central claim is that children are naturally disposed to think charitably of other people as agents whose actions and remarks are best interpreted in light of rational beliefs—even in cases where the children themselves might not subscribe to those beliefs. Is there any empirical evidence for such charitable thinking, especially in young children? Until recently, research in developmental psychology would say no: young children stubbornly impute their own assessment of reality to other people, and have great difficulty in empathizing with the different beliefs that other people might have. However, less verbally oriented tasks have begun to uncover a deep vein of charity—even in infants. Not only do infants work out what other people believe; they also resonate with those beliefs in their own actions. For example, infants stare in surprise when a ball unexpectedly fails to appear where they expect it, but they also stare in surprise when it fails to appear where someone else expects it—even if they did not share that expectation. It is as if infants say to themselves: "Right—no ball! But that's not what he expected—so I guess I'm puzzled too!" (Kovács, Téglás, & Endress, 2010).

Assuming that children do follow this principle of charity, we can ask about its psychological consequences. How is it that children eventually become quite confident of God's existence? Why doesn't their magic detector lead them back to the conclusion that God's extraordinary powers belong to the world of fairy tales? Three interconnected factors are likely to allay any ontological doubts they might have, and make the extraordinary seem ordinary. First, the principle of charity just described is likely to be activated very frequently in some communities, whenever children encounter an utterance or an action that presupposes God's existence and powers. Second, children are likely to suffer from source confusion—to lose track of the many utterances and actions that presuppose God's existence. Third, the so-called "availability" heuristic will come to affect children's estimates of what is probable versus what is improbable.

The impact of the first factor is straightforward. When young children grow up in a community where God's existence and special powers are presupposed in many acts and utterances, they will often be led to deploy the principle of charity—more so than children who grow up in less observant communities. The repercussions of such community variation on children's beliefs are evident early in development. In her study of explanations for the origin of species, Margaret Evans (2001) found that the invocation of God as a creator of species was frequent among 6-year-olds. However, 6-year-olds growing up in a fundamentalist community and receiving a Christian education offered this form of explanation much more often than any other type. By contrast, 6-year-olds growing up in nonfundamentalist community were equally likely to offer a natural explanation: they spoke of species simply "appearing" or "growing from the earth."

Lane and his colleagues examined the understanding of God's extraordinary knowledge among children attending religious schools and those attending secular preschools (Lane et al., 2010 and in press). The developmental pattern was similar in both groups. Initially, as they came to realize that knowledge is constrained by perceptual access, children claimed that God would be constrained like any mortal. But subsequently, the religiously schooled children were quicker to recognize God's exceptional status—to grasp that he would not be bound by such constraints. They also voiced more explanations invoking those special abilities ("He can see through everything"; "He's super smart").

A similar community effect emerged in a study of children's afterlife beliefs. Bering, Hernández Blasi, and Bjorklund (2005) interviewed children aged 5–12 in Spain. Children attending a Catholic school were more likely than children attending a secular school to claim that various functions would continue after death, and were less likely to claim that almost all functions cease at death. These group differences are even more striking in that the children were interviewed about a dead mouse. Apparently, the Catholic-school children concluded that what they had learned about Heaven was applicable to mice as well as men.

Finally, the pattern of judgment discussed earlier—children's assertion that religious stories recount actual events—should be especially marked among children growing up in a religious environment. Some of the children tested by Woolley and Cox (2007) were attending a religious preschool, and they were especially likely to say that the events in the religious stories could really happen. Even among children recruited via a laboratory database, those with more religious parents were more likely to say that the events in the religious stories could really happen. Vaden and Woolley (2011) obtained parallel findings. Despite children's recognition that the story events could not ordinarily happen, the presence of God in the narrative prompted the children from more religious families to accept the story as historical rather than fictional. In short, children growing up in religious communities are often called upon to exercise the principle of charity. Not surprisingly, their faith in the miraculous is augmented.

Source confusions were initially studied in the context of eyewitness memory. In an influential study, Loftus (1975) found that adults who had observed a particular scene—such as an accident—were prone to incorporate objects or events into their memory of the scene that had not actually been present but were implied in later discussion. For example, if asked, "How fast was the white sports car going when it passed the barn while traveling along the country road?" when no barn was actually present in the original scene, adults were prone to "remember" that there was indeed a barn. Subsequent research has pointed to the role played by such source confusion. Adults find it difficult to distinguish between nonexistent entities that they are prompted to think about in the context of discussion—such as the barn in the example just given—and entities that they actually saw for themselves. Unable to pinpoint the source of their thought about the barn, they end up assuming that there really was a barn.

Children are prone to similar source confusions. Ceci and his colleagues asked preschoolers to think about highly improbable events that had never taken place. For example, children might be asked: "Think real hard. Did you ever get your hand caught in a mousetrap and go to the hospital to get it off?" (Ceci, Huffman, Smith, & Loftus, 1994). They were asked these same questions repeatedly over several weeks. At first, few children agreed that such an unlikely event had befallen them; but as the weeks went by, almost half said that it had occurred. Presumably, with repeated invitations to think about the same improbable event, the mental image of it that children retrieved each time they were asked the question became more and more familiar. As a result, they increasingly overlooked the fact that they had merely created that image in the context of the interviewer's question, and they started to believe that the event had actually occurred.

It seems feasible that a similar process occurs with respect to God. Admittedly, children are not deliberately asked misleading questions or repeatedly invited to "think real hard" about a miracle. Nevertheless, if the analysis of the principle of charity set out above is correct, children growing up in religious communities will frequently be led to entertain the idea of God and his miraculous powers, so as to make sense of the many acts and utterances that they encounter. Such prompts will be especially frequent in highly observant communities. Granted the likelihood of source confusion, the mental representations that they trigger will seem increasingly familiar and increasingly disconnected from their original source. Children will come to think of their representations of God and his powers not as exogenous ideas, initially activated when interpreting other people's acts and utterances, but as their own altogether familiar ideas.

Finally, with regard to the third element, we may invoke another body of classic work in cognitive psychology: that concerning the "availability heuristic." An adult who has recently read about a plane disaster, and can therefore easily bring such an episode mind, is likely to regard the likelihood of a similar disaster as greater than someone who cannot readily bring one to mind (Tversky & Kahneman, 1973; Kahneman, 2011). This idea can be linked to the two preceding assumptions in the following way. First, children will vary in the frequency with which they are prompted to entertain—via the principle of charity—the notion of the existence of God and his extraordinary powers. Second, children who are frequently prompted will be especially prone to source confusion—especially likely to lose sight of the fact that the idea of God and his extraordinary powers is an idea that has been repeatedly cued by the acts and utterances of other believers. Finally, and as a result, children growing up in observant communities will readily bring the idea of God and his miraculous powers to mind. That mental availability will eventually reduce their perception of its improbability. Its very availability will lull them into regarding the idea as less extraordinary than they would consider it otherwise.

## Conclusions

It is no coincidence that the word for history and the word for story are equivalent in many languages. Much of what children learn about the past is conveyed to them through stories. As a result, they face a conceptual challenge: they must differentiate between narratives that aim at an accurate, factual rendition of the historical past and those that do not—those that are fictional. At around 5–6 years of age, children spontaneously make use of one major clue in separating history from fiction: if a story includes magical or fantastic elements, they judge that the protagonist is fictional, not real. Conversely if the story is stripped of such elements, they are ready to say that the protagonist is real, not fictional. By implication, young children can conceptualize a key difference between history and fiction. They recognize that even if history is full of peculiar, exciting, and even rare events, it includes no magic. Fiction, on the other hand, especially the fiction that is made available to children and is popular with them, frequently does include magic. Its main characters, good and evil, are endowed with special powers that defy ordinary biology and psychology.

Children's reliable sifting of narrative material underlines the fact that they have some insight into the causal constraints on what can ordinarily happen. They recognize magic for what it is: something that defies ordinary causality. At the same time, and despite the availability of this magic detector, when adults frame an extraordinary outcome for children as something that can indeed happen—thanks to some magical power—children accept it as such. For them, the testimony of adults authenticates a mode of causal explanation that they rarely resort to when left to their own devices.

Religious stories about miracles confront children with a hybrid genre. On the one hand, children's magic detector should indicate that the reported miracle cannot really happen—it defies everyday causal constraints. At the same time, religious stories are not ordinarily presented to children as fairy tales. Especially in religious households, they are presented as accounts of actual events. By approximately 5 years of age, children appear to accept this framing. They accept that religious stories are different from fairy tales. They regard the events in religious stories as real, not fictional. That acceptance of miracles is part of a much broader faith in God's extraordinary powers. Even though children are lucid about the fact that God is credited with extraordinary powers that no mortal possesses, they are relatively confident of his existence. Indeed, they are relatively confident about other people's confidence. We can sum up by saying that despite their cautious and generally skeptical stance toward magic, many children routinely believe in miracles.

Where does this dual stance come from? In keeping with the general argument of this book, I argue that its ultimate source is the testimony provided by other people. The potency of the testimony surrounding the miraculous warrants analysis, not least because it persuades children that even if magic is ordinarily confined to fairy stories, miracles can really happen. Nevertheless, that testimony meets a psychologically receptive audience. Confronted by the otherwise extraordinary actions and utterances of the faithful, children charitably entertain the presuppositions that guide them—namely, that God and his special powers exist. For example, seeing an adult at prayer, children will view the adult not as clasping his or her hands in an empty gesture, but as praying to God.

The psychological repercussions of this principle of charity are likely to be strengthened in three convergent ways. First, children living in observant communities will be prompted on many occasions and by many different people to apply the principle of charity—to entertain the thought that God and his miraculous powers actually exist. Second, adults as well as children easily lose track of the source of their mundane beliefs. A similar process is likely to occur for religious beliefs. God's existence—like the existence of germs—will appear to be an established fact, rather than an idea that has been entertained thanks to the testimony of others. Finally, the ease with which children can bring God to mind is likely to allay ontological doubt. Possibilities that we can easily bring to mind strike us as plausible even if, by the yardstick of observed causal regularity, they are decidedly improbable.

# CHAPTER 11

# Going Native

✦

Stonehenge and the Pyramids offer silent proof of an ancient human capacity for coordinated action. Other primates have left no such monuments. We find evidence of individual tool use—for example, the debris left behind by successive generations of chimpanzees, skilled at hammering nuts—but no enduring signs of cooperation. In view of this vast difference among species in cultural organization, we might expect a comparably vast difference in cognitive ability. But the characterization of that divide, and of what gave rise to it in the course of evolution, has been challenging.

In an eloquent essay, Nick Humphrey pointed to a new direction for comparative research (Humphrey, 1976). Many studies of monkeys and apes had concentrated on the scope of their practical intelligence— their ability to solve problems in the physical world. Yet in thinking about the deployment of that practical intelligence, Humphrey underlined a paradox. Primates have a simple tool kit, and they learn to use much of it through various forms of observational learning, not through individual problem-solving. Admittedly, under experimental conditions, they display a capacity for autonomous reflection and insight in solving various practical problems (Köhler, 1925), but that intellectual capacity is rarely called upon outside the laboratory. How then did it arise in the course of evolution? What endowed primates with such "spare" intellectual capacity?

Watching a group of monkeys housed in a barren cage at Madingley in Cambridge, Humphrey was struck by the fluidity and complexity of their social interaction. He began to think about the evolutionary pressures that such an intense social life might generate. Here is what he wrote: "If intellectual prowess is correlated with social success, and if social success means high biological fitness, then any heritable trait which increases the ability of an individual to outwit his fellows will soon spread through the gene pool." Once set in motion, this process would not be reversible: "An evolutionary ratchet has been set up, acting like a self-winding watch to increase the general intellectual standing of the species."

Humphrey's essay set the stage for a new era of comparative and developmental work on the social, as opposed to the practical, intelligence of primates. In the next few years, landmark studies were published examining the chimpanzee's theory of mind (Premack & Woodruff, 1978), the incidence of deceptive ploys across various primate species (Whiten & Byrne, 1988), and the child's grasp of mental states (Wimmer & Perner, 1983). In their different ways, these investigations vindicated Humphrey's prescient speculation: primates' social intelligence is complicated and worthy of analysis. Certainly, it warrants as much study as their practical intelligence. Moreover, as might be expected, it gradually became clear that even if apes share with human beings a working psychological theory—an intuitive grasp of what other members of their group see, want, and intend—it is also true that human beings, including young children, are more socially astute than their primate cousins, especially when it comes to figuring out what others might believe—rightly or wrongly. For example, children realize that if someone sees an object put in one container, but the object is surreptitiously moved elsewhere during their absence, the person, upon returning, will mistakenly think it is still where he or she left it. Chimpanzees, by contrast, do not seem to grasp the psychological consequences of such ploys (Call & Tomasello, 2008).

However, this new focus on social intelligence—highlighting, as it did, the competitive, even Machiavellian, aspects of primate social interaction—was of limited help when it came to thinking about the vast gulf between human civilization and ape culture. It does not seem very plausible to attribute the unique complexities of human civilization to our undeniable capacity for misleading one another. Stonehenge and the Pyramids surely speak to loftier, collective concerns.

Research conducted by Mike Tomasello and his colleagues has offered a major corrective (Tomasello, 2009). It has targeted our prosocial intelligence—our more benign and collaborative inclinations toward one another. Human beings lend a hand to those in need, and
they coordinate their efforts toward a common purpose. Even toddlers display an altruistic and cooperative spirit. By contrast, although
chimpanzees sometimes offer help, especially in cases where another's
goal is plain to see, their capacity for cooperative projects is minimal
(Warneken, Chen, & Tomasello, 2006; Warneken & Tomasello, 2006;
2009). Based on such results, Tomasello and his colleagues have argued
that a capacity for shared intentionality—a meeting of minds in some
common enterprise—distinguishes the social cognition of humans
from that of primates (Tomasello et al., 2005). Indeed, this sophisticated, prosocial intelligence does seem like a much more plausible
foundation for the explanation of various collaborative human
achievements, including the communication of information, the exchange and sharing of goods, and the collective honoring of all sorts of
social conventions (Tomasello, 2011).

Nevertheless, in addition to this emphasis on children's highly developed, prosocial intelligence, I think it is important to highlight another
distinctive aspect of children's relationship to their fellow human beings. Children are predisposed to live not just in a socially complex and
collaborative world, but in a cultural world, a world that invariably includes language and tools. As such, that cultural world cannot be reduced to the physical environment, and it cannot be understood via
the type of practical intelligence that is applied to problems in the
physical environment. Moreover, the cultural world, even if it depends
on the social world, cannot be reduced to social interaction or cooperation. Words and tools are created and used by human beings—but
they transcend any specific group of individuals, and they cannot be
fully understood by a purely social intelligence, whether Machiavellian
or beneficent. To the extent that children easily immerse themselves in
a cultural world, it looks as if we can and should credit them with an
anthropological intelligence—a form of understanding that is aimed
neither at the physical environment nor at social interaction, but at the
extraordinary phenomenon that is human culture. Indeed, immersion

in a particular culture will ultimately infuse the way that children view both their physical and social environment.

Children do not grow up in a global or universal culture. They are raised in a particular culture, with its own language, technology, institutions, and history. Because of that specificity, children need to look to fellow members of their culture for guidance about its particular rules and regularities. Admittedly, humans are far from unique in looking to other members of their species for information. Such "social learning," as it is called by biologists, is widespread among nonhuman animals and indeed among birds and fishes (Rendell et al., 2011; van Schaik & Burkart, 2011). However, social learning in nonhuman animals is typically aimed at navigating the physical or natural world. There is no cultural universe for them to decode. By contrast, social learning among children is frequently directed at learning about the culture in which they live. Consider some of the apparently simple questions posed by young children: "What's that called?" "What does it do?" "What kind of car is that?" "Whose coffee is that?" "Can I go outside?" (Chouinard, 2007). These questions make sense only in the context of a cultural world—one in which there are names for things, there are tools and artifacts, and there are conventions of ownership and permission.

## The "Artificiality" of Culture

In a wide-ranging survey of human institutions and achievements, Herb Simon analyzed what he called the "artificial"—as distinct from the "natural" (Simon, 1996). He identified several key features of artificial systems: they are created—synthesized—by human beings, but not necessarily with full forethought; they can be characterized in terms of functions and goals; and their operation can be discussed and evaluated in normative terms, rather than purely descriptive terms. Simon's analysis is panoramic. It applies to a variety of cultural systems—financial, political, legal, and so forth. It also applies to language. Any given language has been created by human beings; it serves a variety of human purposes; and it may be used properly or improperly, successfully or unsuccessfully. Similarly, Simon's analysis applies to human technology. Any given tool is created by human beings; it serves human purposes; and its design and use can be normatively evaluated.

Some of the most important regularities in children's lives are governed not by the laws of physics, biology, or psychology, but by the various cultural systems that are passed down to them via successive generations. Despite the "artificiality" of such systems—in Simon's distinctive sense—young children readily adapt to them. For example, children are naturally disposed to treat language as a communication device. They rapidly grasp that language is a complex technology with a boundless stock of mini-apps: a lexicon and a variety of pragmatic devices. Language users—even very young children—can assert, request, and interrogate about a great range of topics. Of course, Noam Chomsky and his followers have long claimed that children have a natural disposition toward language—they do not have to be formally taught how to speak. My point is different, however. When children have an opportunity to engage in a dialogue with a responsive partner, they display an intuitive grasp of what language is *for*. In the same way that they need no formal instruction in the rules of grammar, they need no formal instruction in the complexities of language as a means of communication. They instinctively want to talk to someone about something. Indeed, as Bruner (1978) emphasized, children's rapidly emerging skill at doing things with words is, in certain respects, more precocious and striking than their gradual mastery of its syntax.

Children also treat many physical objects as tools. They understand that all sorts of inanimate entities have been fashioned for human purposes. Even as toddlers, they quickly become accustomed to cups, bottles, spoons, and chairs and put them to appropriate use. This stance toward the physical world is pervasive. As discussed in Chapter 2, James Sully claimed that children overextend this way of thinking—they regard many natural phenomena as having a purpose or design: "The world is a sort of big house where everything has been made by someone, or at least fetched from somewhere" (Sully, 1896/2000, p. 79). Piaget and indeed contemporary investigators have followed in Sully's footsteps, emphasizing the tenacity of such teleological thinking in young children and even adults (Kelemen, 2004; Kelemen & Rosset, 2009). It could be argued that this design stance reflects the naïveté of young children—their failure to grasp that there often is no deus ex machina, that things are the way they are because of the laws of nature, and not because they fulfill some human purpose. Yet children's teleological stance is profoundly helpful. As members of a culture, they actually do inhabit a designed world, one in which all manner of tools and artifacts have been created, many of them over multiple generations, to further human goals. Again, this stance toward the artificial is not something that we need to deliberately teach children. Although they are helped by a demonstration or suggestion to figure out how to use a particular tool and learn the end for which it is best suited, the fact that it has a purpose is not something that children puzzle over. It is an assumption that comes naturally to them.

## An Ancient Tutorial System

Although children everywhere live in an "artificial" cultural world, one in which language and tools are invariably found, there is much for them to learn about the particular culture in which they live. Many of the findings presented in this book make sense if we think of young children as engaged in an ancient tutorial system that helps them to make sense of that specific cultural world. As a species, we depend for our survival on the cumulative maintenance of a local cultural heritage. Accordingly, selection will have favored developmental mechanisms for the transmission of that heritage from one generation to the next. It is plausible, then, that children will be receptive pupils and that caregivers will be engaged and deliberate teachers.

The study of early cognitive development has frequently taken a different tack. It has been impressed by how much intellectual progress children can make when they learn about nature in the way that Rousseau deemed authentic and desirable—namely, on the basis of their own observation and reflection. That influential research program has steadily revealed how infants and young children arrive at intuitive theories about the workings of the physical world. Still, it is worth noting that such learning, at least in the early years, proceeds in approximately the same way in children and in nonhuman primates. Nonhuman primates also have a cogent understanding of the spatial and physical world. For example, when rewards are hidden under some containers but not others, they remember where to search. If one container has, say, five rewards and another has two, they choose the one with more. On the other hand, even when engaged with the physical environment, they have difficulty with the type of tutorial learning that is so conspicuous in human children. When 2-year-olds watch someone dislodge an object that is stuck inside a tube by poking it out with a stick or by rapping the end of the tube on the floor—they promptly do likewise when it is their turn. But when chimpanzees watch the same demonstration, they ignore it and vainly try to get at the object with their finger (Herrmann et al., 2007 and 2010). Thus, with the honorable exception of Vygotskian approaches to cognitive development (Rogoff, 2005; Vygotsky, 1978), the standard developmental strategy has often focused on aspects of cognitive development—the early understanding of the spatial and physical world—that children share with other primates. It has neglected what is uniquely human in human cognitive development.

Children's early conversations nicely illustrate the operation of this ancient tutorial system. As we have seen, children's beliefs about the world can be altered on the basis of another person's say-so. When children hear about a transformation that they have not observed, they register that information and they act upon it. Admittedly, they sometimes ignore what they have been told in favor of their prior knowledge. Still, granted the psychological complexity of the tutorial process, it is remarkable that even 2-year-olds can engage in it and benefit from it. Moreover, children not only listen to what they are told and act upon it—they seek out information from other people. Faced with a puzzle or anomaly, they ask a question. This socially directed search for information is deeply intellectual. It is not restricted to immediate, practical goals, such as finding some food or opening a container. Children display a wide-ranging curiosity, uncoupled from any current pragmatic agenda. They probe the how and why of things, sometimes tenaciously, even if it yields no tangible rewards. Again, many of these persistent questions are not about the natural or physical world, or about people's reasons and motives; they are about the complexities of the culture in which the child lives. They ask why the window cleaner needs to be paid, why roofs have slopes, why we milk cows but not pigs, and whether Grandma is in Heaven.

Children's curiosity, and the willingness of those who care for them to feed it, enable them to enjoy their cultural heritage. Instead of studying the world on their own, with each successive generation returning to Year One and beginning afresh, children can construct a view of their world as seen through the lens of multiple, successive generations. They effectively acknowledge, rightly or wrongly, that their own appraisal of the world may be less accurate, less complete, less deep, than the wisdom passed on to them by their forebears. This does not mean that children are indiscriminately credulous. As we have seen, they resist claims that flatly contradict what they can observe for themselves; but when they are uncertain, they are ready to listen.

Signs of this tutorial system are apparent even in preverbal infants. Csibra and Gergely (2009) point out that human caregivers indicate— via expressive signals—when they intend to provide pedagogic information. They make eye contact, they talk directly to the infant, and offer a demonstration of an object's function. For their part, infants are sensitive to those signals and treat them as conveying generic information (Futó, Téglás, Csibra, & Gergely, 2010). For example, when offered such expressive signals plus a demonstration of how a novel object flashes when its handle is pulled, infants treat the "lesson" as being about that kind of object, not about that particular object. Csibra and Gergely (2011) plausibly argue that this mode of communication constitutes a distinctively human type of pedagogy, one that has evolved to facilitate children's learning, especially when a procedure or tool is hard to decipher without help from other people. Although some forms of teaching do occur in nonhuman animals, there is no compelling evidence that teachers offer generic information to be used in later, comparable situations, even if teachers facilitate their young pupils' opportunity to learn something within a given encounter. For example, adult meerkats initially present young pups with dead scorpions to handle, and only gradually provide live ones. Nevertheless, extrapolation to later, equivalent encounters appears to be left to the learner, rather than being part of the pedagogic message (Thornton & Clutton-Brock, 2011).

It has sometimes been claimed that children's learning in traditional or preliterate cultures proceeds without such a two-way tutorial system. Instead, the learner merely watches an expert over and over again (Lancy & Grove, 2010). In fact, however, adults in traditional rural communities also engage in the deliberate instruction of young children. Even if such teaching is informal and intermittent, it happens. For example, a Kpelle father in Liberia explains how he guides his son: "If I am cutting brush, I give him the machete for him to know how to cut brush. If work becomes hard, I'll show him how to make it easier" (Lancy, 1996, p. 76). Hewlett and his colleagues have documented similar examples of guided tool use in hunter-gatherer communities of the Congo basin. Adults will show infants how to chop or dig with suitable implements (Hewlett, Fouts, Boyette, & Hewlett, 2011). By implication, we should not think of the deliberate teaching of young children as a modern offshoot of formal instruction, something that overrides children's true cognitive predilections. Preschool is part of our biological endowment. It underpins our cultural heritage, rather than being a modern practice foisted on unreceptive pupils.

The provision of generic information—information that can be applied across a wide variety of circumstances—is especially obvious when we look at verbal testimony rather than nonverbal demonstrations. Lexical categories—"fish," "bird," and so forth—signal that similar, and indeed not-so-similar, entities have properties in common, including some inner, invariant essence (Gelman, 2003). As we saw in Chapter 4, when children are told that an unfamiliar creature belongs to a familiar category, they can use that information to infer its properties—where it lives, what it eats—and they are willing to do so in a deferential fashion, setting aside their own perception-based intuitions about what category the creature belongs to. Indeed, as we saw in Chapter 8, children will accept the existence of a category—such as germs—and apply it to particular circumstances, even when they have seen no members of that category and acknowledge that they know nothing about their visible properties.

Language also enables children to receive information that explicitly goes beyond any particular member of a category that might be visible or under discussion. Statements can be explicitly generic, in the sense that they refer to all members of a category. For example, when children are told that "fishes have gills" or that "birds have feathers," it is appropriate for them to apply that conclusion to all the fishes and birds they have encountered—or will encounter. In effect, as Gelman (2009) points out, lexical categories and the generic statements that describe their properties present children with a body of expert opinion accumulated over generations.

Children's willingness to set aside their own intelligent appraisal is also vividly illustrated by the phenomenon of overimitation. Left to their own devices, children can often solve simple, practical problems in a straightforward fashion; but shown a more elaborate and indirect procedure, they faithfully reproduce it—especially in the presence of the person who showed it to them. Indeed, children readily infer a normative component to a demonstration—treating it as an indication not just of how to act, but also of how one *should* act. Our taste for rules and rituals—as well as preschool—comes naturally.

In short, the tutorial system is not just a supplementary source of empirical data for children's otherwise autonomous learning. Between authority and self-sufficiency, authority often prevails. It leads children to revise conclusions that they have reached autonomously. This is just what we would expect if children have some appreciation, however tacit, that human life is lived not in some state of nature, but within a cultural group. In that context, vital information about what to think and what best to do is gained by listening to other people and paying careful attention to their practices. A self-sufficient Emile, who figures out the way the world works in a solitary fashion, does not recover our human nature, but denies it.

Once this tutorial process is set in motion, children are running risks. If they defer to others, despite what they have observed for themselves, they may adopt impractical or maladaptive strategies uncoupled from any immediately observable outcomes. But children's willingness to defer does not amount to blind or indiscriminate credulity. They pay careful attention to the identity of would-be teachers, favoring those who are familiar, who are members of their own cultural group, and who abide by its norms. They pay special attention to proposals made by people who elicit agreement from others, and they mistrust those made by deviants or dissenters. Note that children are not just conformists. They do not simply reproduce a claim or a practice that is widespread, as do conformists. They display a type of higher-order conformity. They identify those who are endorsed by other people, and from them they are willing to learn a new—and from their own perspective uncommon—practice. In effect, children learn best from those who are good cultural learners. Conversely, good cultural learners are more likely to succeed in transmitting what they have learned. For better or for worse, this symbiosis between teacher and pupil is likely to facilitate the transmission of received wisdom and to handicap the unorthodox.

## Beyond Enlightenment

As mentioned in the foreword, the seeds for this book were sewn in an earlier book about the imagination. I claimed that at some point in the evolution of the human species, a confluence occurred between two psychological functions: the ability to communicate via language and the ability to represent unobserved agents and events via the imagination. Without the imagination as its partner, communication is confined to an exchange about things that are visible or imminent. Without communication as its partner, the imagination is confined to solitary rumination. It cannot reach out to conjure up the experiences and ideas of other people. It is unclear how that confluence came about in the course of human evolution. Were human beings capable of rudimentary communication about the here-and-now before the imagination came onstream, or did they enjoy a rich imaginative life before the gift of speech was conferred? Were both functions available but psychologically sealed off from each other for some tantalizing period, and, when conjoined, did each amplify the other? We do not know. What is more or less certain, however, is that that confluence emerged at some point in evolution, with the multifarious consequences set out in this book.

Here, I want to underline two overarching conclusions about the relationship between communication and the imagination. At first glance, because of our associations with the concept of imagination, it is tempting to think that any confluence between the two has its primary impact on the child's engagement in the fantastic and the fictional. For example, the child can conjure up the extraordinary creatures and events that are described in a fairy story, even when they do not conform to anything that the child has seen or ever will see. However, the child is also invited to conjure up, via the testimony of others, the allegedly factual as well as the evidently fictional—the invisible change of state that an object might have undergone, the unexpected motion of a ball down a twisted tube, unseen but potent agents such as germs and oxygen, the hidden operations of the brain and bodily organs, the heroes and villains of the historical past, and the miracles and saints of religious narratives. In short, it would be a mistake to underestimate the degree to which, prompted by the testimony of others, children come to entertain in their imagination what they regard as actual beings and actual events. The confluence between communication and the imagination enables children to envisage multiple unseen realities, and not just unseen fictions.

The second point follows from the first. Children hear about a multiplicity of creatures and events primarily via the testimony of others, and so they face a challenge in differentiating between what is factual and what is fictional. Adults speak and act in ways that take for granted the reality and power of unseen agents. In seeking to make sense of what adults say and do, children charitably entertain those same agents in their imagination, to the point where the agents are easily brought to mind and become familiar, whatever their initial implausibility. As a result, children end up believing in the existence of all sorts of invisible agents. Some of them (germs, for example) definitely exist, whereas others (such as the malicious cave spirits of Tenejapa) presumably do not.

Yet it is unlikely that young children mark a firm conceptual boundary between the two types of entity. Even if they have greater confidence in the existence of germs as compared to cave spirits, this likely reflects children's social antennae—their sensitivity to the pattern and distribution of beliefs in their community—and not some autonomous reflection on what is objectively plausible and what is not. Indeed, where the boundary is drawn between the fictional and the factual is not just a matter of private mental housekeeping. The same type of agent can be located on either side of the boundary, depending on the pattern of beliefs in the surrounding culture.

Consider a particular case study. When young children who are growing up in Europe or North America think about witches, they typically conceive of those agents as fictions, the stuff of fairy tales and bestsellers, but not of real life. Their stance reflects the commitments of their culture. Once we step into another cultural framework, the status of witchcraft can shift dramatically. For example, adolescents—and indeed adults—living in South Africa do not regard witchcraft as a fairy story. Despite efforts to increase public understanding of the AIDS virus and the way in which it is transmitted, efforts that have been in part successful, witchcraft is still widely endorsed and invoked as an explanation for the disease, and traditional healers are routinely consulted to combat its effects. There is little evidence that the Western medical model has displaced local, culturally grounded beliefs in supernatural transmission. Indeed, the two conceptions often coexist within the same individual. Many adolescents and adults invoke both the Western model of AIDS transmission and the power of witchcraft, emphasizing now one and now the other, depending on exactly how a given case is presented to them (Legare & Gelman, 2008; Legare, Evans, Rosengren, & Harris, in press).

The coexistence of these two modes of thinking does not easily fit with a common assumption in developmental psychology—namely, that intellectual development can be best characterized in terms of the type of conceptual shifts that we discern in the development of science. I am skeptical about this analogy. Scientific communities and their distinctive modes of investigation are extreme latecomers, when viewed against the protracted backdrop of human history. It would be odd if cognitive development were to mirror such a recent and distinctive institution. We may all be hardwired for preschool and ritual, but probably not for hypothesis testing or Karl Popper's notion of falsifiability.

It could be argued that children's willingness to embrace the testimony supplied by other people is not so radically different from the data-sharing that we routinely see in science. It is true that scientific endeavors rarely depend on the observations of a single scientist. Even revolutionary scientists rely on data supplied to them by trusted colleagues (Browne, 2002; Shapin, 1995). However, there is a crucial difference between the data supplied to a child and those supplied to a scientist. In the majority of cases, scientists are offered replicable data about observable events. The scientific community is protected from misleading data: those who misreport what they observe face severe penalties in terms of subsequent reputation and influence—they are effectively excommunicated. Children enjoy no such protection. In addition to reliable testimony about observable events, they are routinely presented with claims by people whom they trust concerning spiritual and supernatural events. To the extent that children accept such claims and their implications, their conceptual development will deviate from the pattern that we ordinarily see in science.

Children's ideas about death provide a compelling illustration. Thanks to reliable information about the ordinarily invisible functioning of organs inside the body, children come to understand that death is the consequence of a breakdown in those hidden organs. They further realize that this breakdown stops all bodily and mental processes. However, children's conception of the life cycle goes beyond this biologically grounded account. Children construct a religious conception of death in which they conclude that some processes continue into the afterlife. Depending on the particular practices and beliefs of the culture in which they live, they may accept that the dead join God, join the Ancestors, or undergo reincarnation. Arguably, this religious conception of death is more comprehensive than the earlier naturalistic or biological account that dominates the thinking of younger children. But it is not based on empirical data gathered by the children themselves, or on empirical data supplied by trusted informants in the community. Accordingly, although we might regard the expansion of children's thinking about death as a form of conceptual change, it is markedly different from conceptual change in science.

Even if this later conception of death is more comprehensive than the younger child's, it is hardly more coherent. Recall that in the studies of death conducted in Spain and Madagascar, respondents were more likely to say that living processes continue after death when they were questioned in the context of a religious narrative, as opposed to a medical narrative. Essentially, this meant that mutually inconsistent conclusions were reached in the context of the two narratives. In the medical narrative, a dead person cannot see; but in the religious narrative, he can. Faced with the tension between these two conceptions of death—the biological and the religious—children do not acquire or construct a more coherent conception of death that resolves the contradiction between them. For the most part, they recruit each conception as appropriate. They think in biological terms in a medical or secular context, and in spiritual terms in a religious context. Nevertheless, the unresolved tension between the two conceptions becomes apparent if they are invited to think about both. When their implications are juxtaposed and the tension between them is highlighted, children end up denying the biological facts.

Piaget claimed that although young children's ideas about causation are infused with magical thinking, they gradually adopt a more naturalistic and objective grasp of causal mechanisms (Piaget, 1928). That early paper illustrates a theme that recurred throughout Piaget's writing. He saw cognitive development as a gradual movement in the direction of greater rationality and objectivity. Since then, neo-Piagetian investigations—and indeed more contemporary investigations of the young child as a theorist or scientist—have often disagreed with the timetable or mechanisms that Piaget proposed, but they have generally endorsed his vision of the direction of cognitive development.

In his influential book *The Whig Interpretation of History*, Herbert Butterfield criticized the traditional method adopted by historians, including historians of science: "The total result of this method is to impose a certain form upon the whole historical story, and to produce a scheme of general history which is bound to converge beautifully upon the present—all demonstrating throughout the ages the workings of an obvious principle of progress" (Butterfield, 1931). His observation captures the orthodox conception of cognitive development for the past century or more. In that conception, too, earlier stages of thinking are seen through the lens of later stages, and a subtle form of teleology pervades the narrative. Simply put, it is assumed that cognitive development is progressive. Young children are routinely seen as budding scientists headed toward rationality and objectivity—toward Enlightenment (Harris, 2009).

Children's conception of death highlights the limitations of this approach. Both with respect to their understanding of death and more generally in their increasingly elaborate religious and supernatural concepts, it is difficult to insist that children shed magical thinking and move toward Enlightenment. Instead, they might be described as shedding Enlightenment and moving toward magical thinking.

Margaret Mead made a parallel point soon after Piaget's paper on causal thinking was published. The interviews that she conducted among the Manus led her to the conclusion that animism—the explanation of natural phenomena in terms of supernatural forces—did not come easily to young Manus children, even if a belief in sorcery was widespread in the adult population: "The Manus child is less spontaneously animistic and less traditionally animistic than is the Manus adult" (Mead, 1932). When we read Mead's paper, it is easy to miss its wider application—to conclude that she is describing a developmental trajectory that is found in traditional communities—for example, in Tenejapa, Mexico, or in the impoverished townships and rural areas of South Africa—where beliefs in supernatural forces, including witchcraft, are widespread in the adult population. But we do not need to look so far afield. We find the same pattern in modern, industrialized communities throughout Europe and the United States. There, too, the majority of adults invoke supernatural powers. They believe in God and in an afterlife, and so do their children.

If it distorts the nature of cognitive development to think of young children as scientists, making progress toward objectivity in various subdisciplines—physics, biology, and psychology—is there a more appropriate metaphor? As a graduate student in developmental psychology, I was sometimes disconcerted by what I learned from fellow students studying anthropology. They were dubious about the scientistic picture of cognitive development that prevailed in psychology. Local mentors, such as E. E. Evans-Pritchard and Godfrey Lienhardt, specialists on the complex beliefs systems to be found in Africa, had pointed them toward a less rationalistic alternative. Eventually, when I delved into one or two of the magisterial ethnographies on their reading lists, I began to understand their doubts.

Another aspect of their experience impressed me. Regularly, on weekday afternoons, I drove to the postnatal clinics of Oxford in search of babies to test. My expeditions took me away from the heart of the old city to suburban housing estates. But the journeys of my fellow students were much more adventurous. They traveled to remote Himalayan villages in Nepal or to the rain forests of Amazonia, going native for months or years on end. This immersion sometimes made for a difficult readjustment when they came back. Like migrants who had become fluent in a new language and culture, the return home was sometimes jarring. What was once so natural had an eerie, artificial quality.

The classic method in social anthropology is not the scientific method in the way that experimental scientists conceive of it. It includes no experiments or control groups. Instead, when anthropologists want to understand a new culture, they immerse themselves in the language, learn from participant observation, and rely on trusted informants. Of course, this method has an ancient pedigree. Human children have successfully used it for millennia across innumerable cultures. Indeed, judging by their methods and their talents, we would do well to think of children not as scientists, but as anthropologists.

Notes

References

Acknowledgments

Index

# Notes

## 1. Early Learning from Testimony

1. A positive feature of this focus on specific versus fuzzy mental representations is that it helps to explain a puzzling discrepancy. Recall that 22-month-olds successfully chose an altered (wet) exemplar of Lucy on the basis of verbal testimony. They updated effectively (Ganea et al., 2007). By contrast, 23-month-olds often went back to the first hiding place. Thus, they failed to update effectively (Ganea & Harris, 2010). We can invoke the notion of a nonspecific or fuzzy initial representation to explain children's successful updating in the case of wet Lucy. Presumably, children did not register and encode Lucy's dry state when they put her "to sleep" before leaving the room. After all, stuffed animals are dry by default. So Lucy's dry state would not call for any explicit encoding. Similarly, when the object was left visible in the middle of the room, no particular encoding was needed to indicate its exact location. In each case, therefore, the initial file would carry fuzzy or nonspecific information, reducing the likelihood of any subsequent competition with a file updated via testimony.

2. It is tempting to think that the initial file will interfere with later testimony only when that initial file is derived from firsthand experience—children see the toy hidden at the first hiding place, or hide it there themselves. In fact, however, even when 23-month-olds are simply told that an object is at an initial hiding place and then told that it has been moved to a new hiding place, they frequently search for it at the initial hiding place (Ganea & Harris, 2011).

3. In all three cases (updating, enrichment, revision), there is an issue of file management: What should be done with the preexisting file? As discussed, in the case of updating, there are good ecological reasons for retaining the earlier file. It contains true information about a past state of affairs—and it may prove useful if information about the past needs to be retrieved, or if the earlier state of affairs is likely to be reinstated. By contrast, in the case of enrichment and revision, there is no compelling epistemic reason for retaining the preexisting file. It was incomplete in those cases where enrichment was called for, and it was inaccurate in those cases

where revision was called for. However, the actual psychological process of file management may not correspond to any epistemological ideal. For example, in the case of revision, we might find that children—and adults—are prone to retain demonstrably inaccurate files. Getting rid of an old mental file may be no easy task, even when subsequent testimony clearly indicates that it is wrong. Conversely, there are likely to be cases where new testimony diminishes rather than augments children's accuracy. A relatively accurate memory for a past episode can often be inappropriately altered in the wake of suggestive questioning (Bruck, Ceci, Francouer, & Barr, 1995) or as the result of eavesdropping on a misleading conversation (Principe, Kanaya, Ceci, & Singh, 2006).

## 2. Children's Questions

1. This proposal would fit other theoretical proposals regarding the period of late infancy that claim children become capable of constructing more than one mental model of a given situation (Perner, 1991; Suddendorf & Whiten, 2001).

2. For a thoughtful discussion of the way that toddlers might use indicative gestures, notably pointing, primarily as a way to seek information, see Southgate, van Maanen, & Csibra (2007).

3. A possible explanation for this negative result is that when children fail to receive an adequate answer, they simply reiterate the question. By contrast, when they receive an adequate answer, they ask a follow-up question. Frazier et al. (2009) provide persuasive evidence for exactly this pattern. This would mean that explanatory adequacy has little impact on the raw frequency of children's questions, but does have an impact on the proportion of repeated versus novel or follow-up questions.

## 3. Learning from a Demonstration

1. Note that the receptive-pupil hypothesis might, in principle, imply that children are "super-receptive"—that they will even overimitate actions they assume to be causally ineffective, because they grant quasi-magical powers to the demonstrator. By implying that children will not reproduce actions that they regard as causally ineffective, Lyons et al. (2007) appear to invoke a more conservative form of receptivity. I am grateful to Hannes Rakoczy for drawing my attention to this point.

### 4. Moroccan Birds and Twisted Tubes

1. Research on motor development has demonstrated a parallel phenomenon. Given an opportunity to walk down a slope, 18-month-olds do so confidently when the slope is gentle, but resist if it is too steep. Adult guidance has little impact on their decision to descend or stay put. However, if the slope is intermediate and they are unsure about what to do, adult guidance can be decisive. Given maternal encouragement, they will descend, but given maternal discouragement, they will not (Tamis-LeMonda, Adolph, Lobo, Karasik, Ishak, & Dimitropoulou, 2008). Moreover, 18-month-olds rapidly adjust their receptivity to advice if their perception of uncertainty alters. When wearing slippery, Teflon-soled shoes that make any surface more difficult to negotiate, they heed their mothers' discouragement—even on a flat surface, where they would ordinarily ignore her advice (Adolph, Karasik, & Tamis-LeMonda, 2010). Overall, these data nicely illustrate how, even in the second year of life, children defer to adult guidance but only when they are unsure of their own judgment.

2. Still, we might wonder whether children truly accept the unexpected label. Maybe they simply go along with the experimenter's alternative but do not really believe it. One way to check on children's acceptance is to question them later. Asked to identify the object, will they label it in the way they've been told, or will they revert back to their original intuition? In particular, what will they do if another person arrives and asks them what the object is called? Will they use the unexpected label as their reply? Jaswal, Lima, and Small (2009) report that when allowances were made for the fact that children sometimes forgot what they had been told, they did use the unexpected label.

3. This type of testimony-guided search is similar to the pattern discussed in Chapter 1. Recall that children left a toy in one location, briefly went to the next-door room, and were told on their return that the toy had been moved to another location. Thirty-month-olds were able to resist searching where they had last seen the object. Instead, they searched where they were told to search: at the object's new location. Similarly, the 30-month-olds in this tubes task resisted their inclination to search in the gravity cup—and searched instead where the experimenter had indicated. Both studies reveal how toddlers can search where they are told an object is located, and not where they presume it is located on the basis of where they last saw it.

4. Joh, Jaswal, and Keen (2011) report evidence pertinent to this interpretation. Some 3-year-olds were asked before each trial, "Can you imagine the ball rolling down the tube?" and these children made fewer gravity errors than children in a

control condition who were simply told, "The ball is going to roll down the bumpy tube." Signs that the children were, as instructed, imagining the ball's invisible trajectory were noticeable as they made their choice. They often made an incorrect prediction but then corrected it, whereas control children had fewer second thoughts of this kind. Moreover, children became more accurate over repeated trials. These data clearly show that children benefit from being prompted to use their imagination—although we do not know whether children would continue to do so if they no longer received verbal instruction.

5. Further studies reported by Jaswal (2010) used clear rather than opaque tubes, so that children could watch the ball's downward, curved path. Most children allowed this visible path to guide their search toward the correct cup. Indeed, if the ball ended up in a transparent cup so that its final location was fully visible, few children could be tempted to search in the "gravity cup" even when the experimenter "advised" them that this was where the ball was. However, if the ball traveled down a clear tube and disappeared into an opaque cup, "advice" from the experimenter easily misled the children. Told that the ball had ended up in the gravity cup, children mostly searched there. Indeed, they followed this misleading advice over several trials—even though the gravity cup proved empty every time. Thus, faced with unequivocal, perceptible evidence—the visible presence of an object in a cup—children rejected an adult's proposal that they search elsewhere (just as they rejected the claim that a cup is a shoe). But when the evidence was more equivocal—if the object had disappeared from sight—children turned into trusting disciples.

One further point is noteworthy. When children followed the experimenter's misleading advice and searched in the gravity cup, they obviously failed to find the object. Subsequently, they often went back to search in the correct cup. Apparently, even though they had encoded and acted upon the adult's misleading verbal claim, they had not mentally deleted their own, perception-guided intuition about the true location of the object. These data are again nicely consistent with the claims made in Chapter 1: information that is encoded on the basis of verbal testimony will not automatically lead to the overwriting or deletion of earlier conclusions.

### 5. Trusting Those You Know?

1. Richerson and Boyd (2005) emphasize two different learning biases: a *prestige bias,* in which individuals are prone to imitate those with social prestige, and a *conformist bias,* in which individuals are prone to imitate behaviors that are fre-

quent or common in their group. Preschoolers may have difficulty in gauging variation in certain aspects of social prestige, such as wealth or political influence. Yet, as Richerson and Boyd (2005, p. 252) emphasize, prestige is a many-splendored thing. Preschoolers are certainly able to assess the accuracy and competence of individuals. In that broad sense, as discussed later in this chapter, they display a prestige bias, preferring to learn from those with a history of relative accuracy or competence. Furthermore, as discussed in Chapter 6, there is considerable evidence for a conformist bias in early childhood.

2. A fourth group of children with *disorganized attachment* were also tested, but are not discussed here.

3. It is interesting to note that a preference for each of the two familiar preschool caregivers was widespread among the children in their care, consistent with the fact that the caregivers themselves reported having a good relationship with almost all the children that they cared for (Corriveau & Harris, 2009a). By implication, few if any of the children had an avoidant relationship with their preschool caregiver.

4. The exact mechanism by which children's early attachment is linked to their later pattern of trust calls for more research. One possibility is that the foundations for selective trust are laid down early in life—for example, in the course of interactions between mother and infant during the first year or two of life. However, an equally plausible interpretation is that characteristics of the mother that nurture a particular type of attachment also serve, in parallel, to nurture a given pattern of selective trust. Whatever the exact interpretation, the results displayed in Figures 5.3, 5.5, and 5.6 are a surprising testimony to the long-term predictive power of early-attachment classifications. Keep in mind that the attachment classification was made when children were approximately 15 months of age, whereas the two tests of selective trust were conducted when children were 50 months and 61 months, respectively.

5. By 4 years of age, children do not view all accurate informants as equally capable of providing reliable information in the long term. Four-year-olds placed more trust in an informant whose accurate responses had been self-generated than in an informant whose accuracy had relied on help from a no-longer-available third party (Einav & Robinson, 2011). Thus, as well as tracking whether or not someone has been accurate in the past, young children consider how that accuracy was achieved and give credit only where it is due.

6. Note that mistrust of informants who offer false information can be found among even younger children. Having encountered an informant who provided incorrect rather than correct information about an object's location, 36-month-olds were subsequently less likely to update their belief about its location on the

basis of what that person told them (Ganea, Koenig, & Gordon Millett, 2011). In addition, toddlers aged 24 months were less likely to retain new names supplied by an informant if her prior naming of common objects had been inaccurate rather than accurate (Koenig & Woodward, 2010). Thus, toddlers are less likely to learn from an unreliable source, whether about matters of fact (object location) or matters of convention (object names).

7. It remains to be seen exactly what type of relationship is needed for eliciting trust. I have stressed the bond that preschoolers create with caregivers, but it is plausible that children favor information from a variety of people they know, including friends, classmates—and even familiar cartoon characters (Danovitch, Mills, & Harfmann, 2011).

### 6. Consensus and Dissent

1. Four-year-olds who passed a standard test of false belief showed the most systematic differentiation between the two speakers in the test phase. A plausible interpretation of this finding is that such children are better able to treat bystander reactions as a comment on the trustworthiness of each informant (and not just as a comment on the particular names that they propose).

2. Jaswal and his colleagues told preschoolers about two friends who differed in the way that they produced various familiar plural nouns (Jaswal, McKercher, & VanderBorght, 2008). For example, children were shown a picture of two dogs, and told that one friend said there were "two dogs" whereas the other friend said there were "two dag". Next, the two friends provided conflicting names for unfamiliar objects, and the children could endorse one or the other. Three, 4-, and 5-year-olds strongly endorsed the names offered by the orthodox rather than the deviant "pluralizer." Here, too, we have a case of selective trust, where it is difficult to argue that children were monitoring the two informants in terms of whether or not they made true or false claims. It seems more likely that children were reacting to the conventionality of one informant and the unconventionality of the other.

3. Four- and 5-year-olds also prefer to learn the rules of a novel game from a reliable rather than an unreliable informant. Indeed, in experiments offering persuasive evidence that children regard informants as cultural models who provide normative information, children protested more at the unreliable informant's way of playing the game than at the reliable informant's way of playing (Rakoczy, Warneken, & Tomasello, 2009).

4. Corriveau, Kinzler, and Harris (2012) report that 3-year-olds favor a native

speaker, even one who has proven inaccurate, whereas 4- and 5-year-olds favor a nonnative speaker if she has proven accurate.

5. In line with the notion of "respectful" deference, these group differences were evident when the children reported their judgments publicly, but they disappeared when they reported them privately.

### 7. Moral Judgment and Testimony

1. Author Judith Smetana confirmed that the study used pictures showing the victim in tears (personal communication, July 21, 2009).

2. Note that young children will protest against moral transgressions even when the perpetrator is a stranger from a different group (Schmidt, Rakoczy, & Tomasello, 2011).

3. I am grateful to Tyler Dogget for calling my attention to this point.

### 8. Knowing What Is Real

1. The majority of the younger children had never heard of the scientific entities, highlighting the fact that they were typically learning about them at school, rather than in the home.

2. A study by Canfield and Ganea (2011) provides support for the claim that the pattern of testimony concerning scientific entities is subtly different from the pattern concerning special beings. The substance of parental talk was similar for both—for example, parents often provided generalizations about what scientific entities (such as germs and electricity) or special beings (God, Santa Claus) can do. However, parents were more likely to voice doubt and uncertainty, or a lack of consensus, when talking about special beings.

### 9. Death and the Afterlife

1. A similar, context-bound, differentiation between the individual considered as a physical body and the individual considered as a whole person with a personality, a history, and a social identity has emerged in research on the understanding of AIDS. Legare and Gelman (2008) presented adolescents and adults in South Africa with different narratives concerning an AIDS victim. Sometimes the narrative included events consistent with the idea that the victim had been a target of witchcraft. Sometimes, however, the narrative included events consistent with the idea

that the victim had suffered from a purely viral infection. The key finding was that participants were likely to offer different causal explanations for the illness, depending on the narrative context. On the one hand, they could conceive of AIDS as an affliction of the whole person—a sickness brought about by witchcraft. On the other hand, they could conceive of AIDS as an affliction of the person's bodily processes—a sickness brought about by the mixing of blood products. Strikingly, although many of the adolescents and adults who were interviewed had been exposed to government health programs, stressing the critical role played by transmission of the AIDS virus and the associated risks of unprotected sex, there was little indication that exposure to this medical model led to any reduction in witchcraft beliefs. Instead, individuals voiced both types of causal interpretation, depending on the narrative that they were given. More generally, everyday practices for the prevention or treatment of AIDS drew on both causal interpretations. People sought help from doctors trained in Western medicine, as well as from traditional healers.

2. It is important to note that the relationship between the two conceptions is asymmetrical. Even if the religious stance concedes but goes beyond the biological stance, the reverse is not true. The biological stance makes no concession to the religious stance.

3. Rita Astuti (personal communication) is inclined to think that the Vezo respondents were slower to give nonbiological "theologically correct" replies ("Yes, it still works") than strictly biological replies ("No, it no longer works"). This would fit with the claim that ideas based on the afterlife override (developmentally speaking) biological ideas. It would also be consistent with the conclusion that the two conceptions are not, strictly speaking, separate.

### 10. Magic and Miracles

1. Woolley and Cox (2007) also asked children about the status of story characters. Surprisingly, children mostly judged that each character was just a person "in the book" rather than a "real person," and this type of judgment increased with age. There was no sign that children used the story events to help them decide whether the story character was real or not. The most likely explanation for this finding is that children used the interpersonal setting to draw a blanket conclusion about the story characters. Children listened to the stories being read from books. For preschoolers, it is likely that such reading aloud is intimately—if not inextricably—linked to the activity of listening to a parent or preschool teacher reading them a fictional story. By contrast, in the studies conducted by Corriveau, Kim, et al.

(2009), children were shown a picture and then heard a narrative about the person (the experimenter did not read from a book). Presumably, this reduced the likelihood that children would jump to the conclusion that they were being told a fictional story.

2. In the United States, children are likely to hear about, or directly observe, adults engaging in prayer. The majority of U.S. adults (86 percent) report having a religious preference or affiliation; and among those, approximately three-quarters pray several times a week or more. Even among the small minority of people who express no religious preference and very rarely go to church, approximately one-third pray several times a week or more (Hout & Fischer, 2002).

# References

Adamson, L. B., & Bakeman, R. (2006). Development of displaced speech in early mother-child conversations. *Child Development, 77,* 186–200.

Adolph, K. E., Karasik, L. B., & Tamis-LeMonda, C. S. (2010). Using social information to guide action: Infants' locomotion over slippery slopes. *Neural Networks, 23,* 1033–1042.

Ainsworth, M. D. S., Blehar, M. C., Waters, E., & Wall, S. (1978). *Patterns of attachment: A psychological study of the strange situation.* Hillsdale, NJ: Erlbaum.

Applebee, A. N. (1978). *The child's concept of story: Ages two to seventeen.* Chicago: University of Chicago Press.

Asch, S. E. (1956). Studies of independence and conformity. A minority of one against a unanimous majority. *Psychological Monographs, 70* (9, Whole No. 416).

Astuti, R. (2007). What happens after death? In R. Astuti, J. P. Parry, & C. Stafford (Eds.), *Questions of anthropology* (pp. 222–247). London School of Economics Monographs. Oxford: Berg.

Astuti, R. (2011). Death, ancestors and the living dead: Learning without teaching in Madagascar. In V. Talwar, P. L. Harris, & M. Schleifer (Eds.), *Children and death: From biological to religious conceptions.* New York: Cambridge University Press.

Astuti, R., & Harris, P. L. (2008). Understanding mortality and the life of the ancestors in Madagascar. *Cognitive Science, 32,* 713–740.

Au, T. K., Sidle, A. L., & Rollins, K. B. (1993). Developing an intuitive understanding of conservation and contamination: Invisible particles as a plausible mechanism. *Developmental Psychology, 29,* 286–299.

Baillargeon, R. (1994). Physical reasoning in young infants: Seeking explanations for impossible events. *British Journal of Developmental Psychology, 12,* 9–33.

Barrett, J. L., Richert, R. A., & Driesenga, A. (2001). God's beliefs versus mother's: The development of non-human agent concepts. *Child Development, 72,* 50–65.

Bascandziev, I., & Harris, P. L. (2010). The role of testimony in young children's solution of a gravity-driven invisible displacement task. *Cognitive Development, 25,* 233–246.

Bering, J. M., Hernández Blasi, C., & Bjorklund, D. F. (2005). The development of "afterlife" beliefs in religiously and secularly schooled children. *British Journal of Developmental Psychology, 23,* 587–607.

Bering, J. M., & Parker, B. D. (2006). Children's attributions of intentions to an invisible agent. *Developmental Psychology, 42,* 253–262.

Bettelheim, B. (1991). *The uses of enchantment: The meaning and importance of fairy tales.* London: Penguin Books. (Original work published 1975.)

Birch, S. A. J., Vauthier, S. A., & Bloom, P. (2008). Three- and four-year-olds spontaneously use others' past performance to guide their learning. *Cognition, 107,* 1018–1034.

Bonawitz, E. B., Ferranti, D., Saxe, R., Gopnik, A., Meltzoff, A. N., Woodward, J., & Schulz, L. (2010). Just do it? Investigating the gap between prediction and action in toddlers' causal inferences. *Cognition, 115,* 104–117.

Bond, R., & Smith, P. B. (1996). Culture and conformity: A meta-analysis of studies using Asch's (1952b, 1956) line judgment task. *Psychological Bulletin, 119,* 111–137.

Bowlby, J. (1969). *Attachment and loss: Vol. 1. Attachment.* New York: Basic Books.

Boyer, P. (2001). *Religion explained: The evolutionary origins of religious thought.* New York: Basic Books.

Brent, S. B., Speece, M. W., Lin, C., Dong, Q., & Yang, C. (1996). The development of the concept of death among Chinese and U.S. children 3–17 years of age: From binary to "fuzzy" concepts? *Omega, 33,* 67–83.

Browne, E. J. (2002). *Charles Darwin: Vol. 2. The Power of Place.* London: Jonathan Cape.

Bruck, M., Ceci, S. J., Francouer, E., & Barr, R. (1995). "I hardly cried when I got my shot!" Influencing children's reports about a visit to their paediatrician. *Child Development, 66,* 193–208.

Bruner, J. S. (1978). Learning how to do things with words. In J. S. Bruner & A. Garton (Eds.), *Human growth and development*. Oxford: Oxford University Press.

Butcher, C., Mylander, C., & Goldin-Meadow, S. (1991). Displaced communication in a self-styled gesture system: Pointing at the nonpresent. *Cognitive Development, 16,* 315–342.

Butterfield, H. (1931). *The Whig interpretation of history*. London: G. Bell and Sons.

Call, J. (2010). Do apes know that they could be wrong? *Animal Cognition, 13,* 689–700.

Call, J., & Carpenter, M. (2001). Do apes and children know what they have seen? *Animal Cognition, 4,* 207–220.

Call, J., & Tomasello, M. (2008). Does the chimpanzee have a theory of mind? 30 years later. *Trends in Cognitive Sciences, 12,* 187–192.

Callanan, M. A., & Oakes, L. M. (1992). Preschoolers' questions and parents' explanations: Causal thinking in everyday activity. *Cognitive Development, 7,* 213–233.

Canfield, C. F., & Ganea, P. A. (2011). "I guess you could call it magic": Talking to preschoolers about unobservable entities. Paper submitted for publication.

Cavalli-Sforza, L. L., & Feldman, M. W. (1981). *Cultural transmission and evolution: A quantitative approach*. Princeton, NJ: Princeton University Press.

Ceci, S. J., Huffman, M. L. C., Smith, E., & Loftus, E. W. (1994). Repeatedly thinking about non-events: Source misattributions among preschoolers. *Consciousness and Cognition, 3,* 388–407.

Chen, E. E., Corriveau, K. H., & Harris, P. L. (2011). Children as sociologists. *Anales de Psicología, 27,* 625–630.

Chen, E. E., Corriveau, K. H., & Harris, P. L. (in press). Children trust a consensus composed of outgroup members but do not retain it. *Child Development.*

Chouinard, M. (2007). *Children's questions: A mechanism for cognitive development* (Monographs of the Society for Research in Child Development, Serial No. 286, 72, No. 1).

Clément, F., Koenig, M., & Harris, P. L. (2004). The ontogenesis of trust in testimony. *Mind and Language, 19,* 360–379.

Cohen, L. B. (2009). The evolution of infant cognition: A personal account. *Infancy, 14,* 403–413.

Corriveau, K. H., Fusaro, M., & Harris, P. L. (2009). Going with the flow: Preschoolers prefer non-dissenters as informants. *Psychological Science, 20,* 372–377.

Corriveau, K. H., & Harris, P. L. (2009a). Choosing your informant: Weighing familiarity and recent accuracy. *Developmental Science, 12,* 426–437.

Corriveau, K. H., & Harris, P. L. (2009b). Preschoolers continue to trust a more accurate informant 1 week after exposure to accuracy information. *Developmental Science, 12,* 188–193.

Corriveau, K. H., & Harris, P. L. (2010). Preschoolers (sometimes) defer to the majority in making simple perceptual judgments. *Developmental Psychology, 46,* 437–445.

Corriveau, K. H., Harris, P. L., Meins, E., et al. (2009). Young children's trust in their mother's claims: Longitudinal links with attachment security in infancy. *Child Development, 80,* 750–761.

Corriveau, K. H., Kim, A. L., Schwalen, C. E., & Harris, P. L. (2009). Abraham Lincoln and Harry Potter: Children's differentiation between historical and fantasy characters. *Cognition, 113,* 213–225.

Corriveau, K. H., Kim, E. B., Song, G., & Harris, P. L. (2011). *Young children's deference to a majority varies by culture.* Manuscript submitted for publication.

Corriveau, K. H., Kinzler, K. D., & Harris, P. L. (2012). *Accuracy trumps accent when children learn words.* Manuscript submitted for publication.

Corriveau, K. H., Meints, K., & Harris, P. L. (2009). Early tracking of informant accuracy and inaccuracy. *British Journal of Developmental Psychology, 27,* 331–342.

Corriveau, K. H., Pickard, K., & Harris, P. L. (2011). Preschoolers trust particular informants when learning new names and new morphological forms. *British Journal of Developmental Psychology, 29,* 46–63.

Csibra, G., & Gergely, G. (2009). Natural pedagogy. *Trends in Cognitive Sciences, 13,* 148–153.

Csibra, G., & Gergely, G. (2011). Natural pedagogy as evolutionary adaptation. *Philosophical Transactions of the Royal Society B, 366,* 1149–1157.

Danovitch, J. H., Mills, C. M., & Harfmann, E. (2011, March). *Preschoolers trust familiar characters despite inaccuracy and prefer low-quality products with character images.* Poster presented at the meeting of the Society for Research in Child Development, Montreal.

Davidson, D. (1984). On the very idea of a conceptual scheme. In *Inquiries into truth and interpretation.* Oxford: Clarendon Press.

Debré, P. (1998). *Louis Pasteur.* Baltimore, MD: Johns Hopkins University Press.

DeLoache, J. S., Miller, K. F., & Rosengren, K. S. (1997). The credible shrinking room: Very young children's performance with symbolic and non-symbolic relations. *Psychological Science, 8,* 308–313.

Diamond, A. (1985). Development of the ability to use recall to guide action, as indicated by infants' performance on AB. *Child Development, 56,* 868–883.

Dias, M. G., & Harris, P. L. (1988). The effect of make-believe on deductive reasoning. *British Journal of Developmental Psychology, 6,* 207–221.

Dias, M. G., & Harris, P. L. (1990). The influence of the imagination on reasoning by young children. *British Journal of Developmental Psychology, 8,* 305–318.

Einav, S., & Robinson, E. J. (2011). When being right is not enough: Four-year-olds distinguish knowledgeable informants from merely accurate informants. *Psychological Science, 22,* 1250–1253.

Esbensen, B. M., Taylor, M., & Stoess, C. (1997). Children's behavioral understanding of knowledge acquisition. *Cognitive Development, 12,* 53–84.

Evans, E. M. (2001). Cognitive and contextual beliefs factors in the emergence of diverse belief systems: Creation versus evolution. *Cognitive Psychology, 42,* 217–266.

Flavell, J. H. (1978). The development of knowledge about visual perception. In C. B. Keasey (Ed.), *Nebraska symposium on motivation: Vol. 25.* Lincoln: University of Nebraska Press.

Frazier, B. N., Gelman, S. A., & Wellman, H. M. (2009). Preschoolers' search for explanatory information within adult-child conversation. *Child Development, 80,* 1592–1611.

Fusaro, M., Harris, P. L., & Pan, B. A. (in press). Head nodding and head shaking gestures in children's early communication. *First Language.*

Fusaro, M., & Harris, P. L. (2008). Children assess informant reliability using bystanders' non-verbal cues. *Developmental Science, 11,* 781–787.

Futó, J., Téglás, E., Csibra, G., & Gergely, G. (2010). Communicative function demonstration induces kind-based artifact representation in preverbal infants. *Cognition, 117,* 1–8.

Ganea, P. A. (2005). Contextual factors affect absent reference comprehension in 14-month-olds. *Child Development, 76,* 989–998.

Ganea, P. A., & Harris, P. L. (2010). Not doing what you are told: Early perseverative errors in updating mental representations via language. *Child Development, 81,* 457–463.

Ganea, P. A., & Harris, P. L. (2011). A robust error: 23-month-olds perseverate when verbally updating mental representations. Manuscript submitted for publication.

Ganea, P. A., Koenig, M. A., & Gordon Millett, K. (2011). Changing your mind about things unseen: Toddlers' sensitivity to prior reliability. *Journal of Experimental Child Psychology, 109,* 445–453.

Ganea, P. A., Shutts, K., Spelke, E. S., & DeLoache, J. S. (2007). Thinking of things unseen: Infants' use of language to update mental representations. *Psychological Science, 18,* 734–739.

Gauvain, M., & Munroe, R. L. (2009). Contributions of societal modernity to cognitive development: A comparison of four cultures. *Child Development, 80,* 1628–1642.

Gelman, S. A. (2003). *The essential child: Origins of essentialism in everyday thought.* New York: Oxford University Press.

Gelman, S. A. (2009). Learning from others: Children's construction of concepts. *Annual Review of Psychology, 60,* 115–140.

Gergely, G., Bekkering, H., & Király, I. (2002). Rational imitation in preverbal infants. *Nature, 415,* 755.

Giménez-Dasí, M., Guerrero, S., & Harris, P. L. (2005). Intimations of immortality and omniscience in early childhood. *European Journal of Developmental Psychology, 2,* 285–297.

Goy, C., & Harris, P. L. (1990). *The status of children's imaginary companions.* Unpublished manuscript, Department of Experimental Psychology, University of Oxford.

Greeley, A. M., & Hout, M. (1999). Americans' increasing belief in life after death: Religious competition and acculturation. *American Sociological Review, 64,* 813–835.

Greenfield, P. M., & Savage-Rumbaugh, S. (1990). Grammatical combination in *Pan paniscus:* Processes of learning and invention in the evolution and development of language. In S. T. Parker and K. R. Gibson (Eds.), *"Language" and intelligence in monkeys and apes: Comparative developmental perspectives* (pp. 540–578). Cambridge: Cambridge University Press.

Greenfield, P. M., & Savage-Rumbaugh, S. (1993). Comparing communicative competence in child and chimp: The pragmatics of repetition. *Journal of Child Language, 20,* 1–26.

Guerrero, S., Enesco, I., & Harris, P. L. (2010). Oxygen and the soul: Children's conception of invisible entities. *Journal of Cognition and Culture, 10,* 123–151.

Guidetti, M. (2005). Yes or no? How young French children combine gestures and speech to agree and refuse. *Journal of Child Language, 32,* 911–924.

Haake, R. J., & Somerville, S. C. (1985). Development of logical search skills in infancy. *Developmental Psychology, 21,* 176–186.

Harris, P. L. (1973). Perseverative errors in search by young infants. *Child Development, 44,* 28–33.

Harris, P. L. (1989). *Children and emotion.* Oxford: Blackwell.

Harris, P. L. (2000). *The work of the imagination.* Oxford: Blackwell.

Harris, P. L. (2002). What do children learn from testimony? In P. Carruthers, S. P. Stich & M. Siegal (Eds.), *The cognitive basis of science* (pp. 316–334). Cambridge: Cambridge University Press.

Harris, P. L. (2007). Trust. *Developmental Science, 10,* 135–138.

Harris, P. L. (2009). Piaget on causality: The Whig interpretation of cognitive development. *British Journal of Psychology, 100,* 229–232.

Harris, P. L. (2011). Conflicting thoughts about death. *Human Development, 54,* 160–168.

Harris, P. L., Abarbanell, L., Pasquini, E. S., & Duke, S. (2007). Imagination and testimony in the child's construction of reality. *Intellectica, 2–3,* 69–84.

Harris, P. L., Brown, E., Marriott, C., Whittall, S., & Harmer, S. (1991). Monsters, ghosts and witches: Testing the limits of the fantasy-reality distinction in young children. *British Journal of Developmental Psychology, 9,* 105–123.

Harris, P. L., & Giménez, M. (2005). Children's acceptance of conflicting testimony: The case of death. *Journal of Cognition and Culture, 5,* 143–164.

Harris, P. L., & Kavanaugh, R. D. (1993). *Young children's understanding of pretense* (Society for Research in Child Development Monographs, 58, Serial No. 231, No. 1).

Harris, P. L., Koepke, M., Jackson, R., Borisova, I., & Giménez, M. (2010). *Children's beliefs about death: Confronting the claims of religion and biology.* Unpublished manuscript, Harvard Graduate School of Education.

Harris, P. L., & Koenig, M. A. (2006). Trust in testimony: How children learn about science and religion. *Child Development, 77,* 505–524.

Harris, P. L., & Leevers, H. J. (2000). Reasoning from false premises. In P. Mitchell & K. Riggs (Eds.), *Children's reasoning and the mind* (pp. 67–86). Hove, U.K.: Psychology Press.

Harris, P. L., Pasquini, E. S., Duke, S., Asscher, J. J., & Pons, F. (2006). Germs and angels: The role of testimony in young children's ontology. *Developmental Science, 9,* 76–96.

Harris, P. L., & Want, S. (2005). On learning what not to do: The emergence of selective imitation in tool use by young children. In S. Hurley & N. Chater (Eds.), *Perspectives on imitation: From neuroscience to social science* (Volume 2, pp. 149–162). Cambridge, MA: MIT Press.

Hart, B., & Risley, T. (1992). American parenting of language-learning children: Persisting differences in family-child interactions observed in natural home environments. *Developmental Psychology, 28,* 1096–1105.

Henrich, J., Heine, S. J., & Norenzayan, A. (2010). The weirdest people in the world? *Behavioral and Brain Sciences, 33,* 61–83.

Herrmann, E., Call, J., Hernández-Lloreda, M. V., Hare, B., & Tomasello, M. (2007). Humans have evolved specialized skills of social cognition: The cultural intelligence hypothesis. *Science, 317,* 1360–1366.

Herrmann, E., Hernández-Lloreda, M. V., Call, J., Hare, B., & Tomasello, M. (2010). The structure of individual difference in the cognitive abilities of children and chimpanzees. *Psychological Science, 21,* 102–110.

Herrnstein, R. J., Loveland, H., & Cable, C. (1976). Natural concepts in pigeons. *Journal of Experimental Psychology: Animal Behavior Processes, 2,* 285–302.

Hewlett, B. S., Fouts, H. N., Boyette, A. H., & Hewlett, B. L. (2011). Social learning among Congo Basin hunter-gatherers. *Philosophical Transactions of the Royal Society B, 366,* 1168–1178.

Hockett, C. F. (1960). Logical considerations in the study of animal communication. In W. E. Lanyon & W. N. Tavolga (Eds.), *Animal sounds and communication.* Washington, DC: American Institute of Biological Sciences.

Hollis, M., & Lukes, S. (1982). *Rationality and relativism.* Cambridge, MA: MIT press.

Hood, B. (1995). Gravity rules for 2- to 4-year-olds. *Cognitive Development, 10,* 577–598.

Hood, B. (1998). Gravity does rule for falling events. *Developmental Science, 1,* 59–63.

Hood, B., Santos, L., & Fieselman, S. (2000). Two-year-olds' naïve predictions for horizontal trajectories. *Developmental Science, 3,* 328–332.

Horner, V., & Whiten, A. (2005). Causal knowledge and imitation/emulation switching in chimpanzees (*Pan troglodytes*) and children (*Homo sapiens*). *Animal Cognition, 8,* 164–181.

Horner, V., & Whiten, A. (2007). Learning from others' mistakes? Limits on understanding of a trap-tube task by young chimpanzees and children. *Journal of Comparative Psychology, 121,* 12–21.

Horton, R. (1970). African traditional thought and Western science. In B. R. Williams (Ed.), *Rationality.* Oxford: Blackwell.

Hout, M., & Fischer, C. S. (2002). Why more Americans have no religious preferences: Politics and generations. *American Sociological Review, 67,* 165–190.

Huang, I. (1930). Children's explanations of strange phenomena. *Psychologische Forschung, 14,* 63–183.

Hume, D. (1742/1987). *Essays: Moral, political and literary.* Indianapolis, IN: Liberty Fund.

Hume, D. (1748/1902). *An enquiry concerning human understanding* (L. A. Selby Bigge, Ed.), pp. 114–116. Oxford: Clarendon Press.

Humphrey, N. K. (1976). The social function of intellect. In P. P. G. Bateson & R. A. Hinde (Eds.), *Growing points in ethology.* Cambridge: Cambridge University Press.

Hunter, W. S. (1917). The delayed reaction in a child. *Psychological Review, 24,* 74–87.

Hussar, K., & Harris, P. L. (2010). Children who choose not to eat meat: A demonstration of early moral decision-making. *Social Development, 19,* 627–641

Huttenlocher, J. (1974). The origins of language comprehension. In R. L. Solso (Ed.) *Theories in cognitive psychology: The Loyola Symposium.* Oxford: Lawrence Erlbaum.

Isaacs, N. (1930). Children's "why" questions. In S. Isaacs, *Intellectual growth in young children.* London: George Routledge & Sons.

Isaacs, S. (1930). *Intellectual growth in young children.* London: George Routledge & Sons.

Jaakkola, R. O., & Slaughter, V. (2002). Children's body knowledge: Understanding "life" as a biological goal. *British Journal of Developmental Psychology, 20,* 325–342.

Jaswal, V. K. (2004). Don't believe everything you hear: Preschoolers' sensitivity to speaker intent in category induction. *Child Development, 75,* 1871–1885.

Jaswal, V. K. (2007). The effect of vocabulary size on toddlers' receptiveness to unexpected testimony about category membership. *Infancy, 12,* 169–187.

Jaswal, V. K. (2010). Believing what you're told: Young children's trust in unexpected testimony about the physical world. *Cognitive Psychology, 61,* 248–272.

Jaswal, V. K., Lima, O. K., & Small, J. E. (2009). Compliance, conversion, and category induction. *Journal of Experimental Child Psychology, 102,* 182–195.

Jaswal, V. K., & Markman, E. (2007). Looks aren't everything: 24-month-olds' willingness to accept unexpected labels. *Journal of Cognition and Development, 8,* 93–111.

D. A., & VanderBorght, M. (2008). Limitations on reli-
English plural and past tense. *Child Development, 79,*

A. (2006). Adults don't always know best: Preschoolers
ge in learning new words. *Psychological Science, 17,*

Joh, A. S., Jaswal, V. K., & Keen, R. (2011). Imagining a way out of the gravity bias: Preschoolers can visualize the solution to a spatial problem. *Child Development, 82,* 744–750.

Johnson, C. N. (1990). If you had my brain, where would I be? Children's understanding of the brain and identity. *Child Development, 61,* 962–972.

Johnson, C. N., & Harris, P. L. (1994). Magic: Special but not excluded. *British Journal of Developmental Psychology, 12,* 35–51.

Jones, K. (1999). Second-hand moral knowledge. *Journal of Philosophy, 96,* 55–78.

Kahneman, D. (2011). Thinking, fast and slow. New York: Farrar, Straus and Giroux.

Kaiser, M. K., McCloskey, M., & Proffitt, D. R. (1986). Development of intuitive theories of motion: Curvilinear motion in the absence of external forces. *Developmental Psychology, 22,* 67–71.

Kaiser, M. K., Proffitt, D. R., & McCloskey, M. (1985). The development of beliefs about falling objects. *Perception and Psychophysics, 38,* 533–539.

Keesing, R. M. (1982). *Kwaio religion: The living and the dead in a Solomon Island society.* New York: Columbia University Press.

Keil, F. C., Stein, C., Webb, L., Billings, V. D., & Rozenblit, L. (2008). Discerning the division of cognitive labor: An emerging understanding of how knowledge is clustered in other minds. *Cognitive Science, 32,* 259–300.

Kelemen, D. (2004). Are children "intuitive theists"? Reasoning about purpose and design in nature. *Psychological Science, 15,* 295–301.

Kelemen, D., & Rosset, E. (2009). The human function compunction: Teleological explanation in adults. *Cognition, 111,* 138–143.

Kellert, S. R., & Felthouse, A. R. (1985). Childhood cruelty toward animals among criminals and noncriminals. *Human Relations, 38,* 1113–1129.

Kenward, B., Karlsson, M., & Persson, J. (2010). Over-imitation is better explained by norm learning than by distorted causal learning. *Proceedings of the Royal Society B, 278,* 1239–1246.

Kenyon, B. L. (2001). Current research in children's conceptions of death: A crit'cal review. *Omega, 43,* 63–91.

Kim, A. L., & Harris, P. L. (2009, July). The role of testimony as compared to direct observation of suffering in young children's moral judgment. Paper presented at the Multimod 2009 International Conference, Toulouse, France.

Kim, E., Song, G., Corriveau, K. H., & Harris, P. L. (2011, March). Cultural differences in children's deference to authority. Paper presented at the meeting of the Society for Research in Child Development, Montreal.

Kinzler, K. D., Corriveau, K. H., & Harris, P. L. (2010). Children's selective trust in native-accented speakers. *Developmental Science, 14,* 106–111.

Koenig, M. A., Clément, F., & Harris, P. L. (2004). Trust in testimony: Children's use of true and false statements. *Psychological Science, 10,* 694–698.

Koenig, M. A., & Echols, C. (2003). Infants' understanding of false labeling events: The referential roles of words and the speakers who use them. *Cognition, 87,* 179–208.

Koenig, M. A., & Harris, P. L. (2005). Preschoolers mistrust ignorant and inaccurate speakers. *Child Development, 76,* 1261–1277.

Koenig, M. A., & Woodward, A. L. (2010). Sensitivity of 24-month-olds to the prior accuracy of the source: Possible mechanism. *Developmental Psychology, 46,* 815–826.

Köhler, W. (1925). *The mentality of apes.* New York: Harcourt.

Konner, M. (2010). *The evolution of childhood.* Cambridge, MA: Harvard University Press.

Kovács, Á. M., Téglás, E., & Endress, A. D. (2010). The social sense: Susceptibly to others' beliefs in human infants and adults. *Science, 330,* 1830–1834.

Lancy, D. (1996). *Playing on the mother-ground: Cultural routines for children's development.* New York: Guilford Press.

Lancy, D. F., & Grove, M. A. (2010). The role of adults in children's learning. In D. F. Lancy, J. Bock, & S. Gaskins (Eds.), *The anthropology of learning in childhood* (pp. 145–180). Lanham, MD: AltaMira Press.

Lane, J. D., Wellman, H. M., & Evans, E. M. (2010). Children's understanding of ordinary and extraordinary minds. *Child Development, 81,* 1475–1489.

Lane, J. D., Wellman, H. M., & Evans, E. M. (in press). Socio-cultural input facilitates children's developing understanding of extraordinary minds. *Child Development.*

Legare, C. H., Evans, E. M., Rosengren, K. S., & Harris, P. L. (in press). The coexistence of natural and supernatural explanations across cultures and development. *Child Development.*

Legare, C. H., & Gelman, S. A. (2008). Bewitchment, biology, or both: The coexistence of natural and supernatural explanatory frameworks across development. *Cognitive Science, 32,* 607–642.

Levine, R. A., Levine, S., Schnell-Anzola, B., Rowe, M. L., & Dexter, E. (2012). *Literacy and mothering: How women's schooling changes the lives of the world's children.* New York: Oxford University Press.

Liszkowski, U., Schäfer, M., Carpenter, M., & Tomasello, M. (2009). Prelinguistic infants, but not chimpanzees, communicate about absent entities. *Psychological Science, 20,* 654–660.

Loftus, E. F. (1975). Leading questions and the eyewitness report. *Cognitive Psychology, 7,* 560–572.

Lyons, D. E., Damrosch, D. H., Lin, J. K., Macris, D. M., & Keil, F. C. (2011). The scope and limits of overimitation in the transmission of artifact culture. *Philosophical Transactions of the Royal Society B, 366,* 1158–1167.

Lyons, D. E., Young, A. G., & Keil, F. C. (2007). The hidden structure of overimitation. *Proceedings of the National Academy of Sciences, 104,* 19751–19756.

MacNamara, J. (1972). Cognitive basis of language learning in infants. *Psychological Review, 79,* 1–13.

MacWhinney, B., & Snow, C. (1985). The child language data exchange system. *Journal of Child Language, 12,* 271–296.

McCarthy, D. A. (1930). *The language development of the preschool child.* Minneapolis: University of Minnesota Press.

McCloskey, M., Caramazza, A., & Green, B. (1980). Curvilinear motion in the absence of external forces: Naïve beliefs about the motion of objects. *Science, 210,* 1139–1141.

McCloskey, M., Washburn, A., & Felch, L. (1983). Intuitive physics: The straight-down belief and its origin. *Journal of Experimental Psychology: Learning, Memory, and Cognition, 9,* 636–649.

McGuigan, N., Whiten, A., Flynn, E., & Horner, V. (2007). Imitation of causally opaque versus causally transparent tool use by 3- and 5-year-old children. *Cognitive Development, 22,* 353–364.

Mead, M. (1932). An investigation of the thought of primitive children, with special reference to animism. *Journal of the Royal Anthropological Institute, 62,* 173–190.

Melson, G. F. (2001). *Why the wild things are: Animals in the lives of children.* Cambridge, MA: Harvard University Press.

Meltzoff, A. N. (1988). Infant imitation after a 1-week delay: Long-term memory for novel acts and multiple stimuli. *Developmental Psychology, 24,* 470–476.

Middleton, K. (1999). Introduction. In K. Middleton (Ed.), *Ancestors, power and history in Madagascar* (pp. 1–36). Leiden: Brill.

Milgram, S. (1969). *Obedience to authority.* New York: Harper & Row.

Morford, J. P., & Goldin-Meadow, S. (1997). From here and now to there and then: The development of displaced reference in Homesign and English. *Child Development, 68,* 420–435.

Morison, P., & Gardner, H. (1978). Dragons and dinosaurs: The child's capacity to differentiate fantasy from reality. *Child Development, 3,* 642–648.

Muentener, P., & Schulz, L. (2012). What doesn't go without saying: Communication, induction, and exploration. *Language Learning and Development, 8,* 61–85.

Munroe, R. L., Gauvain, M., & Beebe, H. (2011). Children's questions in cross-cultural perspective: A four-culture study. Paper submitted for publication.

Nielsen, M., & Blank, C. (2011). Imitation in young children: When who gets copied is more important than what gets copied. *Developmental Psychology, 47,* 1050–1053.

Nielsen, M., & Tomaselli, K. (2010). Overimitation in Kalahari Bushman children and the origins of human cultural cognition. *Psychological Science, 21,* 729–736.

Nisbett, R. E., Peng, K., Choi, I., & Norenzayan, A. (2001). Culture and systems of thought: Holistic versus analytic cognition. *Psychological Review, 108,* 291–310.

Olthof, T. (2009, July). How to explain vegetarian children's morally-grounded decision not to eat meat? Paper presented at the 35th Conference of the Association for Moral Education, Utrecht, The Netherlands.

Olthof, T., Postma, A., & Kasperts, A. (2008). The assignment of moral status to animals: Children's use of three mental capacity criteria. Unpublished paper, VU University, Amsterdam.

Olthof, T., Rieffe, C., Meerum Terwogt, M., Lalay-Cederburg, C., Reijntjes, A., & Hagenaar, J. (2008). The assignment of moral status: Age-related differences in the use of three mental capacity criteria. *British Journal of Developmental Psychology, 26,* 233–247.

Pallotta, N. R. (2008). Origin of adult animal rights lifestyle in childhood responsiveness to animal suffering. *Society and Animals, 16,* 149–170.

Pasquini, E. S., Corriveau, K. H., Koenig, M. A., & Harris, P. L. (2007). Preschoolers monitor the relative accuracy of informants. *Developmental Psychology, 43,* 1216–1226.

Pea, R. D. (1982). Origins of verbal logic: Spontaneous denials by two- and three-year-olds. *Journal of Child Language, 9,* 597–626.

Perner, J. (1991). *Understanding the representational mind.* Cambridge, MA: MIT Press.

Piaget, J. (1926). *The language and thought of the child.* New York: Harcourt Brace.

Piaget, J. (1928). La causalité chez l'enfant. *British Journal of Psychology, 18,* 276–301.

Piaget, J. (1954). *The child's construction of reality.* New York: Basic Books.

Plomin, R., Fulker, D. W., Corley, R., & DeFries, J. C. (1997). Nature, nurture and cognitive development from 1 to 16 years: A parent-offspring adoption study. *Psychological Science, 8,* 442–447.

Premack, D. G., & Woodruff, G. (1978). Does the chimpanzee have a theory of mind? *Behavioral and Brain Sciences, 1,* 515–526.

Principe, G. F., Kanaya, T., Ceci, S. J., & Singh, M. (2006). Believing is seeing: How rumors can engender false memories in preschoolers. *Psychological Science, 17,* 243–248.

Principe, G. F., & Smith, E. (2008a). The tooth, the whole tooth, and nothing but the tooth: How belief in the tooth fairy can engender false memories. *Applied Cognitive Psychology, 22,* 625–642.

Principe, G. F., & Smith, E. (2008b). Seeing things unseen: Fantasy beliefs and false reports. *Journal of Cognition and Development, 9,* 89–111.

Quinn, P. C., Eimas, P. D., & Rosenkrantz, S. L. (1993). Evidence for representations of perceptually similar natural categories by 3-month-old and 4-month-old infants. *Perception, 22,* 463–475.

Rakoczy, H., Warneken, F., & Tomasello, M. (2008). The sources of normativity: Young children's awareness of the normative structure of games. *Developmental Psychology, 44,* 875–881.

Rakoczy, H., Warneken, F., & Tomasello, M. (2009). Young children's selective learning of rule games from reliable and unreliable models. *Cognitive Development, 24,* 61–69.

Reid, T. (1764/2000). *An inquiry into the human mind on the principles of common sense* (D. R. Brookes, Ed.). Edinburgh: Edinburgh University Press.

Rendell, L., Fogarty, L., Hoppitt, W. J. E., Morgan, T. J. H., Webster, M. M., & Laland, K. N. (2011). Cognitive culture: Theoretical and empirical insights into social learning strategies. *Trends in Cognitive Sciences, 15,* 68–76.

Richerson, P. J., & Boyd, R. (2005). *Not by genes alone: How culture transformed human evolution.* Chicago: University of Chicago Press.

Rogoff, B. (2003). The cultural nature of human development. New York: Oxford University Press.

Rosenberg, C. (1962). *The cholera years: The United States in 1832 and 1866.* Chicago: University of Chicago Press.

Rosengren, K., Miller, P. J., Gutiérrez, I. T., Chow, P., Schein, S., & Anderson, K. N. (2012). *Children's understanding of death: toward a contextual perspective.* Paper submitted for publication.

Rothbaum, F., Weisz, J., Pott, M., Miyake, K., & Morelli, G. (2000). Attachment and culture. *American Psychologist, 55,* 1093–1104.

Rousseau, J-J. (1762/1999). *Emile.* In *Oeuvres Complètes, Volume 4.* Pléiade Edition.

Russell, B. (1921). *The analysis of mind.* New York: MacMillan.

Rutter, M., Sonuga-Barke, E. J., Beckett, C., Castle, J., Kreppner, J., Kumsta, R., Schlotz, W., Stevens, S., & Bell, C. A. (2010). *Deprivation-specific psychological pat-*

*terns: Effects of institutional deprivation* (Monographs of the Society for Research in Child Development, 75, Serial No. 295, No. 1).

Sachs, J. (1983). Talking about there and then: The emergence of displaced reference in parent-child discourse. In K. E. Nelson (Ed.), *Children's language, Volume 4* (pp. 1–28). Hillsdale, NJ: Laurence Erlbaum Associates.

Savage-Rumbaugh, E. S., Murphy, J., Sevcik, R. A., Brakke, K. E., Williams, S. L., & Rumbaugh, D. M. (1993). *Language comprehension in ape and child* (Monographs of the Society for Research in Child Development, 58, Serial No. 233, Nos. 3–4).

Saylor, M. M., & Baldwin, D. A. (2004). Discussing those not present: Comprehension of references to absent caregivers. *Journal of Child Language, 31,* 537–560.

Schick, K. D., & Toth, N. (1993). *Making silent stones speak: Human evolution and the dawn of technology.* New York: Simon & Schuster.

Schmidt, M. F. H., Rakoczy, H., & Tomasello, M. (2011, March). Young children are moral universalists but conventional parochialists. Paper presented at the meeting of the Society for Research in Child Development, Montreal.

Scribner, S. (1977). Modes of thinking and ways of speaking: Culture and logic reconsidered. In P. N. Johnson-Laird & P. C. Wason (Eds.), *Thinking: Readings in cognitive science* (pp. 483–500). New York: Cambridge University Press.

Shapin, S. (1995). *A social history of truth: Civility and Science in seventeenth-century England.* Chicago: Chicago University Press.

Siegal, M., Butterworth, G., & Newcombe, P. A. (2004). Culture and children's cosmology. *Developmental Science, 7,* 308–324.

Simon, H. A. (1996). *The sciences of the artificial (3rd ed.).* Cambridge, MA: MIT Press.

Singer, P. (1975). *Animal liberation: A new ethics for our treatment of animals.* New York: Random House.

Singer, P. (1981). *The expanding circle.* New York: Farrar, Straus, & Giroux.

Skolnick, D., & Bloom, P. (2006). What does Batman think about SpongeBob? Children's understanding of the fantasy/fantasy distinction. *Cognition, 101,* B9–B18.

Slaughter, V., Jaakkola, R., & Carey, S. (1999). Constructing a coherent theory: Children's biological understanding of life and death. In M. Siegal & C. Peterson

(Eds.), *Children's understanding of biology, health, and ethics* (pp. 71–98). Cambridge: Cambridge University Press.

Slaughter, V., & Lyons, M. (2003). Learning about life and death in early childhood. *Cognitive Psychology, 46,* 1–30.

Smetana, J. G. (1985). Preschool children's conception of transgressions: Effects of varying moral and conventional domain-related attributes. *Developmental Psychology, 21,* 18–29.

Smetana, J. G., Kelly, M., & Twentyman, C. T. (1984). Abused, neglected and non-maltreated children's conceptions of moral and socio-conventional transgressions. *Child Development, 55,* 277–287.

Smith, J. D. (2009). The study of animal metacognition. *Trends in Cognitive Science, 13,* 389–396.

Southgate, V., van Maanen, C., & Csibra, G. (2007). Infant pointing: Communication to cooperate or communication to learn. *Child Development, 78,* 735–740.

Strauss, M. S. (1979). Abstraction of prototypical information by adults and 10-month-old-infants. *Journal of Experimental Psychology: Human Learning and Memory, 5,* 618–632.

Strayer, F. F., & Strayer, J. (1976). An ethological analysis of social agonism and dominance relations among preschool children. *Child Development, 47,* 980–989.

Subbotsky, E. V. (1985). Pre-school children's perception of unusual phenomena. *Soviet Psychology, 23,* 91–114.

Subbotsky, E. V. (1994). Early rationality and magical thinking in preschoolers: Space and time. *British Journal of Developmental Psychology, 12,* 97–108.

Suddendorf, T., & Whiten, A. (2001). Mental evolution and development: Evidence for secondary representation in children, great apes, and other animals. *Psychological Bulletin, 127,* 629–650.

Sully, J. (1896/2000). *Studies of childhood.* London: Free Association Books.

Tamis-LeMonda, C. S., Adolph, K. E., Lobo, S. A., Karasik, L. B., Ishak, S., & Dimitropoulou, K. A. (2008). When infants take mothers' advice: 18-month-olds integrate perceptual and social information to guide motor action. *Developmental Psychology, 44,* 734–746.

Taylor, M., Cartwright, B. S., & Carlson, S. M. (1993). A developmental investigation of children's imaginary companions. *Developmental Psychology, 29,* 276–285.

Taylor, M., Esbensen, B. M., & Bennett, R. T. (1994). Children's understanding of knowledge acquisition: The tendency for children to report that they have always known what they just learned. *Child Development, 65,* 1581–1604.

Thornton, A., & Clutton-Brock, T. (2011). Social learning and the development of individual and group behavior in mammal societies. *Philosophical Transactions of the Royal Society B, 366,* 978–987.

Tizard, B., & Hughes, M. (1984). *Young children learning.* London: Fontana.

Tomasello, M. (2009). *Why we cooperate.* Cambridge, MA: MIT Press.

Tomasello, M. (2011). Human culture in evolutionary perspective. In M. J. Gelfand, C.-Y. Chiu, and Y.-Y. Hong (Eds.), *Advances in Culture and Psychology.* New York: Oxford University Press.

Tomasello, M., Carpenter, M., Call, J., Behne, T., & Moll, H. (2005). Understanding and sharing intentions: The origins of cultural cognition. *Behavioral and Brain Sciences, 28,* 657–691.

Turiel, E. (2006). The development of morality. In N. Eisenberg (Ed.), *Handbook of child psychology, Volume 3* (pp. 789–857). New York: Wiley.

Tversky, A., & Kahneman, D. (1973). Availability: A heuristic for judging frequency and probability. *Cognitive Psychology, 5,* 207–232.

Vaden, V. C., & Woolley, J. D. (2011). Does God make it real? Children's belief in religious stories from the Judeo-Christian tradition. *Child Development, 82,* 1120–1135.

VanderBorght, M., & Jaswal, V. K. (2009). Who knows best? Preschoolers sometimes prefer child information over adult informants. *Infant and Child Development, 18,* 61–71.

Van Schaik, C. P., & Burkart, J. M. (2011). Social learning and evolution: The cultural intelligence hypothesis. *Philosophical Transactions of the Royal Society B, 366,* 1008–1016.

Vygotsky, L. S. (1978). Mind in society: The development of higher mental processes. Cambridge, MA: Harvard University Press.

Want, S. C., & Harris, P. L. (2001). Learning from other people's mistakes: Causal understanding in learning to use a tool. *Child Development, 72,* 431–443.

Warneken, F., Chen, F., & Tomasello, M. (2006). Cooperative activities in young children and chimpanzees. *Child Development, 77,* 640–663.

Warneken, F., & Tomasello, M. (2006). Altruistic helping in human infants and young chimpanzees. *Science, 311,* 1301–1303.

Warneken, F., & Tomasello, M. (2009). Varieties of altruism in children and chimpanzees. *Trends in Cognitive Sciences, 13,* 397–402.

Wellman, H. M., Cross, D., & Watson, J. (2001). Meta-analysis of theory of mind development: The truth about false belief. *Child Development, 72,* 655–684.

Wellman, H. M., & Estes, D. (1986). Early understanding of mental entities: A re-examination of childhood realism. *Child Development, 57,* 910–923.

Whiten, A. (2005). The second inheritance system of chimpanzees and humans. *Nature, 437,* 52–55.

Whiten, A., & Byrne, R. W. (1988). Tactical deception in primates. *Behavioral and Brain Sciences, 11,* 233–273.

Whiten, A., Goodall, J., McGrew, W., Nishida, T., Reynolds, V., Sugiyama, Y., Tutin, C., Wrangham, R., & Boesch, C. (1999). Cultures in chimpanzees. *Nature, 399,* 682–685.

Whiten, A., Horner, V., & de Waal, F. B. M. (2005). Conformity to cultural norms of tool use in chimpanzees. *Nature, 437,* 737–740.

Whiten, A., Horner, V., & Marshall-Pescini, S. (2005). Selective imitation in child and chimpanzee: A window on the construal of others' actions. In S. Hurley & N. Chater (Eds.), *Perspectives on imitation: From neuroscience to social science* (Volume 1, pp. 263–283). Cambridge, MA: MIT Press.

Whiten, A., McGuigan, N., Marshall-Pescini, S., & Hopper, L. M. (2009). Emulation, imitation, over-imitation and the scope of culture for child and chimpanzee. *Philosophical Transactions of the Royal Society B: Biological Sciences, 364,* 2417–2428.

Wimmer, H., & Perner, J. (1983). Beliefs about beliefs: Representation and constraining function of wrong beliefs in young children's understanding of deception. *Cognition, 13,* 103–128.

Wittgenstein, L. (1969). *On certainty.* Oxford: Blackwell.

Woolley, J. D., & Cox, V. (2007). Development of beliefs about storybook reality. *Developmental Science, 10,* 681–693.

Woolley, J. D., & Phelps, K. E. (2001). The development of children's beliefs about prayer. *Journal of Cognition and Culture, 1,* 139–167.

# Acknowledgments

The seeds for this book were planted in the final chapter of an earlier book—*The Work of the Imagination*—in which I speculated about what happens when children begin to coordinate their understanding of language with their imagination. I discussed the possibility that children would then be able to learn from what other people tell them about unobserved—but imaginable—objects or events.

The germination of this basic idea took some time. The late Peter Lipton encouraged me to look at philosophical writing on testimony. A move to Harvard gave me the opportunity to design a course on children's learning from other people's testimony, and I thank several generations of Harvard students who ventured to take the course, despite its weird title (H-180: "Are Children Stubborn Autodidacts?"). In the context of that course, and with generous support from a succession of postdoctoral fellows and visitors—especially Rita Astuti, Fabrice Clément, Shiri Einav, Patricia Ganea, Silvia Guerrero, Laurence Kaufmann, Melissa Koenig, Olivier Mascaro, Francisco Pons, and Rebekah Richert—two ideas took hold: the very testable notion that children might be willing to learn from some people more than from others, and the increasing realization that children learn from others' testimony about a huge range of topics, including everyday events, scientific and historical matters, moral issues, and religious phenomena.

A sabbatical leave in 2006–2007 at the University of Geneva, where the Swiss Center for Affective Sciences was my main host, allowed me to get started on several chapters. Various other opportunities and meetings since then have provided succor and inspiration. For the past several years, I have greatly enjoyed regular visits to the Max Planck Institute for Evolutionary Anthropology in Leipzig, especially to the Department of Developmental and Comparative Psychology, directed by Mike Tomasello. My paper on children who choose not to eat meat had a lively and helpful reception at Yale University in 2009. In 2010, I enjoyed a wonderful conference in London—entitled "Culture Evolves"—that underlined important connections between the empirical research described in this book and broader issues in the evolutionary analysis of cultural learning. I am especially grateful for Andy Whiten's panoramic vision at that conference.

A variety of friends and colleagues have been kind enough to comment on selected chapters. I would especially like to thank Greg Currie, Tyler Doggett, Susan Engel, Carl Johnson, Mark Nielsen, Tjeert Olthof, Hanus Rakoczy, and Sandy Waxman.

Finally, a core group of doctoral students have helped immeasurably in developing new hypotheses, in gathering data, and in offering critical feedback. I warmly thank Linda Abarbanell, Igor Bascandziev, Peter Blake, Diyu Chen, Eva Chen, Kathleen Corriveau, Suzanne Duke, Maria Fusaro, Julia Hayden, Angie Kim, Larisa Heiphetz, Karen Hussar, Katie Kinzler, Elizabeth Pasquini, Andrew Shtulman, and Craig Smith. I am especially grateful to Kathleen Corriveau, who was vital in maintaining a productive and collaborative laboratory.

# Index

Snow, C., 26
Social learning. *See* Cultural learning
Somerville, S. C., 71
Song, G., 110
Sonuga-Barke, E. J., 79
Soul, 140, 143, 144, 154, 157, 170
Source confusion, 188, 190–191, 193
South Africa, 53, 206, 209, 219n1. *See also* Africa
Southgate, V., 214n2
Spain, 142–144, 149, 150, 155, 162–169, 182, 187, 207. *See also* Europe
Speece, M. W., 154
Spelke, E., 14
Stein, C., 95
Stevens, S., 79
Stoess, C., 138
Stories, 4, 6, 8, 12, 115–117, 127, 155–158, 160, 163–166, 173, 175, 181, 183, 185, 190, 192, 219n1, 220n1; fantasy stories, 136, 178, 180, 181, 183, 187, 188, 192, 193, 205–206; historical stories, 173, 175–177, 179–180, 190, 192; religious stories, 181, 190, 192–193
Strangers, 5, 32, 78, 79–88, 92, 96, 145, 219n2
Strauss, M. S., 64
Strayer, F. F., 114
Strayer, J., 114
Subbotsky, E. V., 184
Suddendorf, T., 214n1
Suffering, 6, 115–117; of animals, 120–131
Sugiyama, Y., 45
Sully, J., 24–26, 31, 37, 39–40, 198
Supererogatory acts, 123–124

Taiwan, 101–102, 104
Tamis-LeMonda, C. S., 215n1
Taylor, M., 132, 138
Teachers, 1, 27, 36, 38, 59–60, 81, 92,
95, 112, 117, 138, 142, 149, 199, 201, 203, 204, 220n1
Téglás, E., 188, 201
Teleological thinking, 24–25, 198–199
Testimony, 1–4, 6, 7, 81, 135; and displaced speech, 9, 11, 13, 18–19, 20–21; and questions, 23–24, 31, 41; and categorization, 63–64; and naïve physics, 63, 73–75, 76, 81; and simple perceptual judgments, 106–112; and moral judgment, 113–131; and invisible entities, 148–151, 152–154
Theory of mind, 91, 96, 195, 218n1
Thornton, A., 201
Thucydides, 173, 176
Tizard, B., 32–34, 36, 40, 41
Tomaselli, K., 53, 55
Tomasello, M., 9, 58, 195, 196, 218n3, 219n2
Tool use, 5, 45–47, 61, 64, 103, 105, 106, 194, 196, 198, 199, 201, 202; questions as a tool, 23–24, 45. *See also* Ratchet effect in tool-making
Tooth fairy, 3, 136–139, 142, 146–150
Toth, N., 46
Trap-tube task, 56–58
Trust, 5–7, 36, 77–79, 136, 147, 216n7; in familiar caregivers, 79–91; in accurate informants, 88–92; in familiar vs. accurate informants, 92–96; in a consensus, 98–112
Turiel, E., 113, 120
Tutin, C., 45
Tversky, A., 191
Twentyman, C. T., 114

United Kingdom, 32, 43. *See also* Europe
United States, 27, 32, 34, 43, 110, 128, 154, 168, 171, 209, 221n2. *See also* Boston
Unobservable entities, 134, 137, 143